S0-CAB-267

PENGUIN BOOKS

THE NERO WOLFE COOKBOOK

Rex Stout wrote more than sixty Nero Wolfe stories before his death in 1975 at the age of eighty-eight. He could claim only a fraction of Nero Wolfe's bulk, but he was an excellent cook and enjoyed eating as much as his characters did, though he admitted to a secret passion for the humble hot dog.

THE NERO WOLFE COOKBOOK

by

REX STOUT

and
the Editors of
The Viking Press

PENGUIN BOOKS

Penguin Books Ltd, Harmondsworth,
Middlesex, England
Penguin Books, 625 Madison Avenue,
New York, New York 10022, U.S.A.
Penguin Books Australia Ltd, Ringwood,
Victoria, Australia
Penguin Books Canada Limited, 2801 John Street,
Markham, Ontario, Canada L3R 1B4
Penguin Books (N.Z.) Ltd, 182–190 Wairau Road,
Auckland 10, New Zealand

First published in the United States of America by
The Viking Press 1973
Published in Penguin Books 1981

LIBRARY OF CONGRESS CATALOGING IN PUBLICATION DATA
Stout, Rex, 1886–1975.
The Nero Wolfe cookbook.
Includes index.
1. Cookery. I. Viking Press, Inc., New York.
II. Title.
[TX715.S886 1981] 641.5 80-24421
ISBN 0 14 00.5754 4

Printed in the United States of America by
Command Web Offset, Inc., Secaucus, New Jersey
Set in Baskerville

Thanks

The only part of this book that is all mine is the excerpts from the stories which precede the recipes. All the dishes mentioned in TOO MANY COOKS were cooked twice—some three times or more—by the late Sheila Hibben and me. For years she wrote regularly for *The New Yorker* on food and cooking and restaurants, and she was my dear and valued friend. (A bit of her: One day in January when I was driving her to my house from the station she said, "The country is so wonderful like this, without all those goddam leaves obstructing the view.")

Barbara Burn's name should be on the title page. The comments and explanations in italics are all by her, as well as the final wording of most of the recipes. Without her there would have been no Nero Wolfe cookbook. She also tested, or supervised the testing of, many of the dishes. I thank her warmly.

I thank Michael S. Romano, who tested more than half of the dishes and wrote the first draft of many of the recipes. I thank Helen Taylor, who chose and collected the excerpts from the stories and tested a few of the recipes. And I thank Marshall Best and Laurie Colwin and Mary Chambers and Barbara Morris and Susan Mabon.

That's gratitude for you!

—Rex Stout

Contents

Note

I beg you not to entrust these dishes to your cook unless he is an artist. Cook them yourself, and only for an occasion that is worthy of them.

They are items for an epicure, but are neither finicky nor pretentious; you and your guests will find them as satisfying to the appetite as they are pleasing to the palate. None is beyond your abilities if you have the necessary respect for the art of fine cooking—and are willing to spend the time and care which an excellent dish deserves and must have.

Good Appetite!

—Nero Wolfe, TOO MANY COOKS

Personal

I have never completely understood Wolfe's attitude on food and eating and probably never will. In some ways it's strictly personal. If Fritz presents a platter of broiled squabs and one of them is a little plumper or a more beautiful brown than others, Wolfe cops it. If the supply of wild-thyme honey from Greece is getting low, I am given to understand that American honey on griddle cakes is quite acceptable. And so on. But it really pains him if I am out on a prolonged errand at mealtime because I may insult my palate with a drugstore sandwich and, even worse, I may offend my stomach by leaving it empty. If there is reason to believe that a caller is hungry, even if it is someone whom he intends to take apart, he has Fritz bring a tray, not scraps. As for interruptions at meals, for him there is absolutely nothing doing; when he is once in his chair at the table he leaves it only when the last bite of cheese or dessert is down. That's personal, but he has tried off and on to extend it to me, and he would if I would stand for it. The point is, does he hate to have my meal broken into because it interrupts his, or because it interrupts mine, or just on general principles? Search me.

—Archie Goodwin, THE FINAL DEDUCTION

Foreword

I am happy that my friend Mr. Archie Goodwin will have pleasure with the money he gets from this book. Also I am willing for his literary agent, Mr. Rex Stout, to receive his usual share. Also I am not surprised that my employer, Mr. Nero Wolfe, approves of its publication because he has a great belief in the influence of printed words in books.

But I have not a great hope that many people will eat superior meals because they buy this book and use it. On that I could say much but I will not write much and I will give only one case. There are a man and a woman, married, at whose home I eat sometimes. They own fourteen cookbooks, good ones which they have asked me to suggest, and they have many times asked me for information and advice about cooking which I have been happy to give, but the dishes they serve are only fit to eat. They are not fit to remember after I come away. Those people should not try to roast a duck, and especially they should never try to make Sauce Saint Florentin.

The facts about food and cooking can be learned and understood by anyone with good sense, but if the feeling of the art of cooking is not in your blood and bones the most you can expect is that what you put on your table will be *mangeable*. If it is sometimes *mémorable* that will be only good luck. Mr. Wolfe says that the secrets of the art of great cooking, like those of any art, are not in the brain. He says that no one knows where they are.

But I do not think this book will make your food any the worse. At least it should help with some of the facts.

—Fritz Brenner

THE NERO WOLFE COOKBOOK

1

BREAKFAST IN
THE OLD BROWNSTONE

The house rules in the old brownstone on West Thirty-fifth Street are, of course, set by Wolfe, since he owns the house, but any variation in the morning routine usually comes from me. Wolfe sticks to his personal schedule: at eight-fifteen breakfast in his room on the second floor, on a tray taken up by Fritz, at nine o'clock to the elevator and up to the plant rooms, and down by eleven. My schedule depends on what is stirring and on what time I turned in. I need to be flat a full eight hours and at night I adjust the clock on my bedstand accordingly.

[THE MOTHER HUNT]

I descended a flight to Wolfe's room, tapped on the door, and entered. He was in bed, propped up against three pillows, just ready to attack the provender on the breakfast table which straddled his mountainous ridge under the black silk coverlet. There was orange juice, eggs *au beurre noir,* two slices of broiled Georgia ham, hashed brown potatoes, hot blueberry muffins, and a pot of steaming cocoa.

[OVER MY DEAD BODY]

EGGS AU BEURRE NOIR

6 tablespoons butter   1 teaspoon dry sherry
4 large eggs

Preheat the broiler. Melt 1 tablespoon butter in each of 2 shirred-egg dishes and add the eggs, yolks unbroken, 2 to a dish. Cook over medium heat for 1 or 2 minutes until the eggwhite is set. Spoon the butter over the eggs. Put the dishes under the hot broiler for another minute until the eggs have filmed over. Remove from the oven and let stand in a warm place. In a skillet melt the remaining 4 tablespoons of butter over medium heat. When white waxy particles have settled to the bottom, pour the clear liquid off into a bowl. Return the clarified butter to the pan and continue to cook until it has turned a deep golden brown. Watch it carefully to be sure that the butter does not burn. Add the sherry and stir until blended. Pour the butter sauce over the eggs and serve immediately. (Serves 2)

This is a favorite dish at West Thirty-fifth Street and is served in several of the stories. In one of them, Nero Wolfe cooks the dish himself, using tarragon wine vinegar instead of sherry: Sunday morning a smell woke me—at least it was the first thing I was aware of—a smell I knew well. It was faint, but I recognized it. I got erect and went out to the head of the stairs and sniffed; no doubt about it. I went down three flights to the kitchen and there he was, eating breakfast in his shirt sleeves. Eggs *au beurre noir.* He was playing house.

He said good morning. "Tell me twenty minutes before you're ready."

"Sure. Wine vinegar, I presume?"

He nodded. "Not very good, but it will do."

[THE MOTHER HUNT]

BROILED GEORGIA HAM

1 thin slice Georgia ham
  (5 x 8 inches approximately)
1 cup milk
1 tablespoon vinegar

½ teaspoon mustard
1 teaspoon currant jelly
1 grinding fresh black pepper

Soak the ham in the milk for about 1 hour. Mix the remaining ingredients together and heat. Drain, dry, and broil the ham under a hot flame for 2 or 3 minutes on each side. Pour the sauce over the ham and serve. (Serves 2)

In TOO MANY COOKS *Wolfe explains what is special about the Georgia ham he serves:* "A pig whose diet is fifty to seventy per cent peanuts grows a ham of incredibly sweet and delicate succulence which, well cured, well kept, and well cooked, will take precedence over any other ham the world affords." *Archie gives Inspector Cramer a somewhat less elegant description in* DISGUISE FOR MURDER: "Georgia pigs fed on peanuts and acorns. Cured to Mr. Wolfe's specifications. It smells good but it tastes even better."

HASHED BROWN POTATOES

¼ cup butter	watercress
2 cups diced raw potatoes	salt and pepper to taste
1 teaspoon minced shallots	

Melt the butter in a skillet. Mix the potatoes and shallots together and add. Cook over medium heat without stirring for 3 or 4 minutes. Run a spatula under the potatoes to prevent sticking, and continue to cook until the bottom is browned slightly. Turn the potatoes and cook until the other side browns. Fold out onto a warmed serving dish as you would an omelet, garnish with watercress, and sprinkle with salt and freshly ground black pepper. (Serves 3 to 4)

> *Please note that these potatoes are not fried, as they usually are in American homes. As Archie points out in* THE FATHER HUNT, *eggs are never fried in Wolfe's and Fritz's kitchen, and neither are potatoes.*

BLUEBERRY MUFFINS

⅓ cup butter	4 teaspoons baking powder
(at room temperature)	½ teaspoon salt
⅔ cup sugar	1 cup milk
2 large eggs	1 cup fresh blueberries,
2 cups all-purpose flour	washed and drained

Preheat oven to 375°. Cream the butter and sugar together until fluffy. Beat the eggs and add to the butter mixture. Blend well. Sift the flour, baking powder, and salt together in a smaller bowl and add to the butter mixture alternately with the milk. Stir in the blueberries and spoon into greased muffin tins until two-thirds full. Bake for 25 minutes. (Makes 12 muffins)

On rainy mornings, or even gray ones, Wolfe breakfasts in bed, after tossing the black silk coverlet toward the foot because stains are bad for it, but when it's bright he has Fritz put the tray on a table near the window. [THE GOLDEN SPIDERS]   . . . Entering, I blinked. The morning sun was streaking in and glancing off the vast expanse of Wolfe's yellow pajamas. He was seated at a table by the window, barefooted, working on a bowl of fresh figs

with cream. When I was listing the cash requirements of the establishment, I might have mentioned that fresh figs, in March, by air from Chile, are not hay. [CHAMPAGNE FOR ONE]   . . .
What with grocery bills, including such items as the fresh caviar which Wolfe sometimes stirred into his coddled eggs at breakfast, the minimum monthly outgo of that establishment averaged more than five grand. [TOO MANY CLIENTS]

FRESH FIGS WITH CREAM (see index)

CODDLED EGGS

4 large eggs
  (at room temperature)
2 slices black bread

1 tablespoon sweet butter
2 ounces fresh sturgeon
  caviar (chilled)

Bring 2 cups of water to a simmer in a saucepan and, with a slotted spoon, place eggs in the water and allow them to simmer *very gently* for 4 to 6 minutes, depending on your taste. Remove the eggs from the heat and run cold water over them to cool. Toast the bread, quarter each slice, and spread with butter. Arrange the slices in 2 shallow bowls. Peel the eggs without breaking them and place gently in the center of the toast, 2 to a bowl. Serve the caviar separately, to be stirred into the eggs. (Serves 2)

He was a sight, as he always was when propped up in bed with his breakfast tray. Already down the gullet were the peaches and cream, most of the unrationed bacon, and two-thirds of the eggs, not to mention coffee and the green-tomato jam.

[HELP, MAN WANTED]

GREEN-TOMATO JAM

4 cups green tomatoes
2 tablespoons salt
1 lemon
2 cups light brown sugar

1 teaspoon grated lemon rind
1 teaspoon cinnamon
1 teaspoon nutmeg
¼ teaspoon ground cloves

Be sure that the tomatoes have been picked before the first frost, which will harden them. Wash the tomatoes, remove the stem spots, and cut into 1-inch cubes. Put the cubes in a bowl, sprinkle them with the salt, and let stand overnight in the refrigerator. In the morning, rinse and drain the tomatoes thoroughly. Put them into a large enameled pot and add the lemon, sliced as thin as possible, the brown sugar, rind, and spices. Simmer, covered, until the tomatoes are very soft (about 30 to 45 minutes) and remove from heat. Reserve 4 or 5 of the cubes and put the rest through a food mill or purée in a blender. Chop the remaining cubes coarsely and add to the purée. Return the mixture to the pot and simmer for another 20 to 25 minutes, stirring occasionally, until the jam is thick enough to spread. When the jam is cooled, pour it into sterilized Mason jars and seal tightly. (Makes 1 quart)

Archie usually eats the same breakfast as Wolfe does—in quality and in quantity—and he takes it in the kitchen at his breakfast table. The trouble with mornings is that they come when you're not awake. It's all a blur until I am washed and dressed and have somehow made my way down to the kitchen and got orange juice in me, and I'm not really awake until the fourth griddle cake and the second cup of coffee.   [A WINDOW FOR DEATH]

GRIDDLE CAKES

1 cup all-purpose flour	3 tablespoons sugar
1 cup corn meal	2 large eggs
2 teaspoons baking powder	1½ cups sour milk (or more)
1 teaspoon salt	2 tablespoons melted butter

Sift the flour and corn meal, baking powder, salt, and sugar into a bowl. In a separate bowl beat the eggs until lemon-yellow in color and add the sour milk. (Sour milk can be made by adding a few drops of lemon juice to sweet milk and allowing it to stand for a few hours in a warm place.) Add the dry ingredients to the egg-milk mixture and beat with a wire whisk or electric hand beater. Add the melted butter gradually while beating. Ladle out the batter with a dipper onto a hot, lightly oiled griddle. When the bubbles on top have opened and the underside is golden brown, turn each cake and cook for 1 or 2 minutes more. Serve hot with butter and a sweet topping (see note below). (Makes 12 griddle cakes)

VARIATION:

Buckwheat Griddle Cakes: Substitute 1½ cups buckwheat flour and ½ cup all-purpose flour for the flours in the basic recipe, and use buttermilk instead of sour milk.   [TOO MANY CLIENTS]

As for toppings, Fritz serves several different kinds: wild-thyme honey from Greece or Syria, Puerto Rican molasses, blackberry jam, guava butter, and sometimes just brown sugar: At ten o'clock I was in the kitchen at my breakfast table, sprinkling brown sugar on a buttered sour-milk griddle cake, with the *Times* before me on the rack. Fritz, standing by, asked, "No cinnamon?"
"No," I said firmly. "I've decided it's an aphrodisiac."
"Then for you it would be—how is it? Taking coal somewhere."
"Coals to Newcastle. That's not the point, but you mean well, and I thank you."   [THE MOTHER HUNT]

At eight-fifteen Thursday morning I descended two flights, entered the kitchen, exchanged good mornings with Fritz, picked up my ten-ounce glass of orange juice, took that first sour-sweet sip, which is always the first hint that the fog is going to lift, and inquired, "No omelet?"
Fritz shut the refrigerator door. "You well know, Archie, what it means when the eggs are not broken."
"Sure, but I'm hungry."
It meant that when Fritz had taken Wolfe's breakfast tray up to his room he had been told that I was wanted, and he would not break eggs until he heard me coming down again. . . .
By nine o'clock the morning fog had gone entirely, thanks to the apricot omelet, griddle cakes with bacon and honey, and two cups of coffee.   [PLOT IT YOURSELF]

APRICOT OMELET

1 ounce kümmel	½ teaspoon salt
1 cup apricot preserves	2 teaspoons sugar
6 eggs (at room temperature)	2 tablespoons butter
2 tablespoons cold water	1 teaspoon powdered sugar

Blend the kümmel and the apricot preserves, and set them aside. Preheat the broiler to 500°. Break 3 eggs into a small bowl and add 1 tablespoon of water, ¼ teaspoon of salt, and 1 teaspoon of sugar, and beat thoroughly with a fork or whisk until the eggs are foamy. Heat a 9-inch prepared omelet pan over medium heat until it is hot. To test for the proper heat, shake a few drops of water into the pan. If they jump around and disappear, the pan is ready. Add 1 tablespoon of butter, tilting the pan so that the bottom is covered completely with melting butter. When the foam has subsided, pour the eggs into the pan and with the flat side of a fork, stir the eggs with a circular motion. With the other hand shake the pan back and forth to keep the eggs from sticking. When the eggs are set on the bottom and still moist on top, put 2 to 3 tablespoons of the apricot mixture into the middle of the omelet. Roll the omelet or fold it in half and turn it onto a warm plate. Sprinkle it with ½ teaspoon of powdered sugar and run it under a hot broiler to glaze. Serve immediately, and repeat the operation for the second omelet. (Serves 2)

VARIATIONS:

Bacon and Apricot Omelet: Prepare the omelet in the same way, adding 1 tablespoon of kirschwasser and 2 crumbled strips of cooked bacon to the 3-egg mixture instead of water and sugar. Omit the filling and glaze the finished omelet with heated apricot preserves instead of sugar.

[TOO MANY CLIENTS]

Strawberry Omelet: Prepare the filling by crushing a pint of fresh strawberries, adding 1 tablespoon of sugar, the juice of 1 lemon, and ½ ounce of kirschwasser. Refrigerate the mixture for 1 hour to draw out the strawberry juice. Drain off the juice and heat it in a small pan. Just before you cook the eggs, whip ¼ cup heavy cream and fold it into the crushed, drained berries. When the omelet is nearly cooked, fold 2 to 3 tablespoons of the chilled berry-cream mixture into the center and finish in the usual way. Pour a little of the heated juice over the omelet and glaze under the broiler. Use the remaining juice as a sauce.

[IF DEATH EVER SLEPT]

As I sat in the kitchen at ten minutes past eight Monday morning, having brioches, grilled ham, and grape-thyme jelly, my mind was hopping around. First, why was Fritz so damn stubborn about the jelly? Why wouldn't he try it, just once, with half as much sugar and twice as much sauterne? I had been at him for years.

[DEATH OF A DOXY]

BRIOCHES

1 cake compressed yeast	2 tablespoons sugar
½ cup lukewarm water	1 cup softened butter
4 cups sifted	6 large eggs
all-purpose flour	1 egg yolk
1 teaspoon salt	

Soften the yeast in the water for 5 minutes. Stir in 1 cup of the flour, mixing until smooth. Place the dough in a large bowl and cover with warm water. Set it aside in a warm place until it doubles in bulk (about 1 hour) and the ball of dough floats in the water. In another bowl combine the remaining flour with the ball of dough and the salt, sugar, and half the butter, mixing well. Add 3 of the eggs, beaten, and beat until smooth. Add the remaining eggs, beaten, and the rest of the butter. Set the dough aside to rise until it has doubled in bulk. Beat it down again, shape it into a ball, and place it in a greased bowl. Cover the bowl with aluminum foil and chill it overnight. Cut off pieces of dough large enough to fill fluted brioche molds halfway. Reserve enough to make topknots for the brioches. Roll the pieces of dough into balls, put into the buttered tins, and cut a crisscross on top of each. Roll small pieces of the reserved dough into balls and insert into each crisscross. Cover the tins and set them aside to rise until double in bulk (about 1 hour). Preheat the oven to 450°. Brush the top of each brioche with a little beaten egg yolk. Bake for 15 to 20 minutes until browned, and serve hot. (Makes 18 to 24 brioches)

GRAPE-THYME JELLY

1 cup sauterne	2 medium apples
1½ tablespoons	4½ cups sugar
fresh thyme leaves	water
(or 1 teaspoon dried leaves)	½ bottle liquid pectin
3 to 4 pounds Concord grapes	

Heat the sauterne in an enamel pan to the boiling point. Put the thyme leaves into a bowl and pour the wine over them. Allow the leaves to steep for 30 to 40 minutes. Then pour the mixture back into the pan and simmer it over a low flame until it reduces to half a cup. Stem the grapes and crush them in a large enamel kettle. Peel and cube the apples and add them to the grapes with 1 cup of sugar. Add enough water so that the grapes are just barely covered (too much water will dilute the flavor). Cook the mixture at a simmer until the fruit starts to lose color and becomes soft (about 1 hour). Pour the mixture into a jelly bag or through several thicknesses of cheesecloth and allow it to drain. Do not squeeze the cloth or the jelly will become muddied and the taste will be affected. You should have 2 cups of juice. Add the sauterne, the remaining 3½ cups of sugar, and the pectin. Bring to a boil and stir constantly and rapidly for 1 minute. Remove the mixture from the heat, skim if necessary, and pour into hot sterile jelly glasses. Seal with melted paraffin. (Makes 2 quarts)

I chewed slowly on my third bite of scrapple, swallowed it, and turned to Fritz.

"Creating again?" I asked.

He beamed at me. "You're learning to taste, Archie, to *distinguer*. In ten years more you'll have a palate. Can you tell me what I did?"

"Certainly not. But you did something. Right?"

"I reduced the sage a little and added a touch of orégano. What do you think?"

"I think you're a genius. Two geniuses in one house, and one of them is easy to live with. . . ."   [THE MOTHER HUNT]

SCRAPPLE

1½ pounds fresh pork shoulder
1 quart cold water
1 teaspoon salt
½ teaspoon black pepper
1¼ cups white corn meal
⅓ cup all-purpose flour

½ teaspoon ground fresh sage
(or 1 teaspoon crushed
dried leaves)
½ teaspoon fresh orégano
leaves (or ⅛ teaspoon dried
leaves)

Simmer the pork in the water for about 2 hours. Add ½ teaspoon salt and ¼ teaspoon pepper just before turning off the heat. Remove the meat from the stock and shred it. Strain the stock and reserve 1 cup; continue to boil the remaining stock. Combine the rest of the ingredients and add the cup of reserved stock very slowly, stirring constantly to avoid lumps. Add the mush mixture and the shredded meat to the boiling stock and cook over a low flame for 1 hour, stirring occasionally to prevent sticking. When done, put the scrapple into a meatloaf pan and chill. Slice thin and brown in a very small amount of bacon fat. Serve with maple syrup. (Makes 1 2-pound loaf)

It was Sunday morning in November, and I knew what had happened when I called down to Fritz that I was out of the bathtub: he had lined a casserole with butter, put in it six tablespoons of cream, three fresh eggs, four Lambert sausages, salt, pepper, paprika, and chives, and conveyed it to the oven.

[THE LEAGUE OF FRIGHTENED MEN]

SHIRRED EGGS

4 breakfast sausages	¼ teaspoon fresh black pepper
1 tablespoon butter	2 dashes paprika
4 tablespoons light cream	½ teaspoon
4 large eggs	chopped fresh chives
½ teaspoon salt	

Preheat the oven to 325°. Brown the sausages in a skillet and set them aside to drain on a paper towel. Butter 2 shirred-egg dishes generously, add 2 tablespoons of cream to each, and slip in the eggs, 2 to a dish, being careful not to break the yolks. Arrange the sausages in each dish and sprinkle with salt, pepper, paprika, and chives. Bake for 10 to 15 minutes or until the eggs are done to the desired firmness. (Serves 2)

VARIATION:

Shirred Eggs with Chives and Sherry: Substitute dry sherry for the light cream, using 1 tablespoon instead of 2.   [A RIGHT TO DIE]

> *Archie has often been known to exaggerate his gastronomic prowess and this, we feel, is the case with his description of shirred eggs above. In* KILL NOW, PAY LATER, *he indicates that a guest has eaten her full portion of shirred eggs, which were two in number, and we have used that as a guideline in preparing this recipe. Lambert sausages, incidentally, are a variation of Fritz's summer sausage (see index).*

At nine o'clock Sunday morning I entered the kitchen, told Fritz good morning, got orange juice from the refrigerator, sat at my breakfast table, yawned, sneered at *The New York Times,* and rubbed my eyes. Fritz came with a piece of paper in his hand and demanded, "Were you drunk when you wrote this?"

I blinked at him. "No, just pooped. I've forgotten what I said. Please read it."

He cleared his throat. " 'Three-twenty a.m. There's a guest in the South Room. Tell him. I'll cook her breakfast. AG.' " He dropped it on the table. "I told him, and he asked who, and what could I say? And you will cook her breakfast in my kitchen?"

I took an economy-size swallow of orange juice. "Let's see if I can talk straight," I suggested. "I had four hours' sleep, exactly half what I need. As for telling him who she is, that is my function. I admit it's your function to cook breakfast, but she likes fried eggs and you don't fry eggs. Let's go to the real issue. There is one man who is more allergic to a woman in this house than he is, and you are it. By God, I *am* talking straight." I drank orange juice. "Don't worry, this woman is allergic to a man in *her* house. As for the eggs, poach them—you know, in red wine and bouillon—"

"Burgundian."

"That's it. With Canadian back bacon. That will show her what men are for. Her usual hour for breakfast is half past twelve. I'm still willing to cook it if—"

He uttered a French sound, loud; maybe it was a word.

[DEATH OF A DOXY]

POACHED EGGS BURGUNDIAN

1 cup Burgundy	1 grinding fresh black pepper
½ cup beef bouillon	2 English muffins
1 small bay leaf	4 large eggs
1½ teaspoons minced shallots	1 tablespoon butter
1 sprig parsley	1 tablespoon
½ teaspoon salt	all-purpose flour

In a shallow pan bring the wine and the bouillon to a boil and reduce the heat so that the liquid simmers gently. Add the bay leaf, shallots, parsley, salt, and pepper. Split and toast the English muffins. Poach the eggs in the simmering liquid and when done remove them with a slotted spoon to the prepared muffins. Keep warm in a holding oven. Make a *beurre manié* by rubbing the butter and flour together into a smooth paste. Stir it into the poaching liquid and continue to simmer for a few minutes, stirring constantly, until the sauce thickens. Strain and pour over the eggs. Serve immediately. (Serves 2)

The client had admitted to Wolfe, in my hearing, that she didn't know how to scramble eggs. . . . He had admitted to her, in my hearing, that forty was more minutes than you could expect a housewife to spend exclusively on scrambling eggs, but he maintained that it was impossible to do it to perfection in less with each and every particle exquisitely firm, soft, and moist.

[THE MOTHER HUNT]

SCRAMBLED EGGS

6 large eggs
1 cup light cream
½ teaspoon salt
2 grindings
    fresh black pepper

2 tablespoons butter
4 tablespoons clarified butter
few drops tarragon
    wine vinegar

Bring water in the bottom of a double boiler to a boil and reduce the heat so that the water barely simmers. Use an asbestos pad if necessary. Break the eggs into a small bowl and add the cream, salt, and pepper. Beat vigorously with a whisk. Melt the butter in the top of the double boiler and add the egg-cream mixture. Cover and place over the simmering water. Allow to cook undisturbed for about 15 minutes. Uncover and stir with a wooden spoon and continue to stir constantly until the desired degree of firmness is achieved. Be sure that the water in the bottom section does not reach a full boil. In the meantime, cook the clarified butter in a heavy-bottomed pan over low heat until it turns a dark brown. Be careful that it does not burn. Add a few drops of vinegar, stir, and serve as a sauce for the scrambled eggs. (Serves 2 or 3)

2

LUNCHEON
IN THE
DINING ROOM

When I went to the kitchen to tell Fritz that lunch would be at one o'clock sharp* because we were leaving at two for an appointment, he had a question. For Wolfe he was going to make a special omelet, which he had just invented in his head, and would that do for me or should he broil some ham? I asked what would be in the omelet, and he said four eggs, salt, pepper, one tablespoon tarragon butter, two tablespoons cream, two tablespoons dry white wine, one-half teaspoon minced shallots, one-third cup whole almonds, and twenty fresh mushrooms. I thought that would do for two but he said my God, no; that would be for Mr. Wolfe and did I want one like it? I did. He warned me that he might decide at the last minute to fold some apricot jam in, and I said I would risk it.   [PLOT IT YOURSELF]

MUSHROOM AND ALMOND OMELET

1 tablespoon tarragon butter
  (see note)
½ teaspoon minced shallots
20 button-sized mushrooms
4 tablespoons butter
⅓ cup whole hulled almonds

4 large eggs
2 tablespoons dry white wine
2 tablespoons light cream
salt and pepper to taste
1 sprig Italian parsley
  (or watercress)

In a prepared omelet pan melt the tarragon butter and sauté the minced shallots until they become transparent. In a separate skillet sauté the

* Luncheon is customarily served in the dining room at one-fifteen.

mushrooms (from which you have removed the stems) in 2 tablespoons of the butter until they are wilted and have lost much of their moisture. Drain the mushrooms and set them aside. Wipe out the skillet and add the remaining 2 tablespoons of butter. Sauté the almonds over low heat until they are browned. Drain and set aside. Break the eggs into a mixing bowl, beat for a minute or two with a whisk, and add the wine, cream, salt, and pepper. Beat until the eggs are frothy. Heat the omelet pan in which you have sautéed the shallots and pour in the egg mixture. Stir the eggs with the flat side of the fork in a circular motion for a moment, tilting the pan with your other hand to keep the eggs from sticking. When the eggs are set on the bottom and still moist on top, put the almonds and twelve of the mushrooms into the center. Using the fork, roll the omelet out onto a hot plate and garnish with the remaining mushrooms and a sprig of Italian parsley. (Serves 1 or 2)

NOTE: Make the tarragon butter by rubbing a ¼ teaspoon of crushed dried tarragon leaves into 2 tablespoons of butter and allowing the mixture to stand for at least 30 minutes.

VARIATIONS:

Mushroom and Watercress Omelet: Omit the wine and shallots and reduce the number of mushrooms to 15. Add ¼ cup minced fresh watercress to the eggs when you add the cream. Use 1 or 2 sprigs of watercress instead of parsley as a garnish, with 5 of the mushrooms.   [A RIGHT TO DIE]

Mushroom and Celery Omelet: Substitute ½ cup diced celery for the almonds and omit the shallots. Mince 15 of the mushrooms and squeeze them in a piece of cheesecloth to remove the juice. Sauté briefly in butter. Add 1 teaspoon of chopped fresh Italian parsley to the eggs when you add the wine and cream. Use the remaining 5 mushrooms, sautéed whole, as a garnish. (*When this omelet was served to guests in* MIGHT AS WELL BE DEAD, *Archie was moved to remark,* "Wolfe tells me there was a man in Marseilles who made a better omelet than Fritz, but I don't believe it.")

Anchovy Omelet: Beat the eggs with cold water instead of cream and wine and season with 1 or 2 drops of Tabasco as well as pepper. Omit the salt and shallots. For the filling fry 2 fresh anchovies until they are crisp and add them to the omelet just before you turn it out. If you prefer, substitute anchovy butter (see index) for fresh anchovies, using 2 teaspoons for each 3- or 4-egg omelet. Garnish with a miniature purple iris.
[THE GOLDEN SPIDERS]

For lunch in the dining room, which was across the hall from the office, Fritz served us with chicken livers and tomato halves fried in oil and trimmed with chopped peppers and parsley, followed by rice cakes and honey. I took it easy on the livers because of my attitude toward Fritz's rice cakes. I was on my fifth cake, or maybe sixth, when the doorbell rang.   [MAN ALIVE]

CHICKEN LIVERS

1½ pounds chicken livers
salt and freshly ground
    black pepper to taste
2 large ripe tomatoes
½ teaspoon basil leaves
    (or ¼ teaspoon dried)

1 green bell pepper
2 tablespoons olive oil
2 tablespoons fresh
    chopped parsley

Wash the livers, cutting away any membranes, and dry thoroughly. Slice them thin and sprinkle with salt and pepper. Peel the tomatoes, cut in half, and sprinkle with basil. Seed the pepper and cut it into small pieces. Heat the oil in a small skillet and sauté the peppers for 3 or 4 minutes; remove with a slotted spoon and reserve. Add the chicken livers and sauté for 3 minutes, remove. Fry the tomatoes open side down for another few minutes until they are browned. Arrange the livers and tomato halves on a warm serving platter garnished with the pepper and parsley. (Serves 4)

RICE CAKES

1 cup long-grain rice
1 tablespoon powdered yeast
½ cup warm water
5 large eggs
½ cup sugar
¼ teaspoon nutmeg

1 teaspoon salt
½ cup all-purpose flour,
    sifted
fat for deep frying
    (at 360°)

Cook the rice in salted water until it is very soft. Drain well, mash with a wooden spoon, and set aside. Soften the yeast in the warm water and add to the rice. Let stand in a warm place for 2 hours. Beat the eggs together with the sugar, nutmeg, salt, and flour. Add to the rice and stir well. Let the mixture rise for another 30 minutes. Heat the fat and when it is hot enough, drop the batter by spoonfuls and fry until brown and crisp. Fry only a few cakes at a time so the fat will remain hot enough. Drain the cakes and serve immediately. (Makes 25 cakes)

When I returned to the office after letting her out, Wolfe had straightened up in his chair to lean forward and, with his head cocked, was sniffing the air. For a second I thought he was pretending that our ex-client had polluted the atmosphere with her perfume, but then I realized that he was merely trying to catch an odor from the kitchen, where Fritz was baking scallops in shells— or probably, since I could catch the odor without sniffing, he was deciding whether Fritz had used only shallots in the sauce or had added an onion.   [DEATH OF A DEMON]

BAKED SCALLOPS

1 cup dry white wine	1 teaspoon salt
1 cup water	1 sprig parsley
1 bay leaf	1 pinch nutmeg
6 black peppercorns	2 tablespoons chopped
1 pound cleaned bay scallops	fresh parsley
5 tablespoons butter	1 tablespoon lemon juice
1 tablespoon minced shallots	½ cup fresh bread crumbs
3 tablespoons	¼ cup freshly grated
all-purpose flour	Gruyère cheese

Preheat the oven to 350°. In a large saucepan, bring the wine and the water to a boil. Add the bay leaf, peppercorns, and the washed scallops and return to the boil. Reduce the heat and simmer for 3 or 4 minutes. Drain the scallops and set aside. In a small, heavy-bottomed pan melt 3 tablespoons of the butter and cook the minced shallots until translucent but not browned. Add the flour and stir constantly until it starts to turn golden. Gradually stir in 1½ cups of the hot broth in which the scallops were cooked. Continue to cook, stirring constantly, until the sauce thickens. Add ½ teaspoon of the salt, the sprig of parsley, and the nutmeg, and cook for a few more minutes. Strain the sauce into a bowl and add the scallops, the chopped parsley, lemon juice, and the remaining salt. Stir well. Butter 4 or 6 baking shells and divide the scallop mixture evenly among them. Combine the bread crumbs and cheese; sprinkle the mixture over the filled shells and dot with the remaining butter. Bake 20 to 25 minutes, or until the tops are golden brown. (Serves 4 to 6 as a first or luncheon course)

VARIATIONS:

You may substitute 1 tablespoon minced onions for the shallots. You may also use milk or light cream instead of the scallop broth in making the sauce.

"I have three things to say to you, Archie. The first is a reminder: we are to have rice fritters with black currant jam, and endive with tarragon, for lunch. The second is a piece of information: you will not have time for lunch here. The third is an instruction: you are to proceed to the McNair establishment, get Miss Frost, and have her at this office by two o'clock. Doubtless you will find opportunity to get a greasy sandwich somewhere. . . ."

[THE RED BOX]

RICE FRITTERS

2 large eggs	2 teaspoons sugar
3 tablespoons heavy cream	salt to taste
1 cup cooked rice	½ cup bread crumbs
1 tablespoon butter	oil for deep frying at 375°

Beat one of the eggs until it is frothy. Add 2 tablespoons of the cream and all the rice. Pour the mixture into a saucepan and cook over low heat, stirring constantly, until it is thickened. Add the butter, sugar, and salt. Stir and set aside to cool. Mix the remaining egg with the tablespoon of cream in a small bowl and spread the bread crumbs in a shallow plate. Form the rice mixture into small, flat cakes, dip them into the egg-cream mixture, and then roll them in the crumbs. Fry in the hot oil for 2 to 5 minutes until golden brown. (Do not cook more than three cakes at a time or the heat of the oil will become too low.) Serve with black currant jam or maple syrup.

VARIATION:

Omit the sugar and add 2 tablespoons of sautéed minced onion and 1 teaspoon of curry powder to serve as a nonsweet accompaniment to a meat dish.

ENDIVE SALAD (see index)

As we finished the clam juice, Fritz came with the first install-ment of dumplings, four apiece. Some day I would like to see how long I can keep going on Fritz's marrow dumplings, of chopped beef marrow, bread crumbs, parsley (chives today), grated lemon rind, salt, and eggs, boiled four minutes in strong meat stock. If he boiled them all at once, of course, they would get mushy after the first eight or ten, but he does them eight at a time, and they keep coming. They are one of the few dishes with which I stay neck and neck with Wolfe clear to the tape.

[TOO MANY CLIENTS]

MARROW DUMPLINGS

¼ pound beef marrow
½ medium onion
1 large egg
½ teaspoon salt
½ teaspoon grated lemon rind
⅛ teaspoon nutmeg

1 tablespoon chopped
    fresh parsley (or chives)
⅔ cup bread crumbs
½ cup sifted all-purpose flour
½ cup milk
2 quarts strong beef stock

Grind together the beef marrow and the onion, using the finest blade on the meat grinder. Add the egg, salt, lemon rind, nutmeg, parsley (or chives), bread crumbs, flour, and milk, and mix well into a soft dough, adding more milk if necessary. Bring the beef stock to a boil in a large pot. Using a teaspoon for small dumplings (or a tablespoon if you prefer larger ones), drop the batter into the simmering stock. Cover the pot and simmer for 10 to 15 minutes, depending on the size of the dumplings. Remove with a slotted spoon and allow to drain for a minute before serving. Serve very hot with a rich béchamel sauce. (Makes 15 to 20 dumplings)

NOTE: *See also the recipe for Quenelles Bonne Femme (Mondor patties) (see index) created by Pierre Mondor, from whom Fritz adapted this version.*

Returning down the hall, I paused for a moment before entering the office to sniff. Fritz, as I knew, was doing spareribs with the sauce he and Wolfe had concocted. [MURDER BY THE BOOK] At lunch Fritz, coming to remove the leavings of the spareribs and bring the salad and cheese, had told Wolfe there was a drop of sauce on his tie, and Wolfe had dabbed at it with his napkin.

[EENY MEENY MURDER MO]

SPARERIBS IN SPECIAL SAUCE

4 pounds pork spareribs
1 medium onion
1 clove garlic
1 small green pepper
¼ cup olive oil
½ cup Italian tomato paste
1 teaspoon salt
1 teaspoon fresh basil leaves
   (or ½ teaspoon dried leaves)
1 teaspoon dried rosemary

1 teaspoon fresh orégano
   (or ¼ teaspoon dried leaves)
1 tablespoon chopped
   fresh parsley
¼ teaspoon Tabasco
2 teaspoons dry mustard
¼ cup Worcestershire sauce
½ cup water
½ cup honey
½ cup dry red wine

Preheat the broiler. Cut the ribs into three-rib sections. Chop the onion, garlic, and pepper and sauté in heated olive oil until slightly browned. Add the tomato paste, salt, basil, rosemary, orégano, parsley, Tabasco, dry mustard, Worcestershire sauce, water, and honey. Allow to simmer for 20 minutes, stirring occasionally. Add the red wine and simmer another 15 minutes. Use the sauce to baste the spareribs as they broil (about 30 minutes) but reserve a little to be served hot at the table.

The next hour, at the lunch table, provided nourishment for both my stomach and brain. For the stomach, sweetbreads amandine in patty shells and cold green-corn pudding. For the brain, a debate on the question whether music, any music, has, or can have, any intellectual content.   [THE FATHER HUNT]

SWEETBREADS AMANDINE

4 pairs veal sweetbreads
2 large eggs
1 cup bread crumbs
8 tablespoons butter

6 tablespoons
   whole shelled almonds
lemon slices

poaching liquid:

2 cups water
1 cup dry white wine
1 small carrot
1 small onion

½ teaspoon salt
6 black peppercorns
1 sprig parsley

Wash the sweetbreads and blanch them in boiling water for 3 or 4 minutes. Drain and trim them of any outer skin or connected tissue. Prepare the poaching liquid and bring it to a simmer. Poach the sweetbreads for about 20 minutes; drain, dry well, and cut them in two. Beat the eggs in a small bowl and put the bread crumbs into a separate, shallow dish. Dip the sweetbread pieces first in the crumbs, then in the egg, and then once again in the crumbs. Melt 2 tablespoons of the butter in a skillet and sauté the breaded sweetbreads for about 5 minutes on each side. When golden brown, place them in baked patty shells on a warm platter. When they are all cooked, wipe out the skillet and add the remaining 6 tablespoons of butter. Brown the almonds lightly in the butter, being very careful that the butter does not burn, and pour almonds and butter over the sweetbreads as a sauce. Garnish with lemon slices. (Serves 4)

BAKED PATTY SHELLS
(see index for Sunday-Morning Crescents variation)

GREEN-CORN PUDDING
(see index)

He passed the time until lunch going through catalogues, and at two-thirty p.m. with a veal cutlet and half a bushel of Fritz's best mixed salad stowed in the hold, he returned to the office and resumed with catalogues.   [INSTEAD OF EVIDENCE]

VEAL CUTLET

6 veal cutlets
1 cup bread crumbs
¼ cup freshly grated
    Parmesan cheese
¼ teaspoon paprika
½ teaspoon fresh orégano
    (or ¼ teaspoon dried leaves)

½ teaspoon fresh basil
    (or ¼ teaspoon dried leaves)
2 large eggs
3 tablespoons butter
3 tablespoons olive oil
lime wedges

Trim the cutlets and pound them thin between pieces of waxed paper. In a shallow dish combine the bread crumbs, cheese, paprika, orégano, and basil. Beat the eggs in a small bowl and dip the prepared cutlets first into the egg and then into the seasoned crumbs. Let the cutlets stand for about 10 minutes. Heat the butter and oil in a large skillet. Sauté the breaded cutlets until they are cooked to a golden brown on both sides. Turn only once, taking care not to dislodge the breading. Serve with lime wedges. (Serves 4 to 6)

> *Whatever your personal preferences, be advised never to ask, within Wolfe's hearing, to have an egg served on top of your veal cutlet. Archie drops the hint in the* THE SILENT SPEAKER: *"Confound it!" Wolfe burst out. He was as indignant and irritated as if he had been served a veal cutlet with an egg perched on it.*

FRITZ'S BEST MIXED SALAD
(see index for Salad with Devil's Rain Dressing)

> Wolfe, in the big chair with arms, at the far end of the table, had just started operating on an eight-inch ring of ham and sweetbread mousse.   [MIGHT AS WELL BE DEAD]

HAM AND SWEETBREAD MOUSSE

3 pairs veal sweetbreads	4 egg whites, beaten stiff
1 cup water	2½ cups heavy cream
1 cup dry white wine	½ pound mushrooms
½ pound boiled Georgia ham	3 tablespoons butter
salt and pepper to taste	1 teaspoon minced onion
1 small onion, grated	2 tablespoons flour
2 tablespoons grated carrot	paprika
1 tablespoon minced fresh parsley	

Soak the sweetbreads in cold water for 1 hour, or blanch in boiling water for 3 or 4 minutes, and drain. Preheat oven to 325°. Return the sweetbreads to the pot and cover with the water and wine. Bring slowly to a boil and simmer for 5 minutes. Drain the sweetbreads and trim them. Continue to boil the poaching liquid until there are 1½ cups remaining. Chop one pair of sweetbreads and the ham coarsely and put them through the finest blade of a meat grinder. Add salt and pepper and the grated onion, carrot, and parsley. Mix well. Add the egg whites and blend well, and then slowly add the heavy cream, working the mixture with a wooden spoon into the consistency of a smooth mayonnaise. Put the mixture into a buttered ring mold and cover with foil. Set the mold in a pan of water and bake until set (about 40 minutes). Remove from the oven and allow to cool for 10 to 15 minutes. Invert the mold onto a warm serving dish. While the mousse is baking, chop the remaining sweetbreads into cubes. Slice and sauté the mushrooms in 2 tablespoons of the butter. Drain and reserve. Add the minced onion to the butter and cook until golden. Add the other tablespoon of butter and, when it has melted, add the flour. Cook for 2 minutes, stirring constantly, and gradually add the poaching liquid. Allow to simmer, stirring, until the mixture thickens. Season to taste. Add the mushrooms and the cubed sweetbreads and heat through. After the mousse is unmolded, pour the sauce into the center. Dust with paprika and serve. (Serves 4)

I took my seat, and Fritz came, and I helped myself to a healthy portion of broiled shad that had been marinated in oil and lemon juice seasoned with bay leaf, thyme, and orégano, and three ladles of puréed sorrel. I took only three ladles because at bedtime I would go to the kitchen, heat the leftover sorrel, spread it on a couple of slices of Fritz's bread, and sprinkle it with nutmeg. Serve with a glass of milk. Have a spoon handy to salvage the purée that dribbles onto the plate when you bite.

[A RIGHT TO DIE]

BROILED SHAD WITH SORREL SAUCE

3 pounds fresh shad fillets	1 grinding black pepper
1/3 cup olive oil	3 pounds fresh sorrel
juice of 1 large lemon	2 tablespoons butter
1 bay leaf	1 tablespoon minced shallots
2 sprigs fresh thyme	1 cup dry white wine
1/2 teaspoon fresh orégano	3/4 cup heavy cream
(or 1/4 teaspoon dried leaves)	salt and freshly ground
1/4 teaspoon salt	black pepper to taste

Marinate the shad in the oil and lemon juice, to which the bay leaf, thyme, orégano, salt, and pepper have been added. Let stand for 1 hour or more. Rinse the sorrel and boil it in a small amount of salted water 5 to 7 minutes until it is very tender. Drain it and rub through a sieve. In a saucepan melt the butter and sauté the shallots until they are golden.

Add the sorrel and the wine. Bring the mixture to a boil and cook for about 10 minutes. Add the cream and lower the heat, simmering the sauce for 5 minutes more. Season with salt and pepper. Makes about 2 cups of sauce. Drain and broil the shad for 7 or 8 minutes on each side under a high flame. Remove to a warm dish and pour the sauce over. (Serves 6)

FRITZ'S BREAD

2 cups milk	1 package yeast
2 tablespoons sugar	1/4 cup warm water
2 teaspoons salt	6 cups sifted
1 1/2 tablespoons	all-purpose flour
softened butter	

Heat the milk in a saucepan; when bubbles form around the edges, remove it from the heat and pour it into a mixing bowl. Add the sugar, salt, and butter. Soften the yeast in the warm water; let stand for 5 minutes until the yeast dissolves and pour into the milk mixture. Stir well, blending all ingredients. Stir in 3 cups of the flour and beat until smooth. Add the remaining flour and stir until a stiff dough is formed. Turn the dough out onto a floured board and knead until smooth and elastic—about 10 minutes. Place the dough ball in a lightly greased bowl and turn it once so that the top is coated with grease. Cover and allow the dough to rise in a warm place until it doubles in size—about 1 1/2 hours. Punch the dough down and allow it to rise once again. Cut it into two parts and shape them into loaves. Place each in a greased bread pan and cover with cloth. Allow to rise a third time, until double in bulk. Preheat the oven to 400°. Just before baking, brush the top of each loaf with a little melted butter. Bake for 40 to 45 minutes. If the tops brown too quickly, cover with aluminum foil. Serve warm with butter and preserves. (Makes 2 loaves)

Mark this recipe well. Archie, in THE MOTHER HUNT, *points out that if Fritz ever dies, Wolfe will probably never eat bread again.*

Wolfe and I moved across the hall to the dining room, to eat fried shrimp and Cape Cod clam cakes. With those items, Fritz serves a sour sauce thick with mushrooms which is habit-forming.

[AND BE A VILLAIN]

FRIED SHRIMP

1 pound fresh	dash nutmeg
medium-sized shrimp	1 large egg
1 cup all-purpose flour	½ cup beer
1½ teaspoons baking powder	oil for deep frying (at 375°)
½ teaspoon salt	

Shell and devein the shrimp. Simmer them in a little water for 3 or 4 minutes, drain, and set aside. Sift the dry ingredients together. Beat the egg with the beer and add to the flour, beating well. Set the mixture aside for 1 hour. Heat the oil. Dip each shrimp into the batter, drop them into the fat, and cook until brown.

CAPE COD CLAM CAKES

1½ cups fresh clams, drained	½ teaspoon fresh marjoram
4 large potatoes	(or ¼ teaspoon dried leaves)
½ cup heavy cream	1 teaspoon minced shallots
4 tablespoons butter	2 large eggs
salt and pepper to taste	oil for deep frying (at 375°)
½ teaspoon fresh orégano	lemon or lime wedges
(or ¼ teaspoon dried leaves)	

Mince the clams and set aside. Peel and dice the potatoes and cook in salted water until tender but not mushy. Drain and return them to the pan over hot flame, shaking the pan so that they dry but do not stick to the bottom. Remove from flame and mash thoroughly, so that no lumps remain, and add the cream, butter, salt, and pepper. Stir in the clams, orégano, marjoram, and shallots. Beat the eggs until they are frothy and blend them into the clams until they are completely incorporated. With your hands shape the mixture into twelve oval cakes and fry them, no more than 3 at a time, in the hot fat until they are golden brown. Garnish with lemon or lime wedges, and serve with sour sauce.

SOUR SAUCE

1 cup sour cream (see index)	1 tablespoon capers, marinated
¼ cup horse-radish	in ¼ cup red wine vinegar
1 tablespoon minced Italian	¼ pound mushrooms
parsley (or watercress)	2 tablespoons butter

Put the sour cream in a mixing bowl and stir in the horse-radish, parsley, and drained capers. Sauté the mushrooms, cleaned and sliced, in the butter. Drain and add to the sour sauce. (Makes 1½ cups)

I asked Wolfe, "What's for lunch?"

"Sweetbreads in béchamel sauce with truffle and chervil. Beet and watercress salad. Brie."

"If there's enough you may have some," I said and headed for the stairs.　　　　　　　　　　　　　　　　[THE MOTHER HUNT]

SWEETBREADS IN BÉCHAMEL SAUCE

1 whole black truffle	3 tablespoons
3 tablespoons sweet butter	all-purpose flour
3 pairs veal sweetbreads	sprigs of chervil

poaching liquid:

2 cups water	½ teaspoon salt
1 cup dry white wine	6 black peppercorns
1 small carrot	1 teaspoon fresh chervil
1 small onion	(or ½ teaspoon dried)

Sauté the truffle in a little of the butter and chop it very fine. Mix the truffle bits into the remaining butter, blend well, and set aside for 1 hour. Meanwhile, soak the sweetbreads in water for 1 hour, drain, and trim. Bring the poaching liquid to a simmer and poach the sweetbreads for about 20 minutes; drain, dry well, and cut into 1-inch pieces. Strain the broth and boil it until reduced slightly. Heat the truffle butter in a saucepan and add the flour. Cook for 2 minutes and pour in 1½ cups of poaching liquid, stirring constantly until the sauce is thickened. Mix the sweetbread pieces into the sauce and heat. Serve hot garnished with a few sprigs of fresh chervil. (Serves 4)

BEET AND WATERCRESS SALAD

1 pound fresh beets	freshly ground black pepper
½ cup wine tarragon vinegar	½ bunch watercress

Remove the greenery from the beets and discard (or use in another salad). Boil the unpeeled beets in salted water until tender but not too soft. Drain them, run them under cold water until cooled, and peel. Cut the beets into julienne slices and put into a bowl with the vinegar. Allow to chill in the refrigerator for at least 1 hour. Drain well and serve cold, sprinkled with pepper, on a bed of freshly washed watercress. (Serves 4)

VARIATION:

Before arranging the beets on the watercress, mix gently with a cup of sour cream (see index).

3

WARM-WEATHER DINNERS

That afternoon, preparing for one of Wolfe's favorite hot-weather meals, Fritz had been collecting eight baby lobsters, eight avocados, and a bushel of young leaf lettuce. When he had introduced them to the proper amounts of chives, onion, parsley, tomato paste, mayonnaise, salt, pepper, paprika, pimientos, and dry white wine, he would have Brazilian lobster salad as edited by Wolfe, and not even Wolfe could have it all stowed away by half past eight.*   [A WINDOW FOR DEATH]

BRAZILIAN LOBSTER SALAD

2 large ripe avocados	3 cups lobster meat
1½ tablespoons chopped fresh chives	2 heads young Bibb lettuce
1 tablespoon minced onion	1½ teaspoons tomato paste
1 tablespoon minced fresh parsley	¾ cup homemade mayonnaise (see following recipe)
½ teaspoon dry mustard	3 pimientos
6 tablespoons dry white wine	paprika

Peel the avocados, cut them in half lengthwise, and slice very thin. Put the slices into a stainless-steel bowl and sprinkle on the chives, onion, parsley, dry mustard, and wine. Refrigerate for 30 minutes or more. Pick over the lobster meat for bits of shell and wash and dry the lettuce leaves. Mix together the tomato paste and 4 tablespoons of the mayonnaise. Arrange the lettuce into round beds on 4 salad plates and place 1 tablespoon of the pink mayonnaise in the center of each. Top with the undrained slices of avocado. Mix the remaining mayonnaise with the lobster meat and heap this on top of the avocado. Slice the pimientos and arrange the slices on the lobster meat. Dust with paprika. (Serves 4)

* Dinner in the dining room is customarily served at seven-fifteen or seven-thirty.

MAYONNAISE

2 egg yolks	1 cup olive oil
½ teaspoon salt	1 cup good salad oil
1 teaspoon dry mustard	1 cup sour cream (see index)
¼ cup tarragon wine vinegar (or lime juice)	

Bring all ingredients to room temperature. In a large stainless-steel bowl beat the yolks with a whisk or electric hand beater until they are lemon-yellow. Add the salt, mustard, and half the vinegar (or lime juice). Combine the oils and, beating the eggs steadily, add the oil drop by drop. As the mixture thickens, add the oil in larger amounts until it is all incorporated. Do not overbeat. Add the remaining vinegar and beat it in quickly. The mayonnaise should not be stiff but soft. Fold in the sour cream and chill.

VARIATION:

Instead of sour cream, add 3 tablespoons of Dijon mustard and the juice of 1 lime to the mayonnaise. Fold in ½ cup of whipped heavy cream. Salt to taste.

At nine o'clock, when Doctor Frederick Buhl arrived, Wolfe and I were through in the dining room, having put away around four pounds of salmon mousse, Wolfe's own recipe, and a peck of summer salad.   [A WINDOW FOR DEATH]

SALMON MOUSSE

1 3-pound piece of fresh salmon	2 tablespoons grated onion
2 cups water	1 tablespoon minced fresh parsley
1 cup dry white wine	¼ cup minced green pepper
1 bay leaf	2 tablespoons diced pimiento
2 sprigs thyme	5 tablespoons butter
1 medium onion stuck with 2 cloves	5 tablespoons flour
juice of 1 lemon	salt and pepper to taste
⅓ cup bread crumbs	⅛ teaspoon powdered sage
½ teaspoon Worcestershire sauce	2 large eggs

Preheat the oven to 325°. Poach the salmon in a court bouillon consisting of the water and wine, to which the bay leaf, thyme, and onion with cloves have been added (about 20 to 30 minutes). Drain the salmon, reserving the stock, and remove skin and bones. Flake the meat and put it in a large mixing bowl with the lemon juice, bread crumbs, Worcestershire, onion, parsley, green pepper, and pimiento. Boil the fish stock until it is reduced to 1½ cups. Make a thick sauce with the butter, flour, and strained stock, seasoning it with salt, pepper, and sage. Blend it into the salmon mixture. Beat the eggs and incorporate them into the salmon. Pour the mixture into a greased baking pan or mold and set it in a pan of hot water. Bake for 45 minutes to 1 hour. When done, the mousse will be firm to the touch. Allow it to stand for 10 minutes, loosen the edges with the point of a knife, and invert onto a warm serving platter. Serve warm, or chilled with a dill sauce.

NOTE: Make the dill sauce by combining a cup of sour cream with a teaspoon of dill weed, a tablespoon of lemon juice, ½ teaspoon parsley, and salt to taste.

SUMMER SALAD

dandelion greens	chicory
watercress	1 cup sour cream (see index)
Belgian endive	1 tablespoon tomato purée
Swiss chard	2 medium ripe tomatoes
collard greens	1 tablespoon chopped chives

Wash all the fresh greens in cold water and dry on a clean cloth or towel. Tear the greens into small pieces, and arrange them in a salad bowl. Mix the sour cream with the tomato purée in a small mixing bowl; beat until creamy and pour over the greens. Toss the salad until the greens are well coated with dressing. Garnish with tomatoes, cut in wedges, and sprinkle the chives over the top.

Although Inspector Cramer spends a good deal of time in the red chair in the old brownstone, he does not often join Wolfe and Archie for meals. Archie does not usually miss the opportunity to make him regret this. In BLOOD WILL TELL, *Archie tells him over the telephone,* "I could come down after dinner. We're having lobsters, simmered in white wine with tarragon, and a white-wine sauce with the tomalley and coral. . . ."

LOBSTERS WITH WHITE-WINE SAUCE

4½ cups dry white wine	4 live lobsters
2 quarts water	(1½ to 2 pounds each)
3 sprigs fresh tarragon	1½ cup chopped mushrooms
1 large onion	2 tablespoons butter
1 lemon, quartered	2 tablespoons
1 stalk celery	all-purpose flour
1 bay leaf	½ cup heavy cream

Put 4 cups of the wine and the water into a large kettle and add the tarragon, onion, lemon, celery, and bay leaf. Bring the liquid to a boil and plunge the lobsters in, head first. Lower the heat and simmer for 15 to 20 minutes. Move the lobsters around in the kettle occasionally. When they are done, remove and drain. Cut the lobsters in half by slitting the undershell down the middle with a sharp knife and crack the claws. Remove and discard the dark vein in the tail and the sac near the head. Reserve the green liver (tomalley) and roe (coral), if any. Keep the lobsters warm. Strain the lobster bouillon and reserve 3 cups. Boil 1 cup of the bouillon over a high flame until it is reduced by half. Add the chopped mushrooms and the remaining ½ cup of white wine, and boil again until the liquid is reduced by half again. Remove from the heat, strain, and keep it warm. In another saucepan melt the butter and when it is frothy add the flour. Mix well and cook until the flour turns a golden brown. Slowly add the remaining 2 cups of bouillon, stirring constantly. Cook until the sauce thickens. Crush the tomalley and coral in a mortar and add to the sauce. Simmer the sauce for another 5 minutes. Add the mushroom-wine liquid, and simmer for another few minutes until thoroughly heated. Remove from heat and stir in the cream. Spoon a tablespoon of sauce over the cut side of each half lobster and glaze under the broiler for a minute or so. Serve the rest of the sauce separately. (Serves 4 to 6)

Wolfe was dishing shrimp from a steaming casserole. . . . "This shrimp Bordelaise is without onions but has some garlic. I think an improvement, but Fritz and I invite your opinion."

[MURDER IS CORNY]

SHRIMP BORDELAISE

2 pounds fresh shrimp	1 bay leaf
2 tablespoons butter	1 teaspoon salt
1 carrot, finely chopped	$\frac{1}{2}$ cup dry white wine
2 shallots, minced	$\frac{1}{4}$ cup cognac
1 clove garlic, minced	1 teaspoon all-purpose flour
1 sprig parsley	1 tablespoon sweet butter

Shell, devein, and wash the shrimp. Melt the butter in a large, heavy saucepan. Cook the carrot, shallots, garlic, parsley, and bay leaf over low heat for about 15 minutes, stirring occasionally. Do not allow the mixture to brown. Add the shrimp, salt, wine, and cognac, and raise the heat until the liquid comes to a boil. Regulate the heat so that the liquid simmers gently and cook the shrimp for 6 to 7 minutes, shaking the pan frequently. Remove the shrimp to a warm serving plate and discard the bay leaf and parsley. Reduce the liquid in the pan over a high heat to half its original quantity. Cream together the flour and the sweet butter and add to the liquid. Cook the sauce for 3 to 4 minutes until thickened, and pour it over the shrimp. (Serves 4 to 6)

VARIATION:

Omit garlic and substitute 1 tablespoon of minced onion, in order to judge the above improvement fairly.

Fritz was there with the stuffed clams, and Wolfe sat and took the spoon and fork. He couldn't have sat before giving me instructions because that would have been talking business during a meal, and by heck a rule is a rule is a rule. . . . As I helped myself to clams I held my breath, because if you smell them, mixed with the shallots, chives, chervil, mushrooms, bread crumbs, sherry, and dry white wine, you take so many that you don't leave enough room for the duckling. . . .

[THE FINAL DEDUCTION]

STUFFED CLAMS

3 dozen cherrystone clams	1 tablespoon minced chives
1 cup fresh bread crumbs	1 teaspoon fresh chervil
3 tablespoons minced shallots	(or $\frac{1}{2}$ teaspoon dried leaves)
	(Continued)

1 teaspoon fresh orégano
  (or ¼ teaspoon dried leaves)
1 teaspoon fresh basil
  (or ½ teaspoon dried leaves)
½ teaspoon freshly ground
  black pepper

2 teaspoons dry sherry
4 tablespoons minced
  mushrooms
2 tablespoons butter
clam broth or dry white wine
4 slices bacon

Preheat the oven to 375°. Scrub the clams. Put them in a large kettle with about half an inch of water. Cover the kettle and cook over a medium flame until all the shells open. Remove the clams and save the liquid. Remove the meat and save half the shells. Mince the clams and put them in a bowl with bread crumbs, shallots, chives, chervil, orégano, basil, pepper, and sherry. Sauté the mushrooms in 1 tablespoon of butter for 2 minutes and add to the clams, along with enough clam broth or dry white wine to moisten the mixture. Butter the shells and fill them with the clam mixture. Cut the bacon into 18 small pieces and put 1 on top of each shell. Bake until the clams are golden brown and the bacon is crisp. (Serves 4 to 6 as a first course)

It was only ten minutes to dinnertime when I got home, so the verbatim report had to wait until we had taken on the curried beef roll, celery and cantaloupe salad, and blueberry grunt, and had gone to the office for coffee.   [THE FATHER HUNT]

CURRIED BEEF ROLL

8 slices top round of beef,
  ½ inch thick
salt and pepper to taste
½ pound fresh spinach
1 cup cooked rice
4 tablespoons raisins
1½ teaspoons curry powder
¼ cup dry vermouth

dash nutmeg
2 tablespoons butter
½ to 1 cup strong beef broth
¼ teaspoon thyme
1 bay leaf
garnish: glazed carrots and
  watercress

Trim the beef. Put the slices of beef between pieces of waxed paper and flatten them with a mallet. Season with salt and pepper. Wash and trim the spinach and remove the thick stems. Bring a small amount of salted water to a boil and add the spinach. When it boils again, cook for 2 minutes. Drain the spinach in a colander and squeeze it as dry as possible. Chop very fine. Put it in a mixing bowl and add the rice, raisins, curry powder, and vermouth. Mix well and spoon it onto each slice of beef. Season with more salt and pepper and a dash of nutmeg. Roll up each slice and fasten with toothpicks or butcher's cord. Sauté rolls in skillet in the butter. When browned on all sides, lower heat and add broth, ½ bay leaf, ¼ teaspoon thyme. Cover skillet and braise gently 25 to 30 minutes, or until tender. When they are done, remove to a warm serving plate and garnish with glazed carrots and watercress. (Serves 4)

CELERY AND CANTALOUPE SALAD

2 tablespoons wine	¼ cup currant jelly
tarragon vinegar	3 celery hearts
6 tablespoons olive oil	1 small ripe cantaloupe
¼ teaspoon salt	1 tablespoon chopped chives
⅛ teaspoon freshly ground	½ teaspoon poppy seeds
black pepper	½ teaspoon coriander seeds

Put the first 4 ingredients in a jar and shake well. Heat the currant jelly and blend into the dressing; set the mixture aside. Wash and dry the celery hearts and slice them thin. Peel the cantaloupe and cut it into ½-inch cubes. Combine celery hearts and cantaloupe in a salad bowl and toss them very gently with the dressing. Sprinkle the chives, poppy seeds, and coriander seeds over the top and toss again. (Serves 4)

BLUEBERRY GRUNT   (see index)

I got home just at the dinner hour, seven-thirty, and since it takes an earthquake to postpone a meal in that house, and no mention of business is permitted at the table, my full report of the afternoon had to wait. If the main dish had been something like goulash or calves' brains probably nothing unusual in my technique would have been apparent, but it was squabs, which of course have to be gnawed off the bones, and while I was working on the second one, Wolfe demanded, "What the deuce is the matter with you?"

"Nothing. What?"

"You're not eating, you're nibbling."

"Yeah. Broken jaw. With the compliments of Ann Horne."

He stared. "A *woman* broke your jaw?"

"Sorry, no shoptalk at meals. I'll tell you later."

[WHEN A MAN MURDERS]

SQUABS WITH SAUSAGE AND SAUERKRAUT

2 tablespoons butter	3 medium carrots
12 slices Canadian bacon	3 medium yellow onions
6 cups sauerkraut	6 to 10 link herb sausages
(2½ to 3 pounds)	(see index)
3 squabs	2 cups consommé (see index)
1 bouquet garni consisting of 1	1 cup dry white wine (or more)
bay leaf, 1 sprig parsley, 1	
sprig thyme or fennel, 1 stalk	
celery	

Rub the bottom of a large casserole or Dutch oven with the butter and line it with half the bacon. Drain the sauerkraut well and arrange it on top of the bacon. Clean and split the squabs in two and place on top of the sauerkraut, overlapping them slightly if necessary. Add the bouquet garni. Peel and slice the carrots and onions and distribute them over the top, putting the sausages in last with the remaining slices of bacon. Pour in the consommé and enough white wine so that the mixture is half submerged. Cover the casserole tightly and simmer on a low heat for 1¾ to 2 hours. When the squabs are tender, drain the casserole of liquid and discard the bouquet garni. Arrange the sauerkraut in the center of a large heated platter and surround it with the bacon and sausage. Put the squab on top and serve with boiled potatoes. (Serves 6)

There was no point in spoiling his dinner, so I waited until after we had finished with the poached and truffled broilers and broccoli and stuffed potatoes with herbs, and salad and cheese, and Fritz had brought the coffee to us in the office.

[FOURTH OF JULY PICNIC]

POACHED AND TRUFFLED BROILERS

2 quarts water	2 teaspoons salt
2 cups dry white wine	2 broilers,
1½ pounds veal bones	1½ to 2 pounds each
1 carrot, chopped	2 truffles
1 stalk celery, chopped	2 tablespoons butter
1 medium onion, chopped	2 tablespoons
2 sprigs parsley	all-purpose flour
1 bay leaf	salt and pepper to taste

Combine the water, wine, and veal bones in a large kettle. Add the carrot, celery, and onion to the pot, along with the parsley, bay leaf, and salt. Simmer for 1½ hours. Meantime, using your fingers, loosen the skin from the breast meat of each broiler. Slice the truffles very thin and insert the slices under the skin so that they form a straight line over each side of both breasts. Salt the cavities and truss the broilers. When the stock is cooked, strain it and return it to the pot with the chickens. Bring the liquid to a simmer and poach the birds for 40 to 45 minutes until the meat is tender but not falling from the bone. Remove, drain, and cool the birds for at least 5 minutes. Split the broilers in half down the backbone and arrange them, overlapping, on a warm platter decorated with sprigs of parsley and surrounded with alternating pieces of broccoli and herbed stuffed potatoes. Reduce about 3 cups of the broth by half over a high heat and make a thick sauce using 2 tablespoons each of butter and flour. Strain. Season to taste. (Serves 4)

BROCCOLI

¼ cup olive oil	5 cups broccoli flowerets
2 cloves garlic, mashed	1½ cups dry white wine
¼ cup minced mushrooms	salt and pepper to taste

In a large skillet, heat the olive oil. Sauté the garlic in the oil for 1 or 2 minutes. Add the mushrooms and cook for another minute. Then add the broccoli, tossing it quickly so that each piece is coated with oil. Pour the wine over the broccoli and add salt and pepper. Stir gently and cook for 3 to 5 minutes, uncovered. Then cover the skillet and simmer until the broccoli is tender—about 5 minutes longer. Remove the broccoli to the serving platter and boil the remaining liquid until it is reduced by half. Pour over the broccoli.

HERBED STUFFED POTATOES

2 large potatoes	2 teaspoons chopped
4 tablespoons butter	fresh chives
¼ cup heavy cream	1 teaspoon chopped
½ teaspoon dry mustard	fresh tarragon (or
1 teaspoon fresh chervil	½ teaspoons dried leaves)
(or ½ teaspoon dried leaves)	salt and pepper to taste
2 teaspoons chopped	
fresh parsley	

Preheat oven to 325°. Rub the potatoes with a little butter and poke with a fork. Bake them for an hour, or until done. Cut in half lengthwise and scoop out the potato into a bowl, taking care not to break the skins. Add the remaining ingredients (reserving 1 tablespoon of butter) to the potatoes and mix thoroughly. Return the mixture to the potato skins and dot the top of each with a bit of butter. Run the potatoes under the broiler to brown the tops.

When I returned to the office Wolfe wasn't there, and I found him in the kitchen, lifting the lid from a steaming casserole of lamb cutlets with gammon and tomatoes. It smelled good enough to eat.   [THE GOLDEN SPIDERS]

LAMB CUTLETS

6 lamb cutlets	6 green tomatoes, sliced
6 tablespoons butter	1 teaspoon salt
1 pound center-cut ham steak	1 tablespoon fresh basil
1 stalk celery, sliced	(or 1 teaspoon dried leaves)
2 medium yellow onions, sliced	½ cup dry white wine
2 medium carrots, sliced	½ cup water

Ask the butcher to cut the lamb cutlets from the leg about ½ inch thick and to cut each piece in half. Preheat the oven to 375°. In a large casserole, melt half the butter and brown the cutlets very quickly on both sides. Remove to a warm dish. Cut the ham steak into julienne strips and brown them in the casserole, to which you have added the remaining butter. Remove the ham and drain. Brown the celery, onions, and carrots lightly in the butter and remove. Discard the butter if it has turned brown and add 2 tablespoons more. Line the bottom of the casserole with half the lamb cutlets; then add alternating layers of the vegetables, ham, slices of green tomatoes, and lamb until the casserole is full. The tomatoes should be on the top layer. Add the water and the wine. Sprinkle with salt and basil. Bake at 375° for 45 minutes, or until the tomatoes are tender when pierced with a fork. Serve from the casserole. (Serves 6)

Wolfe always enjoys his food, whether in spite of circumstances or in harmony with them, and after ten thousand meals with him

I know all the shades. The way he spreads pâté on a cracker, the way he picks up the knife to slice the filet of beef in aspic, the way he uses his fork on the salad, the way he makes his choice from the cheese platter—no question about it, this time he had something or somebody by the tail, or at least the tail was in sight.   [IF DEATH EVER SLEPT]

FILET OF BEEF IN ASPIC

4 to 5 pounds boneless beef filet
½ cup sliced carrots
½ cup sliced yellow onions
1 stalk celery, sliced
1 bay leaf
2 sprigs parsley
1 tablespoon salt
5 cups dry white wine

4 to 6 tablespoons oil
2 veal knuckles
    or 2 calves' feet, split
1½ tablespoons gelatin
3 cups brown stock
salt and freshly ground
    black pepper

Marinate the beef overnight in a marinade made of the carrots, onions, celery, bay leaf, parsley, salt, and white wine. Wipe the meat dry and brown it in the oil in a large casserole, turning it every few minutes. Remove the beef, discard the oil, and pour in the marinade. Return the meat to the pan and add the veal knuckles or calves' feet. Simmer over a low heat for 3½ hours, or until the meat is very tender. Turn the meat occasionally. When it is done, transfer the meat and knuckles to a cutting board and allow to cool. Skim off the fat from the braising liquid and strain it through a fine sieve. Pour the liquid into a saucepan and reduce it rapidly to 3 cups. (This step may not be necessary if the liquid has reduced sufficiently during cooking.) Add the gelatin to the brown stock and stir until it is softened. Pour it into the braising liquid and cook over a low heat until all the gelatin has dissolved. Check the seasoning and add salt and pepper if necessary. Let the stock sit for a few minutes while you slice the beef and cut the knuckle meat into julienne strips. Pour the stock into a large pan or mold until the liquid is 1 inch deep. Chill until the gelatin is almost set. At this point you may decorate the aspic by arranging previously cooked slices of carrots, peas, or string beans in some sort of design. Fill the mold with alternating layers of sliced beef and knuckle meat and aspic. Wait for a few minutes between each layer so that the aspic has a chance to set slightly. When the final layer is complete, pour in the remaining aspic and chill until firm, about 4 to 6 hours.

NOTE: If veal knuckles or calves' feet are not available, add another 1½ tablespoons of gelatin to the brown stock.

After lunch I hung around the kitchen for a while, listening to Wolfe and Fritz Brenner, the chef and household jewel, arguing whether horse mackerel is as good as Mediterranean tunny fish for *vitello tonnato*—which, as prepared by Fritz, is the finest thing on earth to do with tender young veal. . . . The argument finally began to bore me because there was no Mediterranean tunny fish to be had anyhow.   [AND BE A VILLAIN]

VITELLO TONNATO

2 7-ounce cans tuna fish
1 5-pound leg of veal,
    boned and rolled
2 medium onions, chopped
2 medium carrots, chopped
2 stalks celery, chopped
1 2-ounce can anchovy
    fillets
3 to 4 leaves fresh basil (or ½
    teaspoon dried leaves)

2 cloves garlic
1 cup white wine
½ teaspoon freshly ground
    black pepper
2 egg yolks
½ cup olive oil
lemon juice to taste
capers
lemon slices

Pour the oil from the tuna into a deep casserole or Dutch oven and heat, browning the veal quickly on all sides. Add the onions, carrots, and celery to the pot with the tuna fish and anchovies, basil, garlic, white wine, and pepper. Cover and simmer for about 2 hours, or until the veal is perfectly tender. When the meat is done, remove to a platter and allow to cool. Put the cooking juices, fish, and vegetables in a blender (or through a food mill) until smooth. Chill. When ready to serve, beat the egg yolks well with a whisk and gradually add the olive oil, beating constantly, until a mayonnaise consistency is achieved. Add the purée of tuna, cooking juices, and vegetables gradually and continue beating until the sauce is creamy and thick. Correct the seasoning, add lemon juice, and chill. Slice the veal and arrange the slices on a platter. Pour the sauce over the meat and garnish with lemon slices and capers. (Serves 6 to 8)

NOTE: Horse mackerel or Mediterranean tunny fish may be substituted for the tuna fish, and olive oil may be used in place of the tuna-fish oil.

4
COLD-WEATHER DINNERS

At the dinner table, in between bits of deviled grilled lamb kidneys with a sauce he and Fritz had invented, he explained why it was that all you needed to know about any human society was what they ate. If you knew what they ate you could deduce everything else—culture, philosophy, morals, politics, everything. I enjoyed it because the kidneys were tender and tasty and that sauce is one of Fritz's best, but I wondered how you would make out if you tried to deduce everything about Wolfe by knowing what he had eaten in the past ten years. I decided you would deduce that he was dead.   [THE FINAL DEDUCTION]

GRILLED LAMB KIDNEYS

8 lamb kidneys	½ teaspoon dry mustard
½ cup olive oil	⅛ teaspoon mace
½ teaspoon salt	4 tablespoons butter
2 grindings fresh black pepper	dash Tabasco
1 teaspoon fresh chopped thyme (or ½ teaspoon dried leaves)	1 tablespoon Worcestershire sauce
	few grains cayenne pepper
	juice of 1 lemon

Wash kidneys, remove skin, and trim off fat. Split and marinate them in a mixture of the oil, salt, pepper, thyme, dry mustard, and mace. Let stand for 30 minutes or more. Preheat broiler. Put the kidneys on skewers and broil them 5 minutes on the skin side. Mix the butter with the Tabasco, Worcestershire, cayenne, and lemon juice. After the kidneys have been cooked on one side, remove from oven and brush with the seasoned butter. Return to broiler, and broil for 3 minutes on the cut side. Remove and brush again with butter, and arrange them on a hot platter. Collect the drippings and add the remaining butter. Stir until the sauce is thoroughly blended and pour over the kidneys. Serve immediately. (Serves 4)

> *Archie describes this dish in some detail in* GAMBIT, *where it is served for lunch to Wolfe, Archie, and a client. Wolfe's mood on that occasion is such that the kidneys aren't appreciated, only chewed and swallowed. As Archie says,* "They might as well have been served to Voltaire." *And everyone knows that Voltaire* "all his life was extremely skinny and in his later years he was merely a skeleton. To call him a great man was absurd; strictly speaking, he wasn't a man at all, since he had no palate and a dried-up stomach. He was a remarkable word-assembly plant, but he wasn't a man, let alone a great man."

═══════════════════════════════════

I couldn't eat early because Fritz was braising a wild turkey and had to convey it to the dining room on a platter for Wolfe to see whole before wielding the knife. Sometimes when I have a date for a game or a show I get things from the refrigerator around six-thirty and take my time, but I wanted some of that hot turkey, not to mention Fritz's celery sauce and corn fritters.

[THE BLACK MOUNTAIN]

BRAISED WILD TURKEY

1 wild turkey	1 bay leaf
4 to 6 slices of pork fat	1 teaspoon fresh rosemary
1 carrot, chopped	(or ½ teaspoon dried
1 onion, chopped	leaves)
2 sprigs parsley	2 cups chicken broth
1 stalk celery, chopped	2 cups dry white wine
1 teaspoon fresh thyme	
(or ½ teaspoon dried	
leaves)	

Preheat the oven to 425°. Clean and truss the turkey so that the legs and wings are held close to the body. Arrange the slices of pork fat over the bird and secure with butcher's cord. (If you prefer, you may use a double layer of cheesecloth saturated with melted butter.) Roast the turkey at 425° for 40 to 45 minutes. Remove the pork slices for the last 15 minutes. Lower the heat to 375° and add the remaining ingredients to the pan (the carrot, onion, parsley, celery, thyme, bay leaf, rosemary, broth, and wine). Cook for 2 to 3 more hours until the turkey is done, basting the bird every 20 minutes. Add more broth or wine as needed. The turkey is done if the juice runs clear when pricked with a fork.

CELERY SAUCE

3 stalks celery, chopped	2 tablespoons butter
1 onion studded with	2 tablespoons
two cloves	all-purpose flour
1 bay leaf	1¼ cups milk
2 sprigs parsley	salt and pepper to taste
1 cup chicken broth	
(or strained turkey broth)	

Put the celery stalks in a saucepan with the onion, bay leaf, parsley, and chicken or turkey broth. Simmer until the celery is tender, about 15 to 20 minutes. Drain (reserve the liquid) and purée the celery in a blender or force through a food mill. Melt the butter in a saucepan, add the flour, cook for a couple of minutes, and gradually add the milk, stirring until the sauce begins to thicken. Season with salt and pepper and simmer for about 10 minutes, stirring occasionally. Add the puréed celery. If the sauce is too thick, add some of the liquid the celery was cooked in. Correct the seasoning.

NOTE: You may use half celery stock and half milk instead of all milk in making the white sauce.

> *This same turkey dish was also served cold as a snack in* THE BLACK MOUNTAIN: In the kitchen Fritz greeted us by putting down his magazine, leaving his chair, telling Wolfe, "Starving the live will not profit the dead," and going to open the refrigerator door.
>
> "The turkey," Wolfe said, "and the cheese and pineapple. I've never heard that before. Montaigne?"
>
> "No, sir." Fritz put the turkey on the table, uncovered it, got the slicer, and handed it to Wolfe. "I made it up. I knew you would have to send for me, or come, and I wished to have an appropriate remark ready for you."
>
> "I congratulate you." Wolfe was wielding the knife. "To be taken for Montaigne is a peak few men can reach."

CORN FRITTERS (see index)

Fritz was at the big table, spreading anchovy butter on shad roe.
"Cross me off for dinner," I told him. "I'm doing my good deed
for the year and getting it over with."

He stopped spreading it to look at me. "That's too bad. Veal
birds in casserole. You know, with mushrooms and white wine."

[CHAMPAGNE FOR ONE]

VEAL BIRDS IN CASSEROLE

8 thin slices of veal
(about 3 × 5 inches)
1 cup chopped cooked chicken
1 tablespoon minced chives
½ cup bread crumbs
¼ cup freshly grated
Parmesan cheese
1 teaspoon fresh orégano
(or ¼ teaspoon dried leaves)
2 or 3 large eggs
1 teaspoon salt

½ teaspoon freshly ground
black pepper
6 tablespoons butter (or more)
18 button mushrooms
¼ cup diced onion
1¼ cups dry white wine
1 cup chopped tomatoes,
drained
4 leaves fresh basil
(or ½ teaspoon dried leaves)

Put the veal slices between sheets of waxed paper and pound them flat
with a mallet. Make a stuffing by mixing the chicken, chives, bread
crumbs, cheese, orégano, 2 eggs, salt, and pepper together. Add another
egg if the mixture seems too dry. Spread a little stuffing on each of the
veal slices. Roll each slice and secure with a piece of cord. Preheat the
oven to 350°. Melt the butter in a casserole on top of the stove over a
medium flame. Sauté the veal birds until they are brown on all sides.
Remove each bird as it is done. When they are all browned, add the
onions and mushrooms to the butter and brown lightly. (Add more
butter if necessary.) Add the wine to deglaze the pan, scraping the
bottom with a wooden spoon to loosen any browned bits, and add the
tomatoes and basil. Stir and simmer for 10 minutes. Return the veal
birds to the pan and baste with the liquid. Bake for 45 minutes, covered.
Remove the birds to a hot serving platter. Correct the seasoning for the
sauce left in the casserole and pour over the meat. If most of the liquid
has evaporated during the cooking time, add another cup of wine and
warm the sauce thoroughly, stirring constantly.

*It is rare that Archie allows personal matters to interfere with
business, but sometimes it just can't be helped:* My prompt ap-

pearance at the scene of a homicide would arouse all of Purley's worst instincts, backed up by reference to various precedents, and I might not get home in time for dinner, which was going to be featured by grilled squabs with a sauce which Fritz calls *Vénitienne* and is one of his best. [DIE LIKE A DOG]

SQUABS WITH SAUCE VÉNITIENNE

6 squabs
1 cup olive oil
4 tablespoons chopped fresh parsley
1 tablespoon chopped fresh chervil (or 1 teaspoon dried leaves)

1 tablespoon fresh tarragon (or 1 teaspoon dried leaves)
1 teaspoon salt
¼ teaspoon freshly ground black pepper

Split each squab down the back without separating the halves. Flatten them with the palm of your hand by gently pressing on the breastbone. Marinate them for 30 to 45 minutes in a marinade composed of the remaining ingredients. Ten minutes before cooking time, preheat the broiler. Put the skin side down first and brush the birds with some of the marinade. Grill for 10 to 15 minutes. Turn and brush on some more marinade. Broil for another 10 or 15 minutes until the squabs are done. Serve with sauce Vénitienne. (Serves 4 to 6)

SAUCE VÉNITIENNE

2½ cups clam juice
¾ cup dry white wine
1½ tablespoons butter
1½ tablespoons flour
1½ teaspoons tomato paste
¼ cup tarragon vinegar
1 tablespoon minced shallots
1 tablespoon chopped fresh parsley

1 grinding of black pepper
3 egg yolks
1 teaspoon fresh chervil (or ½ teaspoon dried leaves)
1 teaspoon fresh tarragon (or ½ teaspoon dried leaves)
1½ tablespoons minced truffles (optional)

In a saucepan mix the clam juice and ½ cup of the white wine. Boil rapidly and reduce the amount by half. Make a *beurre manié* with the butter and flour and add it to the broth. Add the tomato paste, stir, and simmer for 5 minutes. The mixture will start to thicken; stir constantly. In a separate saucepan heat the remaining ¼ cup of wine, the vinegar, shallots, parsley, and black pepper. Boil rapidly and reduce in volume by half. Add to the clam juice–wine sauce and bring to a simmer. Remove from heat and add the egg yolks 1 at a time, beating well after each addition. Return the sauce to the heat and simmer for about 10 minutes *very slowly*, stirring constantly. Strain the sauce and return it to the saucepan. Stir in the chervil, tarragon, and truffles. Heat for a moment, correct seasoning, and serve with grilled squab.

It is more often the case that Archie must forgo Fritz's excellent meals for reasons of business, however, and he never fails to point out his sacrifice when the opportunity arises: "Friday afternoon," I said, "day before yesterday, Orrie phoned and asked me to meet him that evening. You may remember that I wasn't here to help with the capon Souvaroff, which I regretted."
[DEATH OF A DOXY]

CAPON SOUVAROFF

1½ cups *pâté de foie gras*	4 to 6 very thin slices of pork fat
8 whole black truffles	½ cup brown sauce (see below)
3 ounces cognac	½ cup Madeira
2 tablespoons truffle juice	1 cup all-purpose flour
1 capon, weighing 9 to 10 pounds	

Preheat oven to 425°. Mix together the *pâté*, 4 of the truffles, chopped very fine, cognac, and truffle juice. Wash the capon, dry it carefully, and stuff the body cavity with the *pâté* mixture. Slice 2 of the truffles very thin so that there are about 8 to 10 slices. With your fingers, gently loosen the breast skin and arrange the truffle slices down the breast of each bird under the skin. Tie the legs close to the body and tuck the wing tips behind the back of the bird. Place the thin slices of pork over the breast and tie them down with cord. Put the capon on its side in a roasting pan and roast at 425° for 10 minutes. Turn to the other side and cook for another 10 minutes. Take great care not to break the skin. Set the bird upright and cook for 10 minutes more; then reduce the heat to 375° and cook for 1½ hours, basting every 20 minutes with pan drippings. When the capon is done, the juice will run clear when the bird is pricked with a fork. Remove to a large casserole. Skim the fat from the roasting pan and pour the juices into a saucepan. Add the brown sauce, remaining truffles, and Madeira and simmer for 5 minutes. Pour over the capon. While the sauce is still simmering, make a stiff pastry dough with the flour and a little water. Roll it out and cover the top of the casserole with the dough, sealing the edges. Raise the oven heat to 425°, put the casserole in the oven, and bake for 20 minutes. When done, bring the casserole to the table. Unseal the crust and the perfume of truffle sauce will fill the room. (Serves 6 to 8)

BROWN SAUCE

¼ cup butter	2 cups strong beef stock
6 tablespoons all-purpose flour	salt and pepper to taste

Melt the butter in a pan and allow to cook slowly until it has turned brown. Do not let it burn. Add the flour and cook for 1 or 2 minutes. Gradually add the beef stock (or canned beef bouillon) and stir constantly until the sauce thickens. Season with salt and pepper to taste. (Makes 1¾ cups)

Business is taboo at the dinner table, but crime and criminals aren't, and the Rosenberg case hogged the conversation all through the anchovy fritters, partridge in casserole with no olives in the sauce, cucumber mousse, and Creole curds and cream.
[DEATH OF A DOXY]

ANCHOVY FRITTERS

1 cup all-purpose flour	oil for deep frying (at 375°)
¾ cup beer .	fresh parsley sprigs
½ teaspoon salt	black olives
1 small onion	lemon wedges
2 dozen fresh anchovies	

Make a batter by mixing the flour, beer, and salt. Grate the onion and add that, mixing well. Let the batter stand for 5 minutes. Clean and dry the fresh anchovies. Do not remove the heads. Heat the oil. Dip each anchovy into the batter and fry until golden (about 3 to 5 minutes). Drain on paper towels and serve on a bed of fresh parsley garnished with black olives and lemon wedges. (Serves 4 to 6 as a first course)

PARTRIDGE IN CASSEROLE (see index for Perdrix en Casserole)

CUCUMBER MOUSSE

3 large cucumbers
¼ cup dry white wine
1 tablespoon grated onion
1 teaspoon salt
½ teaspoon freshly ground
    black pepper

½ cup mayonnaise (see index)
1 envelope gelatin
2 tablespoons hot water
½ cup heavy cream
4 tablespoons wine vinegar
2 pimientos

Seed 2 of the cucumbers and chop them coarsely. Do not peel. Put the pieces through a fine sieve or purée them in a blender. Add the wine, onion, salt, pepper, and mayonnaise to the purée and mix lightly. Soften the gelatin in the hot water and add it to the cucumber mixture. Whip the cream until stiff and fold it into the mousse. Pour into an oiled, chilled timbale mold or 4 individual molds. Chill until firm. In the meantime, marinate thin slices of the remaining cucumber in the vinegar. Unmold the mousse on a chilled platter and garnish with the marinated slices of cucumber and pimiento strips. (Serves 4)

CREOLE CURDS AND CREAM (see index)

Orrie Cather and Saul Panzer, as Wolfe's steadfast associates, are occasionally invited to dinner, but sometimes they only hear about what is being served. In DEATH OF A DOXY, *Saul misses onion soup and Kentucky Burgoo by a hair, though there was undoubtedly enough of the latter to feed a small army.*

ONION SOUP (see index)

KENTUCKY BURGOO

2 pounds beef cut from the
    shank (plus the bones)
½ pound lamb shoulder, boned
1 medium chicken, disjointed
1 tablespoon salt

1 teaspoon freshly ground
    black pepper
1 small pod red pepper,
    chopped
2 cups peeled, diced potatoes

2 cups diced onions

2 cups fresh butter beans

3 carrots, diced

2 green peppers, seeded and
   diced

3 cups corn cut from the cob

2 cups diced okra

12 tomatoes, seeded and peeled

1 clove garlic

1 cup minced fresh parsley

Put the beef, lamb, and chicken, together with the bones, into a large soup kettle and cover with water. Add salt, black pepper, and red pepper. Bring the water to a boil, reduce the heat, and simmer for about 2 hours, covered. Add the potatoes and onions; and at intervals of 10 minutes, add the butter beans, carrots, green peppers, and corn. After adding the corn, simmer for 2 more hours, or until the mixture is very thick. Watch it carefully and stir occasionally so that it does not stick. Add more water from time to time if necessary, but use as little as possible. Add the okra, tomatoes, and garlic and simmer for another hour, or until these vegetables are done and blended with the others. Remove the pot from the stove and stir in the parsley. This soup improves by standing and can be kept for a long time in the refrigerator. It is delicious when reheated. (Serves 8 to 10)

Fritz entered at eight o'clock to announce dinner, the main item of which was a dish called by Wolfe and Fritz "cassoulet Castelnaudary," but by me boiled beans. I admit they were my favorite beans, which is saying something. The only thing that restrained me at all was my advance knowledge of the pumpkin pie to come.

[INSTEAD OF EVIDENCE]

CASSOULET CASTELNAUDARY

2 cups dried white beans
   (Great Northern)

¼ pound salt pork, sliced thin

1 medium onion stuck with
   2 cloves

1 medium carrot, sliced

4 cloves garlic

2 bay leaves

4 sprigs thyme

4 sprigs parsley

1 pound loin of pork

1 pound loin of mutton

2 tablespoons oil or bacon fat

1 cup sliced onions

1 cup strong beef stock
   (or more)

2 tablespoons tomato purée

3 pieces bacon rind

freshly ground black pepper

1 sausage (see index for recipe
   for Summer Sausage)

¾ cup bread crumbs

Soak the dried beans overnight in water (at least 6 hours) or put them into boiling water and soak for 1 hour. Discard any that are damaged or floating. Put the picked-over beans into a pot with fresh water to cover. Add the salt pork, which you have blanched for a minute or 2 in boiling water and sliced, the onion with cloves, the carrot, 2 of the whole garlic cloves, and a bouquet garni made of 1 bay leaf, 2 sprigs of thyme, and 2 sprigs of parsley. Simmer, covered, until the beans are three quarters done (about 2 hours). In the meantime, cut up the pork and mutton into 2-inch dice and brown them in the oil or bacon fat. Remove the meat from the pan and brown the sliced onions in the oil. If any of the fat has burned, remove it and use fresh oil. Return the meat to the pan. Crush the 2 remaining garlic cloves and make another bouquet garni of the remaining bay leaf, thyme, and parsley. Add them to the pan with the beef stock and tomato purée. Cover and simmer for 1½ hours, adding stock as necessary.

When the beans are almost done, drain them (reserving the liquid) and remove the bouquet garni, garlic, onion, and carrot. Line an earthenware pot (preferably made of Issel clay) with the bacon rind (parboiled in water). Add a layer of beans, then some of the meat with the juices, then beans, and so on, peppering each layer and ending with beans. Put the salt pork slices on top with a sliced sausage. If liquid is not visible, add some of the cooking liquid from the beans. Spread the bread crumbs over the top and dribble melted pork or bacon fat over the top. Bake in a 350° oven for about 1½ hours. (Serves 4 to 6)

VARIATION:

If you are from Toulouse and not Castelnaudary, you may want to add a *confit d'oie* (preserved goose) during the final baking.

PUMPKIN PIE   (see index)

5

DESSERTS

Although desserts are frequently served with luncheon and dinner, not much is made of them in conversation, although it is clear that Wolfe and Archie both find a great deal in them to admire and savor. Archie will occasionally curb his appetite for the main course (even when it is dumplings or fritters) if he knows that there is a pumpkin pie or cherry tart coming up, but Wolfe never speaks of desserts in spite of the fact that Fritz has a large repertoire and some distinguished specialities, such as his personal version of cottage cheese with fresh pineapple soaked in white wine that even a Vishinsky wouldn't veto [THE BLACK MOUNTAIN]. *With the exception of cheese, which usually follows a meal when a sweet does not, Fritz's desserts fall into four principal categories: tarts, pies, fruits, and puddings. They are arranged thus below, with no interrupting comments, as is entirely appropriate.*

Tarts

TART SHELLS

1 cup all-purpose flour	1/3 cup cold sweet butter
1 tablespoon sugar	2 tablespoons cold water
1/2 teaspoon salt	(or more)

Preheat oven to 425°. Sift the flour, sugar, and salt together. Cut the butter into the flour, using a pastry knife, until the mixture resembles corn meal. Sprinkle the water sparingly over the mixture and stir with a fork to moisten until the dough will hold a ball shape. Divide the dough into 6 equal parts and roll each section out on a lightly floured board. Fit each round into a tart pan; press the dough down, crimp the edges, and prick the bottom of each with a fork. Fill each tart with uncooked rice and bake for 12 to 15 minutes. Remove from the oven, discard the rice, and fill with one of the following fillings. (Makes 6 tart shells)

CHERRY TART FILLING   [FER-DE-LANCE]'

¾ cup sugar	2 tablespoons cornstarch
½ cup dry white wine	(or more)
2 tablespoons brandy	¼ cup water
1 teaspoon lime juice	1 cup heavy cream
1 pound pitted sweet cherries	grated lime rind

Put the sugar, wine, brandy, and lime juice in a saucepan. Bring to a boil, stir, and add the cherries. Simmer gently for 7 minutes. Remove from the heat. Mix the cornstarch in a ¼ cup of water and add to the cherries. Return the pan to the heat and stir the mixture until it thickens. Add more cornstarch if necessary, dissolving it in a little water first. Set the mixture aside and cool slightly. Fill each tart with the mixture. Whip the cream and fold in the grated lime rind. Using a pastry tube, decorate the top of each tart with the whipped cream.

NOTE: In making the tart shells, use cherry heering to moisten the dough in place of water.

FIG AND CHERRY TART FILLING   [THE GOLDEN SPIDERS]

2 cups chopped fresh figs	½ cup dry white wine
2 cups pitted sweet cherries	2 tablespoons cornstarch
¾ cup sugar	¼ cup Grand Marnier

Put the fruit, sugar, and wine in a saucepan. Bring to a boil and simmer until the fruit is tender. Blend the cornstarch with Grand Marnier and add it to the fruit. Stir and cook until the mixture thickens. Remove from heat and allow to cool before filling the tart shells.

RHUBARB TART FILLING   [THE FINAL DEDUCTION]

4 cups fresh chopped rhubarb	2 tablespoons cornstarch
½ cup dry white wine	¼ cup orange juice
1⅔ cups sugar	¼ teaspoon nutmeg

Put the rhubarb, white wine, and sugar in a saucepan and bring to a boil. Simmer until the rhubarb is tender. Mix the cornstarch with the orange juice and blend into the rhubarb, stirring over a low heat until the mixture thickens. Remove from heat, add nutmeg, stir, and cool before filling the tart shells.

Pies

PIE CRUST

2 cups sifted all-purpose flour	¼ teaspoon salt
2 egg yolks	1 cup butter
2 tablespoons sugar	ice water

Sift the flour into a mixing bowl and make a well in the center. Put the egg yolks, sugar, salt, and butter in small chunks into the well. Using your fingers or a pastry blender, work the flour into the liquid to form a stiff dough. If more liquid is necessary, add 1 or 2 drops of ice water. Roll the dough into a ball and wrap it in foil or waxed paper; chill in the refrigerator for an hour. Divide the dough into halves. Roll out one piece for the bottom crust and line a 9-inch pan with it. Roll the dough for the top crust into a circle and cut it into ½-inch strips to be used for a lattice crust. Fill the bottom crust with one of the fillings below and arrange the strips for the top crust. Brush with a little milk before baking. Use the baking directions given below for the individual fillings.

APPLE PIE   [FER-DE-LANCE]

6 large Cortland apples	1 teaspoon cinnamon
(see note)	1 tablespoon flour
1 cup sugar	1 tablespoon butter
1 tablespoon lemon juice	¼ cup milk

Preheat oven to 450°. Pare, core, and divide the apples into eighths. Add the sugar, lemon juice, cinnamon, and flour, mixing lightly. Put the mixture into the lined pie plate, dot with butter, and cover with top crust. Brush crust with the milk (or with a little water and granulated sugar). Bake at 450° for 15 minutes; reduce heat to 350° and bake 35 minutes longer, or until the top crust is golden and the filling is bubbling and browned.

NOTE: If Cortland apples are not available, Baldwins, Greenings, and

Gravensteins are all acceptable substitutes; if these apples are used, the lemon juice and flour may be omitted.

BLUEBERRY PIE   [HELP, MAN WANTED *and* A WINDOW FOR DEATH]

3 cups blueberries   juice of 1 lemon
¾ cup sugar   1 tablespoon butter
pinch salt   ¼ cup milk
2 tablespoons all-purpose flour

Preheat oven to 400°. Pick over the berries and discard leaves, stems, and unripe berries. Mix together with sugar, salt, flour, and lemon juice and pour into a 9-inch pan lined with pastry. Dot with butter and put on top crust. Brush with milk and bake for 40 minutes until top crust is golden brown.

GREEN-TOMATO PIE   [OVER MY DEAD BODY]

4 quarts green tomatoes   ½ cup red wine vinegar
2 pounds light-brown sugar   1 teaspoon each ground
1 pound seedless raisins   cinnamon, cloves, nutmeg,
½ pound chopped citron   and allspice
1 cup rendered beef suet   ½ cup brandy
1 tablespoon salt

Chop the green tomatoes coarsely and drain well. Cover with cold water and bring to a boil. Simmer, covered, for 30 minutes and drain. Add the sugar, raisins, citron, suet, salt, and vinegar and cook the mixture until thick (about 2 hours). When cooked, cool thoroughly and add the spices. Store in sealed jars until use. (Makes enough for 4 pies.) When ready to use, fill a prepared pie tin with the mincemeat and pour half the brandy over the filling. Top the filling with strips of pastry to form a lattice. Bake at 350° for 35 to 40 minutes until the top crust is brown. Sprinkle another ¼ cup of brandy over the pie just before serving. Serve warm with a hard sauce made of 1 cup of confectioners' sugar creamed with ¼ pound of sweet butter. Add brandy to taste, blend well, and chill.

VARIATION:

Two quarts of peeled, cored, crisp apples may be substituted for 2 quarts of the tomatoes.

PUMPKIN PIE   [INSTEAD OF EVIDENCE]

4 large eggs
2 cups puréed pumpkin
1 cup light-brown sugar
1 tablespoon blackstrap
  molasses
1 teaspoon salt

1 cup light cream
1 teaspoon cinnamon
1 teaspoon ginger
1/4 teaspoon ground cloves
1/4 teaspoon nutmeg

Beat the eggs and stir all the ingredients together well. Pour into unbaked
pie shell and bake at 400° for 10 minutes. Lower heat to 350° and bake 30
to 40 minutes longer until done. No top crust is necessary, but it is neither
forbidden nor untraditional to add one.

Fruits

APPLES BAKED IN WHITE WINE   [TOO MANY CLIENTS]

6 firm cooking apples
3 tablespoons currants
4 tablespoons chopped pecans

2 teaspoons cinnamon sugar
4 tablespoons butter (1/2 stick)
3/4 cup dry white wine

Preheat the oven to 350°. Wash the apples and core them so that a small
bit is left in the base to act as a stopper for the filling. Mix the currants,
pecans, and 1 teaspoon of the cinnamon sugar together and fill the apples.
Grease a baking pan with 1 tablespoon of the butter. Place the apples
in the pan and dot them with the rest of the butter. Pour the wine over
the apples and sprinkle them with the remaining cinnamon sugar. Bake
until tender, about 30 to 35 minutes. Serve hot or cold with the pan juices
as a sauce. Use whipped cream if you like. (Serves 6)

AVOCADO   [IF DEATH EVER SLEPT]

3 large ripe avocados
1 cup sugar
4 tablespoons lime juice

2 tablespoons green chartreuse
1/2 cup heavy cream
6 slices lemon

Chill the avocados. Cut them in half, removing the pulp and reserving
the skins, taking care not to tear them. To the pulp, add the sugar, lime
juice, and chartreuse. Using a hand mixer, whip all the ingredients to a
smooth consistency. Return the mixture to the skins. Whip the cream

until stiff and serve separately. Garnish each avocado with a slice of lemon. (Serves 6)

SPICED BRANDIED CHERRIES   [DEATH OF A DOXY]

2 pounds dark sour cherries
3 slices pineapple
2 pounds sweet Bing cherries
2 cinnamon sticks

2 tablespoons whole cloves
1 cup sugar
½ cup cognac

Wash the cherries and remove the stems. Cut the pineapple into ½-inch chunks and add to the cherries. Sterilize 2 1-quart Mason jars and fill each one with the fruit up to 1 inch of the top. Push 1 cinnamon stick and 1 tablespoon of the cloves into each jar and add ½ cup of sugar to each. Pour ¼ cup of cognac over the top and seal the lids tightly. Let stand for 1 hour and then turn each jar over. Continue to do this until the sugar is dissolved. Then store the jars in a cool place for 90 to 120 days before serving.

FRESH FIGS AND CREAM   [CHAMPAGNE FOR ONE]

12 fresh figs
1 cup kümmel

2 tablespoons sugar
½ cup heavy cream

Marinate the figs in kümmel for at least 2 hours in the refrigerator. Drain and clean the figs, removing the stems. Arrange in serving dishes; sprinkle with sugar and a little of the kümmel. Whip the cream until stiff and spoon a little on top of each serving. (Serves 3)

VARIATION:

For breakfast, do not whip the cream and do not add the extra kümmel or sugar.

BAKED PEARS   [CHRISTMAS STORY]

6 Bosc pears
¾ cup dry white wine
6 tablespoons sugar
1 teaspoon cinnamon

8 tablespoons butter (1 stick)
¼ pound shredded Cheddar
cheese

Peel, halve, and core the pears. Place the halves in a shallow baking dish and set aside. In a saucepan put the wine, sugar, cinnamon, and butter. Bring the mixture to a boil, lower the heat, and simmer for 5 minutes. Pour over the pears. Bake the pears at 375° for 30 to 35 minutes, basting frequently with the juices, or until the pears can be punctured easily with a fork. Add more wine if necessary. When cooked, remove the pears, allow them to cool, and arrange them on serving dishes, allowing 2 for each serving. Sprinkle on the cheese. Pour the baking syrup into a saucepan, simmer for a few minutes, and spoon over the pears. (Serves 6)

PINEAPPLE AND CHEESE [THE BLACK MOUNTAIN]

8 slices fresh pineapple
½ cup dry white wine

1 cup creamed cottage cheese
mint leaves

Put the pineapple slices in a bowl with the wine and refrigerate for at least 2 hours. Drain and arrange on dessert plates, two slices for each serving. Whip the cottage cheese to a smooth consistency and top each slice of pineapple with a large spoonful. Garnish with mint leaves. (Serves 4)

RASPBERRIES IN SHERRY CREAM [THE FATHER HUNT]

1 quart raspberries
1 cup heavy cream
2 large eggs
2 tablespoons sugar

2 tablespoons dry sherry
½ teaspoon almond extract
pinch salt

Wash and pick over the berries; chill until ready to serve. Heat the cream in the top of a double boiler. Separate the eggs and beat the yolks with the sugar until they are very smooth. Pour a little of the hot cream into the yolks, beating constantly, and put the mixture back into the rest of the cream, beating steadily to avoid lumping. Continue to cook until the mixture has thickened. Add the sherry, almond extract, and salt. Beat the egg whites until they are stiff and fold them into the sauce. Serve warm over the chilled berries. (Serves 4)

STRAWBERRIES ROMANOFF [THE MOTHER HUNT]

1 quart strawberries
6 tablespoons Cointreau
2 tablespoons sugar

½ cup heavy cream
1 cup vanilla ice cream
1 teaspoon lemon juice

Wash and hull the berries. Put them in a bowl and add half the Cointreau; sprinkle on the sugar and refrigerate for 1 to 1½ hours. Whip the heavy cream until stiff. Whip the ice cream in a separate bowl until it is softened; add the lemon juice and the rest of the Cointreau. Add the strawberries to the ice-cream mixture and fold in the whipped cream. Serve in a timbale surrounded with cracked ice. (Serves 4)

Archie notes in A WINDOW FOR DEATH *that he buys ice cream at Schramms on Madison Avenue.*

WATERMELON   [THE FATHER HUNT]

4 cups cubed watermelon, seeded
¼ cup sugar

1 cup dry sherry
mint leaves

Sprinkle the watermelon with the sugar and pour the sherry over the fruit. Chill in the refrigerator. Serve garnished with mint leaves. (Serves 4)

Puddings

ALMOND PARFAIT   [IN THE BEST FAMILIES]

¾ cup sugar
¾ cup water
8 egg yolks

1 cup heavy cream
1 teaspoon almond extract
2 tablespoons minced almonds

Put the sugar and water in a saucepan and bring to a boil, stirring constantly. Continue to cook for 5 minutes. Remove from heat and allow to cool. Pour the syrup into the top of a double boiler. Beat the egg yolks until lemony in color and add 2 or 3 tablespoons of the syrup to the eggs. Beat again and add the egg-yolk mixture to the syrup. Over simmering water cook the mixture, stirring constantly with a wooden spoon, until it begins to thicken and coats the spoon. Remove from heat and continue to stir until the mixture has cooled. Whip the heavy cream into stiff peaks and set aside. Add the almond flavoring and minced almonds to the egg mixture and fold in the whipped cream. Pour the mixture into a parfait mold and freeze it. Unmold just before serving and garnish with more minced almonds. (Serves 6)

BLUEBERRY GRUNT   [THE FATHER HUNT]

4 cups blueberries	4 tablespoons butter
1 cup sugar	8 slices sponge cake (see index)

Wash and pick over the berries. Put them in a saucepan with the sugar and cook over a low heat for 10 minutes, taking care that they do not burn. Line a buttered baking dish with 2 slices of the cake. Ladle a cup of blueberries and juice over the cake. Put on another layer of sponge cake and berries, continuing until the ingredients are used up. Dot each layer with pieces of butter. Bake at 350° for 15 to 20 minutes. Remove pan from oven and allow the dessert to cool. Chill it in the refrigerator for 3 to 4 hours before serving with whipped cream. (Serves 6)

CHESTNUT WHIP   [DEATH OF A DOXY]

1 pound chestnuts	2 tablespoons vanilla
2 cups milk	2 squares bitter chocolate
2 large eggs	½ cup heavy cream
½ cup sugar	

Cut a small cross on the flat side of each chestnut with the point of a knife. Put them into a shallow baking pan and bake at 450° for 5 to 10 minutes, or until the shells start to open. Cool the chestnuts slightly and when they are easy to handle, remove the shells and underlying skin. Purée the chestnut meats in a blender, adding a little milk. Put the rest of the milk in a saucepan with the beaten eggs and sugar. Cook over a low flame, stirring until the mixture starts to thicken. Add the vanilla and chestnut purée and mix thoroughly. Allow to cool slightly while you grate the chocolate. Mix in ¾ of the chocolate; when it is melted, pour into sherbet glasses and chill. Just before serving, whip the cream until stiff. Using a pastry tube, decorate the top of each serving. Grate the remaining chocolate and sprinkle on top. (Serves 6)

CRÈME GÉNOISE   [DEATH OF A DOXY]

2¼ cups milk	2 teaspoons grated orange rind
3 tablespoons sugar	1½ ounces Grand Marnier
4 egg yolks	1 tablespoon butter
3 tablespoons all-purpose flour	2 tablespoons citron, chopped
¼ teaspoon salt	6 macaroons
¼ teaspoon almond extract	

Put the milk into the top of a double boiler over boiling water and scald it until a thin film is formed. In a separate pan over low heat mix the sugar, egg yolks, flour, salt, almond extract, orange rind, and Grand Marnier. Gradually pour in the scalded milk and beat constantly. Cook for 5 to 10 minutes until the mixture is quite thick, stirring steadily. Remove from heat, add the butter and citron, and mix well. Crumble each macaroon into individual sherbet glasses and pour the *crème* over each. Chill. Serve with whipped cream or with a little Grand Marnier. (Serves 6)

CREOLE CURDS AND CREAM   [DEATH OF A DOXY]

2 quarts sour milk
4 tablespoons sugar flavored
   with anise

1 cup heavy cream
2 tablespoons sugar

Allow the sour milk to clabber in a 5-quart crock. Pour the clabber into a long muslin bag and allow it to drain overnight in a cool place. Put a pan below the bag. (A large conical strainer or collander lined with cheesecloth can be used instead of a muslin bag.) An hour or two before serving, remove the curds from the strainer and place them in a mixing bowl. Gently fold in the flavored sugar. Refrigerate until chilled and serve cold with heavy cream and the additional sugar, sprinkled on top. (Serves 6)

FIG SOUFFLÉ   [A RIGHT TO DIE]

7 tablespoons granulated sugar
1½ cups fig purée
   (1 to 2 pounds fresh figs)
3 tablespoons Grand Marnier

5 egg whites
2 tablespoons confectioner's
   sugar

Add 6 tablespoons of the granulated sugar to the fig purée and beat it over hot water until the sugar is dissolved. Off the heat add the Grand Marnier and blend thoroughly. Allow to cool. Beat the egg whites until stiff but not dry and fold them into the purée. Butter a soufflé dish and sprinkle the sides and bottom with the remaining tablespoon of granulated sugar. Make a collar of parchment paper and tie it around the soufflé dish. Pour in the mixture and bake at 350° degrees for 35 to 40 minutes. When it is nicely browned, serve the soufflé sprinkled with confectioner's sugar and with a side dish of heavy cream. (Serves 4)

LEMON-SHERRY PUDDING WITH BROWN-SUGAR SAUCE
[BLOOD WILL TELL]

2 tablespoons cornstarch
½ teaspoon cinnamon
¾ cup sugar
1½ cups heated milk
2 tablespoons butter
½ teaspoon salt

grated rind of 1 lemon
4 egg yolks
juice of 2 lemons
3 tablespoons dry sherry
3 egg whites
brown-sugar sauce (see below)

Put the cornstarch, cinnamon, and sugar in the top of a double boiler, add the milk, and stir until the sugar has dissolved. Add the butter, salt, and grated lemon rind. Stir well over simmering water until the butter has melted. Beat the egg yolks slightly and add them to the mixture, stirring constantly until the mixture thickens enough to coat a wooden spoon. Remove pan from heat and add the lemon juice and sherry, blending well. Beat the egg whites until stiff and fold them in. Pour the pudding into individual buttered baking cups and set in a pan of water. Bake at 325° for 30 minutes, or until a toothpick comes away clean when inserted in the pudding. Remove from oven and cool. Serve chilled. (Serves 6)

BROWN-SUGAR SAUCE

4 tablespoons butter
1 cup brown sugar
½ cup dry white wine
    (or champagne)

¼ cup light cream
⅓ cup chopped Macadamia
    nuts

Put the butter in a saucepan and when it is melted, add the brown sugar. When the sugar is completely dissolved, gradually add the wine, stirring constantly. Bring the mixture to a boil and remove from heat. Add the cream and beat vigorously until smooth. Fold in the chopped nuts and serve warm with the chilled pudding.

PAPAYA CUSTARD
[GAMBIT]

1½ cups light cream
3 large eggs, plus 1 yolk
1½ cups papaya pulp, puréed
    (2 to 3 papayas)
½ teaspoon salt

¼ cup sugar
juice of 1 orange
grated rind of 1 orange
½ cup toasted coconut

Heat the cream, beat the eggs and yolk, and mix together with the papaya purée, salt, sugar, and orange juice and rind. Blend well. Pour into individual custard cups and place in a pan of hot water. Bake at

325° for 40 to 45 minutes, or until a toothpick comes away clean when inserted in the custard. Garnish with toasted coconut.

VARIATION:

Instead of individual cups, use 1-quart baking dish and unmold the custard onto a serving plate. Garnish with slices of papaya and top with the coconut.

WALNUT PUDDING   [PRISONER'S BASE]

3 tablespoons butter
1/2 cup brown sugar
1/4 teaspoon baking soda
1 3/4 cups milk
1/4 cup Marsala

2 large eggs
1/2 teaspoon salt
2 cups bread cubes
1 1/2 cups minced walnuts
whipped cream

In a skillet melt the butter and add the brown sugar, stirring over a low heat to avoid burning. Add the baking soda to the milk and wine and gradually add it to the melted sugar. Simmer for 2 to 3 minutes, then remove from heat and allow to cool. In a mixing bowl beat the eggs; sprinkle with salt and add to the milk/sugar mixture. Butter a 1 1/2-quart baking dish and spread the bread cubes evenly over the bottom of the dish. Sprinkle on 1/2 cup of minced walnuts. Pour in the custard and sprinkle the top with another 1/2 cup walnuts. Bake at 350° for 40 to 45 minutes. Serve with whipped cream and remaining crushed walnuts.

6

THE PERFECT DINNER FOR THE PERFECT DETECTIVE

Although many different kinds of food are served and enjoyed at the old brownstone on West Thirty-fifth Street, there are a few items that appear on the table with fair regularity. We could even assume that an entire meal devoted to these special favorites in one combination or another would strike the great man as the ideal dinner. There are many possible variations, but the main theme would be shad roe followed by duckling in some guise and then a main course of pork with a side dish of corn, the whole array somehow flavored with anchovies.

Shad Roe

Fritz came to announce lunch. That was no time for me to comment or ask a question, with a sautéed shad roe fresh and hot from the skillet, and the sauce, with chives and chervil and shallots, ready to be poured on. [THE FINAL DEDUCTION]

SHAD ROE AUX FINES HERBES

2 pairs fresh shad roe
½ cup butter
2 teaspoons chopped fresh chives
1 teaspoon fresh chervil
   (or ¼ teaspoon dried leaves)

1 teaspoon fresh tarragon
   (or ¼ teaspoon dried leaves)
1 teaspoon minced shallots
salt and pepper to taste

Blanch the roe in salted water, simmering it for about 5 minutes. Drain and separate the pairs. In a large skillet, heat ¼ cup of the butter and add the shad. Cook the roe for a minute on each side over a medium flame, turning them very carefully. Cover the skillet and reduce the heat. Cook for 10 minutes longer. Remove the roe to a heated platter. Add the remaining butter and the herbs to the skillet and heat for 2 minutes. Correct the seasoning and pour over the roe. Serve immediately. (Serves 2 as a main course, 4 as a first course)

Purists will observe that the classic fines herbes *combination always includes parsley. Fritz knows this, of course, and, in fact, made a point of mentioning the omission in* A RIGHT TO DIE; *we must assume that this is a particular stipulation of Wolfe's.*

Another dispute over seasoning occurs in THE MOTHER HUNT, *in which shad roe in casserole is served:* one of the few dishes on which Wolfe and Fritz had a difference of opinion that had never been settled. They were agreed on the larding, the anchovy butter, the chervil, shallot, parsley, bay leaf, pepper, marjoram, and cream, but the argument was the onion. Fritz was for it, and Wolfe dead against. There was a chance that voices would be raised.

SHAD ROE IN CASSEROLE (*without Onion*)

2 pairs shad roe	1 tablespoon minced parsley
4 tablespoons anchovy butter (see note)	salt and pepper to taste
4 thin sheets pork fat	1 teaspoon fresh marjoram (or ½ teaspoon dried leaves)
1 teaspoon fresh chervil (or ½ teaspoon dried leaves)	1 bay leaf
2 tablespoons minced shallots	1½ cups heavy cream

Preheat the oven to 375°. Blanch the roe in salted water for 5 minutes. Drain and separate the pairs. Spread each piece of roe with a spoonful of anchovy butter and wrap each in the pork sheets, securing tightly with a thin cord. Arrange the larded roe in the bottom of a buttered casserole and sprinkle them with chervil, shallots, parsley, marjoram, salt, and pepper. Add the bay leaf to the dish. Pour in the heavy cream and cover the dish with a piece of heavy aluminum foil. Bake for 25 to 30 minutes. Remove the foil and cook uncovered for 5 minutes longer. Correct the seasoning and serve the roe from the casserole or remove to a heated platter, strain the sauce, and pour it over the roe. (Serves 2 as a main course, 4 as a first course)

NOTE: To make 1¼ cups of anchovy butter, mash eight fillets of anchovies with the juice of 1 lemon (or 1 ounce of cognac) in a mortar until all the liquid has been incorporated. Mix in 1 tablespoon chopped fresh parsley. Add the mixture to 1 cup of softened sweet butter and beat well to form a smooth paste. Pack into a small crock and refrigerate for at least 1 hour before using.

The main dish was shad roe with Creole sauce. Creole sauce is all right, and Fritz's Creole sauce is one of his best, but the point is that with that item Fritz always serves bread triangles fried in anchovy butter; and since he had known four hours ago that I would be there, and he was aware of my attitude toward bread triangles fried in anchovy butter, he had proceeded beyond the call of duty. Again I passed up a salad, but only because there wasn't any room for it.   [IF DEATH EVER SLEPT]

SHAD ROE WITH CREOLE SAUCE

2 pairs fresh shad roe
¼ cup butter, plus
   2 tablespoons
¼ cup chopped shallots
¼ cup chopped celery
¼ cup chopped green pepper
¼ cup chopped pimiento
1½ cups tomato pulp without
   seeds or juice

1 tablespoon cornstarch
2 tablespoons water
salt and freshly ground
   black pepper to taste
few grains cayenne
1 tablespoon chopped fresh
   Italian parsley (or
   watercress)

Parboil and sauté the shad roe according to the directions in the recipe for Shad Roe aux Fines Herbes (see index), but use a sauce made as follows: Melt 2 tablespoons of the butter in a large skillet and cook the shallots, celery, green pepper, and pimiento for 5 minutes, or until the shallots are golden. Add the tomato pulp and bring the mixture to a boil. Reduce the heat and simmer, covered, for 1 hour. Mix the cornstarch with the water and add. Cook, stirring, until the sauce is thickened. Correct the seasoning with salt, pepper, and cayenne. Add the parsley.

NOTE: This sauce is also good served over corn or rice fritters or with white fish fillets.

BREAD TRIANGLES FRIED IN ANCHOVY BUTTER

12 slices white bread   ½ cup anchovy butter (see index)

Trim the crusts from the bread and cut the slices into triangles. Butter one side of each slice with anchovy butter and set aside. Heat 2 table-spoons of the butter in a large skillet and arrange as many triangles in the pan as possible. When they are golden on the bottom, turn and cook them on the other side. Add more butter as needed. Serve warm. (Serves 4 or 1 Archie)

Another dish that often appears on both Wolfe's table and at Rusterman's Restaurant, the only place where Wolfe really likes to eat outside his home, is shad-roe mousse Pocahontas. This dish was first cooked by Mr. Crabtree of the Kanawha Spa, for a meeting of Les Quinze Maîtres, *the greatest living masters of the subtlest and kindliest of the arts, in* TOO MANY COOKS. *This important meeting will be further discussed in a later chapter.*

SHAD-ROE MOUSSE POCAHONTAS

1-pound halibut	1 onion
1 pair blanched shad roe	1 carrot
3 egg whites	1 stalk celery
1¾ cups heavy cream	2 sprigs parsley
¾ teaspoon salt	¼ teaspoon freshly ground
½ teaspoon white pepper	black pepper
¼ cup butter	3 egg yolks
2 cups water	1 teaspoon all-purpose flour
1 cup dry white wine	½ teaspoon lemon juice

Remove all skin and bones from the halibut and save them. Put the fish through a meat grinder and then force it through a fine sieve. Mix in gradually the unbeaten whites of eggs and then, also gradually, ¾ cup of the cream. Season with ¼ teaspoon of the salt and a dash of the white pepper. Leave the dish in the refrigerator for 20 minutes. Preheat the oven to 350°. Sauté the roe in the butter; remove the skin and sprinkle with ¼ teaspoon salt and the black pepper. Pull one of the sacs apart with a silver fork into quite small pieces and fold it into the fish mixture. Butter a ring mold well and fill it with the mixture. Set it in a pan of hot water, cover the mold with parchment paper, and bake for 20 minutes. Turn onto a hot platter and fill the inside of the ring with the following sauce, which must be ready when the ring is. Put the skin and bones of the halibut into a saucepan with the water and wine, adding the onion and carrot cut in pieces, the celery, parsley, the rest of the salt, and the black pepper. Beat the egg yolks, flour, and ½ cup of cream together, and pour onto them 1½ cups of the strained court bouillon. Put in a double boiler over simmering water and add the remaining ½ cup cream and the second shad roe broken into medium-sized fragments. Correct the seasoning. Allow the sauce to thicken, stirring constantly. Remove from the fire, add lemon juice, and fill the ring with it. (Serves 4)

Although the shad-roe season is a short one, Wolfe takes full advantage of it every year, often to the disgruntlement of his Mr. Goodwin: It was one of those days. Shad roe again for lunch, this time larded with pork baked in cream with an assortment of herbs. Every spring I get so fed up with shad roe that I wish to heaven fish would figure out some other way. Whales have.

[THE FINAL DEDUCTION]

SHAD ROE IN CASSEROLE (*with Onion*)

2 pairs shad roe	2 tablespoons minced shallots
4 tablespoons anchovy butter (see index)	1 teaspoon fresh marjoram (or ½ teaspoon dried leaves)
4 thin sheets pork fat	salt and pepper to taste
1 teaspoon minced onion	1 bay leaf
1 teaspoon fresh chervil (or ½ teaspoon dried leaves)	1½ cups heavy cream

Follow the instructions for Shad Roe in Casserole (see index), adding the onion with the chervil, shallots, and other seasonings. (Serves 2 as a main course and 4 as a first course)

Duckling

Dinnertime during May and June is likely to feature a duckling in one form or another. In THE FINAL DEDUCTION, *Archie is con-*

*fronted by a dilemma posed by two favorite dishes appearing in
the same meal, stuffed clams and* duckling roasted in cider with
Spanish sauce as revised by Wolfe and Fritz, leaving out the
carrot and parsley and putting anchovies in.

DUCKLING ROASTED IN CIDER WITH SPANISH SAUCE

1 duck, 5 to 6 pounds
1 teaspoon salt
¼ teaspoon freshly ground
　　black pepper
1 cup apple cider
1 anchovy fillet
4 tablespoons butter

2 tablespoons minced onion
½ pound sliced mushrooms
3 tablespoons all-purpose flour
1 cup tomato sauce (see note)
1 teaspoon tomato paste
1 tablespoon paprika
½ cup dry sherry

Preheat the oven to 375° degrees. Wash out the cavity of the duck and remove bits of excess fat from the loose skin. Reserve the liver. Prick the
skin of the duck with a sharp fork in several places to allow the layer of
the fat under the skin to melt and escape during the cooking, which auto-
matically bastes the bird as it cooks. Season with the salt and pepper and
place on a rack in a shallow baking pan. Cover with foil and roast for 1
hour. Remove the pan from the oven and drain off the accumulated fat.
Remove the foil, pour the cider over the duck, and return it to the oven
for another hour, basting with the cider every 15 minutes. Replace the
foil for the last 15 minutes of cooking. While the duck roasts, sauté the
duck liver and the anchovy in the butter for about 10 minutes. Remove
the liver and anchovy and mince. Add the onion to the pan and cook for
5 minutes; add the mushrooms and cook for 5 minutes more. Add the
flour, blend for a minute, then add the tomato sauce and paste, the paprika, and the sherry. Continue to cook, stirring constantly, until the
sauce thickens. Add the liver and anchovy. If the sauce is too thick, add a
little water. Carve the duck and arrange the meat on a heated platter.
Spoon some of the sauce over the meat and serve the rest in a separate
bowl. (Serves 4)

NOTE: To make a cup of tomato sauce, simmer six large, peeled, seeded,
and juiced tomatoes (about 2 cups of pulp) over a low flame for 1 hour
with ¼ cup minced green onions, ½ bay leaf, a sprig of parsley, and 2
cloves. Strain.

*Duckling is occasionally a feature of Sunday dinner, which is
served at midday, and in* THE MOTHER HUNT, *when Archie returns*

to the house too late to eat in the dining room, he is served a warmed-over version of duckling in Flemish olive sauce at his breakfast table in the kitchen.

DUCKLING IN FLEMISH OLIVE SAUCE

2 ducklings,
  3 to 3½ pounds each
juice of 3 lemons
	1 teaspoon salt
	½ teaspoon freshly
	  ground black pepper

Preheat the broiler to 375°. Quarter the ducklings and brush all the pieces with the lemon juice. Sprinkle with the salt and pepper and place skin side down on broiler rack. Broil for about 45 minutes, turning the pieces occasionally and pricking them with a fork, until they are brown, crisp, and tender. (You may also roast the pieces, at 350°, on a rack in a roasting pan, for 1½ hours; be sure to turn the pieces frequently.) Serve with Flemish olive sauce. (Serves 4 to 6)

FLEMISH OLIVE SAUCE

6 tablespoons butter
2 tablespoons chopped
  fresh parsley
2 tablespoons minced shallots
1½ tablespoons all-purpose
  flour
	1½ cups champagne
	½ cup pimiento-stuffed
	  green olives
	1 tablespoon minced truffle
	salt and pepper to taste

Melt the butter in a saucepan. When it is frothy, add the parsley and shallots, but do not allow the butter to brown. Cook slowly for 5 minutes and add the flour. Blend well and cook 3 minutes, stirring constantly. Add the champagne slowly and continue to stir. When the mixture is smooth and thickened (after about 10 minutes), remove from heat and strain the sauce. Slice the olives and add them with the truffles to the sauce. Simmer for 5 more minutes and season with salt and pepper. Serve hot.

Another leftover that sounds good enough to eat is curried duck, which Archie is obliged to decline in THE DOORBELL RANG, *being too tired to chew.*

CURRIED DUCK

5 medium onions, sliced	1 tablespoon curry powder
¼ pound mushrooms, sliced	3 cups chopped cooked duck
3 tablespoons butter	2 cups duck broth (see note)
1 cup cubed apples	2 cups cooked rice
3 tablespoons all-purpose flour	½ cup raisins
½ teaspoon salt	3 tablespoons brandy
¼ teaspoon freshly ground black pepper	

Sauté the onions and mushrooms in the butter in a large saucepan for 10 minutes. Add the apples and sprinkle on the flour, salt, pepper, and curry powder. Blend well. Cook for 5 more minutes, stirring constantly. Add the cooked duck and the broth, and simmer for 30 minutes. Stir occasionally. Correct the seasoning and serve with the rice, into which you have mixed the raisins, soaked for 30 minutes in the brandy.

NOTE: To make the duck broth, put the bones, skin, and leftover bits of meat from the duck carcass into a kettle. Add a bouquet garni of parsley, thyme, and bay leaf, and an onion. Pour in 2½ cups water and ½ cup dry white wine. Bring to a boil, lower the heat, and simmer for 1 hour. Add additional wine or water so that you will have at least 2 cups of liquid.

Archie's immense contributions to the household on West Thirty-fifth Street need not be enumerated here; there are some areas, however, where his willingness to offer assistance is not taken, even with a grain of salt: I went to the kitchen to see how Fritz was getting on with the braised duckling stuffed with crabmeat, because I didn't want to sit and watch Wolfe. . . . When I offered to spread the paste on the cheesecloth which was to be wrapped around the ducklings, Fritz gave me exactly the kind of look Wolfe has given me on various and numerous occasions.

[PLOT IT YOURSELF]

BRAISED DUCKLINGS STUFFED WITH CRABMEAT

2 ducklings, 3 to 3½ pounds each	½ cup minced shallots or scallions
4 tablespoons butter	1½ cups flaked crabmeat

2 tablespoons chopped
  fresh parsley
2 cups soft bread crumbs
1 large egg
salt and pepper

1 carrot, sliced
1 onion, sliced
3 cups strong chicken stock
2½ cups all-purpose flour
1 truffle

Preheat the oven to 425°. Wash out the cavity of each duckling and re-move bits of excess fat from the loose skin. Reserve this fat and the giblets and necks for the stock. Prick the skin of the ducks with a sharp fork in several places. In a small saucepan melt the butter and sauté the shallots until they are soft, about 5 minutes. Toss the crabmeat and parsley in a bowl with the bread crumbs and add the shallots or scallions and butter. Mix in the unbeaten egg and season with salt and pepper. Mix well and stuff the ducklings loosely with the mixture. Truss the birds and place on a rack in a shallow baking pan, into which you have put half the carrot and onion and 1 cup of the chicken stock. Roast the ducks for 1 hour, or until the skin begins to brown. While the ducks are cook-ing, simmer the neck, giblets, and excess fat for 30 minutes in the remain-ing stock, carrot, and onion. Strain and set aside. Make a paste with the flour and enough water to moisten it. Knead it for a few minutes until it is smooth and roll out half the dough on a floured board. Flour the roll-ing pin and gently wrap the dough around the pin. Lay out a double thickness of cheesecloth measuring about 15 by 12 inches. Unroll the dough onto the cloth, leaving 1 or 2 inches of cloth around the edges. Repeat the operation with the rest of the dough. When the ducklings have cooked for 1 hour, remove them from the oven and allow to cool slightly. Wrap each duckling in the cheesecloth and before sealing pour a little duck stock over the bird and arrange a few slices of truffle on top. Seal the pastry, peel off the cheesecloth, and return the birds to the roast-ing pan. Cook for another hour. Remove from the oven, place on serving platter, and with a sharp knife cut open the casing and carve. (Serves 4 to 6)

VARIATION:

Bone the ducklings after braising and arrange them around a platter with the crabmeat stuffing heaped in the center. Serve the sauce sepa-rately.   [CHRISTMAS STORY]

In A RIGHT TO DIE, *a duckling dish affords Wolfe the opportunity to be more than usually cordial to a couple of clients in his in-vitation to dinner:* "No doubt you have information for me, and suggestions, and in less than half an hour it will be dinnertime. If you and Mr. Whipple will dine with us, we'll have the evening for it. Wild duck with Vatel sauce—wine vinegar, egg yolk, tomato paste, butter, cream, salt and pepper, shallots, tarragon, chervil, and peppercorns. Is any of those distasteful to you?"

WILD DUCK IN VATEL SAUCE

2 wild ducks
juice of 3 lemons
1 teaspoon salt
½ teaspoon freshly ground
    black pepper

garnish: parsley sprigs, carrot
    curls, kumquats soaked in
    brandy

Prepare and broil the ducks according to the directions given in the recipe for duckling in Flemish olive sauce (see index). After cooking, separate the legs from the thigh sections and remove the breast meat from the bone, discarding the ribs and backbone. Arrange the meat on a serving platter and garnish with the parsley, carrots, and brandied kumquats. Chill. Serve with hot Vatel sauce. (Serves 4 to 6)

VATEL SAUCE

2 tablespoons minced
    mushrooms
4 tablespoons butter
1½ tablespoons tarragon wine
    vinegar
1½ tablespoons brandy
1 teaspoon minced shallots
1 teaspoon fresh chervil (or
    ½ teaspoon dried leaves)

1 tablespoon minced celery
1 teaspoon fresh thyme (or
    ½ teaspoon dried leaves)
1 tablespoon tomato paste
3 egg yolks
salt and white pepper
dash nutmeg
¾ cup light cream

Sauté the mushrooms in 1 tablespoon of the butter. In a saucepan heat the vinegar, brandy, shallots, chervil, celery, thyme, and mushrooms and bring to a boil. Cook over a high flame until the liquid has been reduced by more than half. Remove from the heat and cool. Mix in the tomato paste and 1 egg yolk at a time, beating vigorously after each addition. Return the pan to a low heat, add the remaining 3 tablespoons of butter, and mix until smooth. Season with salt and pepper to taste and a dash of nutmeg. In the meantime, warm the cream in a separate pan and add it to the sauce, off the heat. Blend in well and serve hot with the chilled duck.

Undoubtedly the greatest duckling dish of all is duck Mondor, which was originated by Pierre Mondor, one of Wolfe's close friends, the owner of Mondor's Restaurant in Paris, and one of Les Quinze Maitres. Although Mondor never cooks the dish himself in any of the stories, Fritz often does, and Wolfe serves it on one occasion to his closest friend, Marko Vukcic, owner of Rusterman's Restaurant in New York City and a great cook in his own right.

DUCK MONDOR

2 ducks, 5 to 6 pounds each	2 egg yolks
2 celery stalks, sliced	1 cup heavy cream
2 onions, sliced	1 ounce cognac
2 medium apples, peeled and diced	1/4 teaspoon nutmeg
1 lemon	salt and pepper to taste
2 tablespoons butter	8 ounces grated Gruyère cheese
2 tablespoons all-purpose flour	crushed pistachio nuts
1 cup dry white wine	

Preheat the oven to 350°. Wash the duck and remove the excess fat from the loose skin. Mix the celery, onions, and apples together. Stuff the duck cavities with the mixture and truss the birds. Rub the skin of each duck with 1/2 of the lemon and prick the skin here and there with a sharp fork. Put the ducks on a rack in a roasting pan and bake for about 1¾ hours. Do not baste. When they are done, remove from oven and remove and discard the stuffing. Cut the ducks into serving pieces, arrange them on an ovenproof platter, and keep warm. Raise the oven temperature to 450°. Melt the butter in a saucepan; add the flour and cook, stirring, for 3 minutes. Add the wine and stir until the mixture begins to thicken. Remove from the heat and add the egg yolks one at a time, beating vigorously after each addition. Return the saucepan to the heat, add the cream, and heat through; do not allow to boil. Add the cognac and nutmeg and correct the seasoning with salt and pepper. Simmer very gently for 3 minutes more. Pour the sauce over the pieces of duck and sprinkle on the cheese. Bake in the hot oven until brown, about 5 minutes. Garnish with the pistachio nuts. (Serves 4 to 6)

For two more superb duckling dishes, see index for boned duckling with sauce Rouennaise and roast duck Mr. Richards. We have reason to believe that versions of each dish have been prepared and served at West Thirty-fifth Street, but they are the original creations of Marko Vukcic, and the recipes properly belong elsewhere in this book.

Pork

Braising is unquestionably the preferred method of dealing with pork in Fritz's kitchen, although the braising liquid may vary from spiced wine [MIGHT AS WELL BE DEAD] *and beer* [METHOD THREE FOR MURDER] *to a "sharp brown sauce."* [AND BE A VILLAIN]

PORK FILLETS BRAISED IN SPICED WINE

1 3-pound pork tenderloin
1 cup good soy sauce
5 cups Burgundy
1 large onion, sliced
1 clove garlic, crushed
12 peppercorns, crushed

1 carrot, sliced
4 tablespoons grated fresh ginger
4 tablespoons butter
2 tablespoons all-purpose flour
2 tablespoons Dijon mustard

Slice the pork into 6 equal strips. Combine the soy sauce and Burgundy in a large saucepan. Add the onion, garlic, peppercorns, carrot, and ginger to the soy-sauce–wine mixture. Bring the liquid to a boil and simmer for 20 minutes. Put the pork strips in a large bowl and pour the marinade over them. Let stand overnight, turning the meat occasionally. Two hours before you plan to serve, preheat the oven to 350°. Remove the pieces of pork from the marinade and wipe them dry with a cloth or paper towel. Put them between sheets of waxed paper and pound flat with a mallet. Melt 2 tablespoons of the butter in a skillet and sauté the fillets briefly. As they brown, transfer them to a casserole. Add enough of the marinade to cover the meat (reserving the rest) and bake for 1½ hours. When the pork is done, remove to a heated platter. In a saucepan make a sauce with the remaining 2 tablespoons of butter, the flour, and 1½ cups of the marinade/braising liquid. When the sauce has thickened, stir in the mustard and simmer for 15 minutes. Stir occasionally. Strain and serve over the pork fillets. (Serves 4)

The main dish at dinner had been pork stewed in beer, which both Wolfe and Fritz know I can get along without. . . . I sat in my working chair and looked across the desk at him. Since he weighs a seventh of a ton he always looks big, but when he's being obnoxious he looks even bigger. "Do you suppose it's possible," I asked, "that pork has a bloating effect?"

"No, indeed," he said, and opened a book.

PORK STEWED IN BEER

3 pounds pork shoulder, boned	4 tablespoons butter
3 tablespoons olive oil (or more if needed)	2 pounds onions, sliced
	1 bay leaf
¼ cup all-purpose flour	1 teaspoon fresh thyme (or
½ teaspoon paprika	½ teaspoon dried leaves)
½ teaspoon salt	1 pint beer
¼ teaspoon fresh ground white pepper	

Trim all the fat and tendons from the pork and cut the meat into 2-inch cubes. Heat the oil in a 2-quart Dutch oven. Mix the flour, paprika, salt, and white pepper together and dredge the pork cubes. Brown the meat in the oil, removing the pieces as they are done. In a skillet melt the butter and brown the onions lightly, stirring occasionally. Remove them with a slotted spoon and put them in the Dutch oven. Return the pork to the pot and add the bay leaf, thyme, and beer. Stir gently, cover the pot, and cook over a low flame for 1½ to 2 hours. (If you prefer, bake the dish in the oven at 275° for 2 hours.) Stir occasionally to prevent sticking. When the pork is tender, the dish is done. If the sauce is not thick enough, add a *beurre manié* (1 tablespoon butter and 1 tablespoon flour kneaded together) to the pot and stir until the desired consistency is reached. (Serves 4 to 6)

Like duckling, pork occasionally provides Wolfe with the chance to display cordial hospitality to his clients: "It just occurred to me—could I prevail upon you to dine with me? You said you were just leaving for the day. I have a good cook. We are having fresh pork tenderloin, with all fiber removed, done in a casserole, with a sharp brown sauce moderately spiced. There will not be time to *chambrer* a claret properly, but we can have the chill off. . . . Do you happen to know the brandy labeled Remisier? It is not common. I hope this won't shock you but the way to do it is to sip it with bites of Fritz's apple pie. Fritz is my cook."

[AND BE A VILLAIN]

FRESH PORK TENDERLOIN IN CASSEROLE

1 2- to 3-pound pork tenderloin	1 sprig parsley
4 cups dry white wine	2 teaspoons salt
1 yellow onion, sliced	4 tablespoons butter
1½ tablespoons tarragon vinegar	1½ cups rice
6 black peppercorns, crushed	1 tablespoon chopped fresh parsley
1 bay leaf	2 cups canned sour cherries (save the liquid)
1 carrot, sliced	1 cup bouillon (see index)
1 stalk celery, sliced	

Place the pork tenderloin in a large mixing bowl. Combine the wine, onion, vinegar, peppercorns, bay leaf, carrot, celery, sprig of parsley, and 1 teaspoon of the salt in a large saucepan and simmer over a low heat for 15 minutes. Pour the liquid over the pork, setting aside 1 cup of the marinade for later use in the sauce. Marinate the pork for 24 hours. Remove the meat, drain, and wipe dry. Melt the butter in a large skillet and brown the meat on all sides, and remove. Add the rice to the skillet and stir until all grains are coated with butter. Cook over a medium heat for 3 minutes. Put the rice into the bottom of a large casserole; add the chopped parsley and the remaining teaspoon of salt. Add the cherries with a cup of the cherry liquid and put the pork tenderloin on top. Pour in the reserved cup of marinade and the bouillon. Cover the casserole tightly and bake at 350° for 1¼ hours, or until the pork is tender and all the liquid is absorbed. Remove the meat and slice it. Fluff up the rice with a fork, replace the meat, and serve from the casserole. (Serves 6)

At times clients are not served in the dining room for one reason or another, so Fritz serves them in the office from trays. In HELP WANTED, MALE, *dinner in the office consists of melon, broiled pork-loin wafers, salad with Wolfe's own dressing (see index), blueberry pie, and coffee.*

BROILED PORK-LOIN WAFERS

3½-pound pork-loin roast	4 tablespoons vermouth
3 tablespoons butter	2 tablespoons wine vinegar
1½ tablespoons flour	1 tablespoon minced sour
1 cup beef stock	gherkins
½ cup dry red wine	1 tablespoon minced chives
2 teaspoons minced shallots	1 teaspoon dry mustard
½ teaspoon fresh tarragon (or	watercress
¼ teaspoon dried leaves)	

Cut ¼-inch-thick slices from the pork loin, and, using half the butter, butter them on both sides. Broil the pork under a hot flame and set aside on a warm platter. In a saucepan melt the remaining butter and add the flour. Stir until the flour turns a golden brown and gradually add the stock and the red wine. Continue to stir until the sauce starts to thicken. Remove from heat and set aside. In a small saucepan put the shallots, tarragon, vermouth, and vinegar. Boil until the liquid is reduced by half. Add it to the sauce and cook over a low heat, stirring, for 3 minutes. Add the gherkins, chives, and dry mustard, which you have made into a paste with 1 tablespoon of the sauce. Simmer the sauce for 5 more minutes. Pour the sauce over the pork and garnish with watercress. (Serves 6)

One of Wolfe's favorite things to do with pork is to have Fritz make a sausage out of it. We have already sampled his scrapple in the breakfast chapter, and we will meet up with the famous saucisse minuit *recipe in Chapter 12, but there is also a summer sausage, of which Saul Panzer, for one, is inordinately fond.*

SUMMER SAUSAGE

2 pounds beef fillet	¼ teaspoon powdered nutmeg
2 pounds lean pork shoulder,	1 teaspoon minced thyme leaves
boned	(or ½ teaspoon dried leaves)
1 pound pork fat	freshly ground black pepper to
2 ounces cognac	taste
3 teaspoons salt	1 onion, grated
¼ teaspoon powdered cloves	sausage casings (see note)

Cube the beef, pork, and pork fat, and put all the meat through the fine blade of a meat grinder. Put the ground meat into a large bowl and sprinkle on the remaining ingredients (except sausage casings). Mix thoroughly. When the spices are completely blended, fill sausage casings with the mixture, tying the sausages into 3-inch lengths. The sausages are now ready to be cooked.

NOTE: Sausage casings, made from pig intestines, can be obtained from most Italian butcher shops.

Because sausage-making is a time-consuming business, Fritz has learned to farm out some of this labor to trusted suppliers, one of whom is a Mr. Howie in New Jersey who makes sausage according to Wolfe's specifications (without allspice but sometimes with cloves) and another of whom is a Swiss named Darst who lives up near Chappaqua and prepares a sausage with ten herbs in it, from homemade pigs.

SAUSAGE WITH TEN HERBS

2 pounds fresh pork
1 pound pork fat
2 pounds lean beef
1 tablespoon salt
1 teaspoon freshly ground
    pepper
1 clove garlic, minced
1 large onion, chopped fine
1 bay leaf, crushed fine
¼ teaspoon powdered cloves

1 teaspoon anise seed
1 teaspoon sweet marjoram
1 teaspoon thyme (or ½
    teaspoon dried leaves)
1½ teaspoons fresh chopped
    parsley
1 teaspoon dry mustard
½ teaspoon mace
¼ teaspoon nutmeg
sausage casings

Cube the pork, pork fat, and beef and run them all twice through the fine blade of a meat grinder. Put the meat in a mixing bowl and add the salt, pepper, garlic, and onion. Mix the remaining herbs and spices together and blend well into the meat. Using the meat grinder with a special sausage-stuffing attachment, fill the casings with the mixture, tying into 3-inch lengths.

One special lunch, in THE SILENT SPEAKER, *featured two favorite dishes together:* Fritz entered to announce lunch, which that day happened to consist of corn cakes with breaded fresh pork tenderloin, followed by corn cakes with a hot sauce of tomatoes and cheese, followed by corn cakes with honey. Fritz's timing with the corn cakes was superb. At the precise instant, for example, that one of us finished with his eleventh, here came the twelfth straight from the griddle, and so on.

BREADED FRESH PORK TENDERLOIN

1 3-pound pork tenderloin	1 stalk celery, coarsely chopped
½ cup all-purpose flour	1 bay leaf
salt and freshly ground black pepper	2 sprigs parsley
1 medium onion, coarsely chopped	1 cup dry white wine
1 medium carrot, coarsely chopped	2 egg yolks
	1 cup fresh bread crumbs
	¼ cup dry sherry

Preheat the oven to 325°. Wipe the meat with a clean cloth and dredge with flour, salt, and pepper. Strew the onion, carrot, and celery on the bottom of a roasting pan with the bay leaf and parsley. Place the pork on top and pour the wine over all. Roast for 1½ hours, basting occasionally with the pan juices. Remove from the oven and cool slightly. Beat the egg yolks and brush over all sides of the pork. Roll the meat in the bread crumbs, moisten with the sherry, and roll again in the crumbs until the meat is completely coated. Raise the temperature of the oven to 400° and return the meat to the pan from which the juices and vegetables have been removed and reserved. Roast for another 15 minutes, or until the crust is browned. In the meantime, skim the fat from the pan juices, strain, and reduce the juices in a saucepan to about half a cup. Pour the sauce over the meat just before serving. (Serves 4 to 6)

Since the main dish in this meal is obviously corn cakes, it appears that we should move on to the subject of corn without further delay.

Corn

CORN CAKES

2 cups yellow corn meal
1 cup all-purpose flour
1 teaspoon baking powder
¼ teaspoon powdered sage
1½ teaspoons salt

4 tablespoons butter
¼ cup minced celery
2 large eggs
3 cups milk

Combine the corn meal, flour, baking powder, sage, and salt in a bowl. In a small skillet melt the butter and sauté the celery until soft. Beat the eggs and add to the corn meal with the celery and butter. Mix well. Gradually add the milk, stirring constantly until the batter is the thickness of heavy cream. Heat the griddle, grease it, and pour out the batter by spoonfuls to make cakes about 2 inches in diameter. Turn once so that they are nicely browned on both sides. Add more milk to the batter if it should begin to thicken. Serve as a side dish with plenty of butter. (Makes about 18 to 20 2-inch cakes)

VARIATION:

Corn Cakes with Tomato and Cheese Sauce: Use white corn meal instead of yellow and omit the celery and sage, substituting freshly ground black pepper.

THE SAUCE

2 tablespoons butter
2 tablespoons all-purpose flour
1½ cups heavy cream, heated
¼ pound Fontina cheese
2 egg yolks

½ cup tomato purée
½ teaspoon salt
2 grindings black pepper
2 dashes Tabasco (optional)

Melt the butter in a saucepan and add the flour. Cook over a low heat for 3 minutes and gradually add the warm cream, stirring constantly. Cube the cheese and add to the sauce, a few cubes at a time, until it is all melted. Remove from heat. Beat the egg yolks with a little of the sauce and then add them to the saucepan. Stir well over a low heat until the sauce has thickened. Add the tomato purée and stir until heated through. Season with salt and pepper. Add the Tabasco if you like a hotter sauce.

Corn Cakes with Honey: Use yellow corn meal, omitting the celery and sage, and adding 2 tablespoons brown sugar. Serve with warm wild-thyme honey.

By an arrangement with a farmer named Duncan McLeod up in Putnam County, every Tuesday from July 20 to October 5, sixteen ears of just-picked corn were delivered. They were roasted in the husk and we did our own shucking as we ate—four ears for me, eight for Wolfe, and four in the kitchen for Fritz. The corn had to arrive no earlier than five-thirty and no later than six-thirty. That day it hadn't arrived at all, and Fritz had to do some stuffed eggplant, so Wolfe was standing scowling at the globe when the doorbell rang.   [MURDER IS CORNY]

LAMB-STUFFED EGGPLANT (see index)

It developed that the delivery boy, who was taking some corn also to Rusterman's Restaurant, was attacked and killed behind the restaurant, and the unraveling of that murder is the story of MURDER IS CORNY, *during the course of which Wolfe explains to Inspector Cramer the best way to cook corn on the cob.*

CORN ON THE COB

Wolfe: It must be nearly mature, but not quite, and it must be picked not more than three hours before it reaches me. Do you eat sweet corn?

Cramer: Yes. You're stalling.

Wolfe: No. Who cooks it?

Cramer: My wife. I haven't got a Fritz.

Wolfe: Does she cook it in water?

Cramer: Sure. Is yours cooked in beer?

Wolfe: No. Millions of American women, and some men, commit that outrage every summer day. They are turning a superb treat into mere provender. Shucked and boiled in water, sweet corn is edible and nutritious; roasted in husk in the hottest possible oven for forty minutes, shucked at the table, and buttered and salted, nothing else, it is ambrosia. No chef's ingenuity and imagination have ever created a finer dish. American women should themselves be boiled in water.

Next to corn served fresh, corn fritters seem to be the most highly prized dish made from this most highly prized of vegetables, appearing more frequently in the stories than any other single food with the exception of beer and milk. Archie puts them, too, in the category of ambrosia: I went on by to the kitchen, and was served by Fritz with what do you think? Corn fritters. There had been eight perfectly good ears and Fritz hates to throw good food away. With bacon and homemade blackberry jam they were ambrosia.

CORN FRITTERS

8 ears fresh corn
1¼ teaspoons salt
¼ cup milk
2 tablespoons all-purpose flour

2 egg whites
½ cup good vegetable oil
   (or more)

Remove the husks from the corn and score each row of ears, letting the corn milk drain into a bowl. Then cut the kernels off into the bowl. Add the salt, milk, and sifted flour, and blend well. Let the mixture stand in the refrigerator for 15 minutes. Beat the egg whites until stiff and fold gently into the batter. Drop by spoonfuls into hot oil (½ inch deep in the skillet) and cook until golden brown, turning once. Serve immediately with homemade blackberry jam (see index). (Makes 12 fritters)

In place of blackberry jam, honey—domestic autumn honey or wild-thyme honey from Syria or Greece—or anchovy butter (see index) may also be used, depending on when and how the fritters are being served. They have been known to be main courses at luncheon, side dishes at dinner, or snacks at any time. In describing a particularly bad Wolfe mood, Archie heightens the drama by employing fritters as the main course: At lunchtime on Thursday, anyone who wanted to know how things were shaping up could have satisfied his curiosity by looking in the dining room and observing Wolfe's behavior at the midday meal, which consisted of corn fritters with autumn honey, sausages, and a bowl of salad. At meals he is always expansive, talkative, and good-humored, but throughout that one he was grim, sullen, and peevish. Fritz was worried stiff.   [AND BE A VILLAIN]

Another corn dish involving the use of fresh corn is green-corn pudding, which is served at lunch in THE FATHER HUNT *with sweetbreads amandine (see index).*

GREEN-CORN PUDDING

6 ears young corn, scraped	3 large eggs
1 tablespoon sugar	4 tablespoons melted butter
1 tablespoon cornstarch	1 cup milk
1 teaspoon salt	
2 tablespoons chopped pimiento	

Preheat oven to 350°. Combine all ingredients in the order given except for the eggs. Separate the eggs, beating the yolks and adding them to the mixture. Beat the egg whites until stiff and fold them in last. Put the mixture into a greased 1½-quart casserole and bake for 35 minutes.

VARIATION:

For chicken and corn pudding, add 1 cup of cooked (preferably poached) chicken meat and omit the sugar.   [TOO MANY COOKS]

Two more favorite corn dishes use corn meal rather than corn taken fresh from the cob, but they all belong in this chapter nonetheless, as does the following starling recipe, certain aspects of which bear an obvious resemblance to corn on the cob.

CORN MUFFINS [A RIGHT TO DIE]

1 cup yellow corn meal	2 tablespoons sugar
1 cup all-purpose flour	1 large egg
4 teaspoons baking powder	1 cup milk
½ teaspoon salt	2 tablespoons melted butter

Preheat the oven to 425°. Sift the corn meal, flour, baking powder, salt, and sugar into a bowl. Beat the egg and add the milk to it. Stir into the dry ingredients and add the melted butter. Stir lightly, only enough to incorporate the butter. With a spoon drop the batter into a buttered cast-iron muffin tin, filling each cup two-thirds full. Bake for 20 to 25 minutes and serve with plenty of butter.

VARIATION:

Add ½ cup chopped, cooked country sausage to the batter and stir thoroughly (see index for Summer Sausage).

Each year around the middle of May, by arrangement, a farmer who lives up near Brewster shoots eighteen or twenty starlings, puts them in a bag, and gets in his car and drives to New York. It is understood that they are to be delivered to our door within two hours after they were winged. Fritz dresses them and sprinkles them with salt, and, at the proper moment, brushes them with melted butter, wraps them in sage leaves, grills them, and arranges them on a platter of hot polenta, which is thick porridge of fine-ground yellow corn meal with butter, grated cheese, and salt and pepper. It is an expensive meal and a happy one, and Wolfe always looks forward to it, but that day he put on an exhibition. When the platter was brought in, steaming, and placed before him, he sniffed, ducked his head, and sniffed again, and straightened to look up at Fritz.

"The sage?"

"No, sir."

"What do you mean, no, sir?"

"I thought you might like it once in a style I have suggested, with saffron and tarragon. Much fresh tarragon, with just a touch of saffron, which is the way . . ."

"Remove it."

Fritz went rigid and his lips tightened.

"You did not consult me," Wolfe said coldly. "To find that without warning one of my favorite dishes has been radically altered is an unpleasant shock. It may possibly be edible, but I am in no humor to risk it. Please dispose of it and bring me four coddled eggs and a piece of toast." [THE GOLDEN SPIDERS]

STARLINGS

18 or 20 starlings	1 cup dry sherry
salt	½ pound butter
chervil	18 or 20 sage leaves (or pieces
basil	of aluminum foil)
thyme	

Dress the birds and sprinkle them with salt. Let them stand for about 5 minutes and then sprinkle them with a pinch each of chervil, basil, and thyme—or whatever other herbs you have fresh, except for tarragon and saffron, which are not advised. Melt the butter and combine with the sherry. Brush each bird with the mixture and wrap individually in sage leaves (or aluminum foil). Seal the edges tightly to keep the juices in. Grill for 15 to 20 minutes in a hot (400°) oven or over coals. Serve them in the wrapping, or arrange on polenta (see recipe below) and pour the juice over each bird before serving.

POLENTA

2 cups yellow corn meal	8 tablespoons butter (1 stick)
4 cups boiling water	½ teaspoon ground sage
1 teaspoon salt	

Sprinkle the corn meal slowly into the boiling water. Add the salt. Stir the meal until it thickens. Cover and continue to cook for 25 minutes over hot water, stirring occasionally with a wooden spoon. Stir in the butter and sage. Serve hot.

VARIATION:

Instead of serving hot, pour the polenta into a buttered mold and chill thoroughly. Unmold and slice. Sauté the slices in butter until browned on both sides. Serve with warm autumn honey.

There is a happy ending to this unfortunate luncheon, and we shall give it to you, even though it involves putting a pork recipe in the wrong place in this chapter. I think that Fritz, who obviously tried to smooth Wolfe's ruffled feathers by putting a favorite concoction before him, would not mind: At the dinner table that evening, neither Wolfe nor Fritz gave the slightest indication that starlings had ever come between them. As Wolfe took his second helping of the main dish, which was Danish pork pancake, he said distinctly, "Most satisfactory." Since that for him was positively lavish, Fritz took it as offered, nodded with dignity, and murmured, "Certainly, sir."

DANISH PORK PANCAKE

1 pound lean pork loin, boned
7 tablespoons butter
3 tablespoons minced shallots
2 cups sifted all-purpose flour
6 large eggs

1 teaspoon salt
1 cup milk (or more)
watercress
cooked pitted prunes

Trim the pork of all fat and cut into tiny cubes. Melt 3 tablespoons of the butter in a skillet and add the pork, sautéing over a low flame until the meat is cooked (at least 20 minutes). Drain the meat and set aside. Add 2 tablespoons of butter to the pan and cook the shallots until golden. Drain. Put the flour in a large mixing bowl and make a well in the center. Break the eggs in a separate bowl, add the salt, and beat lightly. Slowly blend the eggs into the flour, mixing until smooth. Add the milk, the rest of the butter, and beat until all are incorporated. Add more milk if the batter is too thick. Add the pork cubes and shallots and stir well. Drop the batter by spoonfuls on a hot greased griddle and cook the cakes until browned on both sides, turning once. Garnish them with the watercress and the prunes. (Makes about 12 to 15 2-inch cakes)

7

THE RELAPSE

The previous chapter has paved the way for a chapter dealing with the care and feeding of a genius when things have gone wrong; usually Wolfe's bad moods have something to do with a bad case or a client, but in some cases, an extraordinary culinary event is the cause as well as the result of what Archie fondly calls Wolfe's "relapses."

Wolfe sat at the kitchen table with a pencil in his hand and sheets of paper scattered around. Fritz stood across from him, with a gleam in his eye that I knew only too well. Neither paid any attention to the noise I made entering. Wolfe was saying:

". . . but we cannot get good peafowl. Archie could try that place on Long Island, but it is probably hopeless. A peafowl's breast flesh will not be sweet and tender and properly developed unless it is well protected from all alarms, especially from the air, to prevent nervousness, and Long Island is full of airplanes. The goose for this evening, with the stuffing as arranged, will be quite satisfactory. The kid will be ideal for tomorrow. We can phone Mr. Salzenbach at once to butcher one and Archie can drive to Garfield for it in the morning. You can proceed with the preliminaries for the sauce. Friday is a problem. If we try the peafowl we shall merely be inviting catastrophe. Squabs will do for tidbits, but the chief difficulty remains. Fritz, I'll tell you. Let us try a new tack entirely. Do you know shish kebab? I have had it in Turkey. Marinate thin slices of tender lamb for several hours in red wine and spices. Here, I'll put it down: thyme, mace, peppercorns, garlic—"

I stood and took it in. It looked hopeless. There was no question but that it was the beginning of a major relapse.

[THE RED BOX]

SHISH KEBAB

3 pounds shoulder of spring
    lamb, boned
1 pint Burgundy
½ cup olive oil
1 teaspoon fresh thyme (or
    ½ teaspoon dried leaves)
1 teaspoon fresh orégano (or
    ¼ teaspoon dried leaves)
1 teaspoon mace

1 tablespoon black peppercorns
1 clove garlic
1 large onion
mushrooms
eggplant
tomatoes
green peppers
large green olives stuffed with
    pimientos

Trim the lamb of fat and tendons and cut into 2-inch cubes. Make a marinade of the wine, olive oil, thyme, orégano, mace, and peppercorns. Mash the garlic and slice the onion and add these to the liquid. Pour over the lamb and allow the meat to stand for 2 to 4 hours. When ready to cook, drain and pat the meat dry with a cloth or paper towel. Preheat the broiler. Stem the mushrooms and cut in half if they are large; cube the unpeeled eggplant and quarter the tomatoes. Parboil and slice the seeded peppers. Alternate meat and vegetables on skewers and brush with the marinade. Broil them on one side until browned, brush again with the marinade, and turn to broil the other side. (Serves 4)

> The talk at table may be of anything and everything, except business, usually of Wolfe's choosing, but that time I started it by remarking, as I helped myself from the silver platter, that a man had told me that shish kebab was just as good or better with kid instead of lamb. Wolfe said that any dish was better with kid instead of lamb, but that fresh kid, properly butchered and handled, was unattainable in the metropolitan area. Then he switched from meat to words and said it was miscalled shish kebab. It should be spelled seekh kebab. He spelled it. That was what it was called in India, where it originated. In Hindi or Urdu a seekh is a thin iron rod with a loop at one end and a point at the other, and a kebab is a meatball. Some occidental jackass, he said, had made it shish instead of seekh, and it would serve him right if the only seekh kebab he ever got was tough donkey instead of lamb.   [THE FATHER HUNT]

> Wolfe had a relapse. It was a bad one, and it lasted three days. When I got back to Thirty-fifth Street, he was sitting in the kitchen, arguing with Fritz whether chives should be used in tomato tarts.   [FER-DE-LANCE]

TOMATO TARTS

tart crust (see index)
3 tablespoons butter
2 medium onions, chopped, or
   ½ cup minced shallots
2 pounds tomatoes
1 cup heavy cream
3 large eggs

1½ teaspoons salt
½ teaspoon freshly ground
   black pepper
1 teaspoon minced basil leaves
1½ tablespoons minced
   chives (optional)

Melt the butter in a skillet and cook the onions until they are transparent. Peel, seed, and chop all the tomatoes except one and add the tomato pulp to the onions. Cook over a low heat until they have been reduced to a softened mass. Remove from the heat and cool. Add the cream to the eggs and beat well. Mix them with the tomato mixture and season with salt, pepper, basil, and chives. Line the tart pans with the pastry and fill with the tomato mixture. Slice the remaining tomato and place a slice on each tart. Bake at 350° for about 35 minutes, or until the center is set and the tart is nicely browned. Sprinkle on more chives or basil before serving. (Serves 6)

I had never really understood Wolfe's relapses. . . . Nothing that I could say made the slightest dent on him. While it lasted he acted one of two different ways: either he went to bed and stayed there, living on bread and onion soup . . . or he sat in the kitchen telling Fritz how to cook things and then eating them on my little table. He ate a whole half a sheep that way in two days once, different parts of it cooked in twenty different ways. At such times I usually had my tongue out from running all over town from the Battery to Bronx Park, trying to find some herb or root or maybe cordial that they needed in the dish they were going to do next. [FER-DE-LANCE]

ONION SOUP

5 cups thinly sliced onions
3 tablespoons of butter
1 tablespoon of olive oil
1½ teaspoons salt
½ teaspoon sugar

3 tablespoons flour
8 cups strong beef stock
½ cup dry white vermouth
salt and pepper

Slowly cook the onions in the butter and oil, using a heavy, 4-quart covered pot. After 10 minutes, add salt and sugar. Cook for 35 minutes in all, stirring every 10 minutes until the onions have turned an even brown color. Add the flour 1 tablespoon at a time and continue to stir and cook for 3 or 4 minutes longer. Add the stock, 2 cups at a time, stirring after each addition. Add the wine and simmer the soup, partially covered, for 45 to 50 minutes. Skim and stir. Correct seasoning and serve very hot.

NOTE: Do not serve with grated cheese or toasted French bread, which detract from the consistency and flavor of this carefully balanced brew.

LAMB COOKED IN TWENTY DIFFERENT WAYS

We have already had recipes for lamb cutlets, lamb kidneys, Kentucky burgoo, cassoulet, and shish kebab. In later pages we will find recipes for leg of lamb, lamb loaf, and hunkiev beyandi. That makes eight different ways. If you substitute cooked chunks of lamb for duck in curried duck, cubes of boned lamb shoulder for pork in the braised-in-beer recipe, breast of lamb for spareribs, and chopped lamb liver for the chicken livers, you'll have twelve different ways. We will leave it to you to use lamb brains instead of beef when you do your favorite brain recipe the next time (Wolfe does not seem to enjoy brains). And so, at the risk of sending the reader into his own brand of relapse, we will now do our best to supply the seven missing lamb recipes, still working from the same animal. Keep in mind Wolfe's earlier remark that kid, if you can get it, is probably better than lamb in any of the following dishes.

LOIN LAMB CHOPS

1 medium onion, chopped	3 tablespoons flour
½ teaspoon chopped parsley	2 tablespoons melted butter
salt and pepper to taste	2 cups dry white wine
4 double-thick loin lamb chops	1 teaspoon lemon juice

Sprinkle the onion and the parsley over the bottom of a large casserole. Salt and pepper the chops on both sides and rub them with 2 tablespoons of the flour. Dip the chops into the melted butter and arrange them in the casserole (they may overlap slightly). Pour the wine around them. Cover tightly and simmer on top of the stove until the meat is tender (30 to 50 minutes, depending on the age and quality of the meat). Remove the chops to a warm plate, thicken the broth with the remaining tablespoon of flour, add the lemon juice, and strain over the chops. (Serves 4)

LAMB CHOPS WITH WALNUTS

8 rib lamb chops
3 tablespoons clarified butter
salt and freshly ground
   black pepper
2 teaspoons minced shallots

1 large green pepper, finely
   diced
½ cup black walnuts
½ cup dry white wine

Trim the chops of excess fat and scrape off the end of the rib bone. Melt the butter in a skillet and sauté the chops, about 3 minutes to a side, until they are nicely browned. (If you like them well done, cook about 6 minutes on each side.) Remove to a warm platter and sprinkle with salt and pepper. Add the shallots and the green pepper to the pan and cook for 5 minutes. Chop the walnuts and add to the pan. Cook, stirring, for 1 or 2 minutes. Spoon the mixture over the chops and deglaze the pan with the wine. Pour the warm wine over the chops and serve very hot. (Serves 4)

BRAISED LAMB SHANKS

4 lamb shanks, whole
2 tablespoons olive oil
salt and pepper to taste
2 tablespoons all-purpose flour
1 cup beef broth
1 cup red wine
2 tablespoons tomato paste
1 clove garlic

1 sprig thyme
1 bay leaf
1 carrot
2 onions
¼ pound mushrooms
2 tablespoons butter
sprigs parsley

Trim the lamb of excess fat and tendons. As you heat the oil in a heavy kettle on top of the stove, sprinkle the lamb with the salt, pepper, and flour. Brown the shanks in the oil, turning them frequently. Remove from the pot and set aside. Pour out the oil and add the broth and wine to the pot. Bring to a boil, lower the heat, and simmer, adding the tomato paste, garlic clove, thyme, and bay leaf. Return the meat to the pot and simmer over a low heat for 1 hour. Skim the fat. Cut the peeled carrots and onions into chunks and add them to the pot. Simmer for another 20 minutes until the carrots are tender. Meanwhile, clean and stem the mushrooms and sauté them gently in the butter. Just before you serve the stew, add the mushrooms and garnish with the parsley. Serve the lamb shanks from the pot. (Serves 4)

BAKER'S-OVEN CASSEROLE

3 pounds lamb neck, boned
1 pound pork shoulder, boned
4 medium potatoes, sliced
1 large yellow onion, sliced
1 teaspoon salt
½ teaspoon freshly ground
    black pepper

3 tablespoons butter
1 cup dry white wine
2 tablespoons chopped
    Italian parsley
2 tablespoons grated Parmesan
    cheese

Preheat the oven to 300°. Trim the meat and cut the pork into 1-inch cubes. Cover the bottom of a baking dish with 2 of the sliced potatoes. Add the meat and cover with the sliced onion. Season with the salt and pepper. Add the last of the potatoes and top with bits of the butter. Pour the wine over the dish and bring it to a boil on the top of the stove. Sprinkle the dish with the parsley and Parmesan cheese and put on the cover. Bake for 2 hours. (Serves 4)

LAMB-STUFFED EGGPLANT

1¼ pounds ground lamb
1 medium onion, grated
1 cup cooked rice
⅓ cup plus 2 tablespoons
    tomato juice
½ green pepper, chopped fine
¼ cup chopped dill
2 tablespoons currants
salt and freshly ground black
    pepper to taste

1 tablespoon chopped parsley
3 tablespoons pine nuts
3 medium eggplants
¾ cup dry white wine
¾ cup water
4 tablespoons butter
bunch parsley

In a bowl mix the lamb, onion, rice, tomato juice, green pepper, dill, currants, salt, pepper, parsley, and pine nuts. Wipe the eggplants with a damp cloth. Cut them in half and scoop out the inside flesh, leaving a ½-inch shell. Fill each eggplant with equal parts of the lamb mixture. Put a rack in the bottom of a large casserole or Dutch oven and cover the rack with a heavy layer of the parsley. Put the eggplant halves on the parsley. Dot the top of each eggplant with butter. Into the bottom of the pan pour the wine and water. Cover the pot tightly and simmer over medium heat for 1 hour, or until the eggplant is tender. Remove to a warm platter and keep it warm while you make the sauce.

THE SAUCE

1 cup of the cooking stock
2 large eggs, plus 1 yolk

3 tablespoons lime juice
pinch paprika

Strain the cooking stock into a bowl. In another bowl, beat the eggs and the extra yolk until frothy. Add the lime juice, blend well, and put into a saucepan. Gradually add the stock to the saucepan, stirring well. Cook over a low heat until the sauce thickens. Add the paprika and pour the sauce into a sauceboat to serve with the stuffed eggplant. (Serves 6)

This is one of the dishes that can be made with either kid, lamb, or veal. Since Archie fails to pick up the kid as planned at Mr. Salzenbach's, we are led to believe that the fricandeau served at lunch that day was actually made with lamb.   [THE RED BOX]

FRICANDEAU

1 2½-to-3-pound slice loin of
  lamb, approximately
  1½ inches thick
2 garlic cloves, sliced
3 tablespoons butter
2 carrots, sliced
1 onion, sliced

1 stalk celery, sliced
2 sprigs parsley
1 bay leaf
1 cup beef stock
1 cup dry white wine
1 small truffle

Preheat the oven to 325°. Ask the butcher to trim the lamb of excess fat and tendon. Make several incisions in the meat and lard it with slices of garlic. Melt the butter in a large casserole. Sauté the carrots, onion, and celery in the butter until the onions start to brown. Remove the casserole from the heat. Arrange the piece of lamb on top of the vegetables; add the parsley and bay leaf to the pan. Mix the stock and the wine together and pour into the casserole until it comes up to the top but does not cover the meat. Cover the casserole and bake for 1½ hours. Baste frequently with the liquids, adding more stock if necessary. When the meat is tender, remove it from the casserole and keep it warm on a hot serving platter. Strain the gravy, skim off the fat, and measure out 1⅓ cups. Add a little wine or stock if necessary. Place this liquid in a saucepan and reduce to 1 cup over a high flame. Mince the truffle and add it to the sauce; simmer for 5 minutes more. Correct the seasoning and pour over the meat. Serve with braised endive. (Serves 4)

NOTE: Veal may also be used in this dish; be sure to lard it with pork fat or ask the butcher to do it for you. Lamb has a high fat content so that larding is not necessary.

It was after six o'clock when I got there. I went to the kitchen first and commandeered a glass of milk, took a couple of sniffs at the goulash steaming gently on the simmer plate, and told Fritz it didn't smell much like freshly butchered kid to me. I slid out when he brandished a skimming spoon.   [THE RED BOX]

GOULASH

3 pounds stewing lamb, boned
½ cup all-purpose flour
1 tablespoon salt
½ teaspoon freshly ground
    black pepper
½ cup butter

2 tablespoons paprika
4 cups sliced onions
1 green pepper
1 bay leaf
1½ cups strong beef stock
¼ cup Polish vodka

Cut the lamb into 1-inch chunks and dust with the flour, salt, and pepper. Melt the butter in a large casserole and brown the meat, a few pieces at a time. Do not allow the butter to burn. Sprinkle paprika over the meat as it cooks. Add the onions to the pot. Seed and slice the green pepper and add it along with the bay leaf and beef stock. Cover the pot and simmer until tender (about 1 hour). Five minutes before you take the stew off the heat, skim it of fat and stir in the vodka. Serve with noodles or rice. (Serves 4)

This dish, made with lamb instead of kid, is served for dinner on the day that fricandeau has appeared on the table at lunch. Since the two dishes are very similar, this may seem to be rather too much of a good thing, but remember, this is a relapse.

At ten minutes past nine in the evening of that long day I went to the kitchen. Wolfe was at the center of the table with Fritz, arguing about the number of juniper berries to put in a marinade for venison loin chops.

Wolfe: Very well, proceed. I say three, but proceed as you will. If you put in five, I won't even have to taste it; the smell will tell me. With four it might be palatable.   [THE DOORBELL RANG]

VENISON LOIN CHOPS

4 large venison loin chops	1 sprig tarragon
2 tablespoons minced shallots	4 tablespoons red wine vinegar
4 juniper berries, crushed	2 tablespoons olive oil
2 small carrots, sliced	1 cup dry vermouth
2 sprigs Italian parsley	2 tablespoons butter
½ teaspoon salt	1 cup sour cream (see index)
8 black peppercorns	1 tablespoon minced chives
1 small bay leaf	

Put the trimmed chops into a large bowl with the shallots. Add the juniper berries and carrots to the bowl with the parsley, salt, peppercorns, bay leaf, tarragon, vinegar, olive oil, and vermouth. Cover the bowl and marinate for at least 24 hours in the refrigerator. When ready to cook, remove the chops from the marinade, reserving ½ cup, wipe dry, and sauté in the butter in a large skillet for 4 to 5 minutes a side. Remove the chops as they are done to a heated platter and keep hot in a slow oven. Pour the reserved strained marinade into the sautéing pan and bring it to a boil, deglazing the pan by scraping up any of the meat bits that have adhered to the bottom. Stir in the sour cream and chives, heating thoroughly. Do not allow the sour cream to boil. Correct the seasoning and serve with the chops. (Serves 4)

Sometimes I thought it was a wonder Wolfe and I got on together at all. The differences between us, some of them, showed up plainer at the table than anywhere else. He was a taster, and I was a swallower. Not that I didn't know good from bad; after seven years of education from Fritz's cooking, I could even tell, usually, superlative from excellent. But the fact remained that what chiefly attracted Wolfe about food in his pharynx was the affair it was having with his taste buds, whereas with me the important point was that it was bound for my belly. To avoid any misunderstanding, I should add that Wolfe was never disconcerted by the problem of what to do with it when he was through tasting it. He could put it away. I have seen him, during a relapse, dispose completely of a ten-pound goose between eight o'clock and midnight, while I was in a corner with ham sandwiches and milk, hoping he would choke. At those times he always ate in the kitchen.   [LEAGUE OF FRIGHTENED MEN]

GOOSE

1 10-pound goose	4 teaspoons salt
3 leeks, sliced	8 black peppercorns
1 large carrot, sliced	1 cup dry white wine
1 cup chopped celery	1 cup water
1 tablespoon chopped parsley	3 cups milk
½ teaspoon powdered sage	8 cloves garlic, crushed
½ teaspoon fresh tarragon (or	4 egg yolks
¼ teaspoon dried leaves, crushed)	2 teaspoons dry mustard

Cut the goose into 12 pieces and place them in a large saucepan. Add the leeks and carrots to the pan along with the celery, parsley, sage, tarragon, 2 teaspoons of the salt, and the peppercorns, wine, and water. Bring the mixture to a boil, cover the pan, lower the heat, and simmer for 1 to 1¼ hours, until the goose is done. Remove the meat from the broth and keep warm. In the top of a double boiler scald 2½ cups of the milk, to which you have added the garlic. Remove from heat. Beat the egg yolks with the remaining ½ cup of milk and slowly add to the hot milk, stirring constantly. Return the mixture to the heat; over boiling water, add the remaining 2 teaspoons of salt and the dry mustard. Continue to cook, stirring constantly, until the sauce is thickened. Pour over the goose and serve immediately. (Serves 6)

HAM SANDWICH (see index for Georgia-Country-Ham Sandwiches)

Fritz was in the kitchen, on his third bottle of wine, absolutely miserable. Added to the humiliation of a homicide in the house he kept was the incredible fact that Wolfe had passed up a meal. He had refused to eat a bite.   [EENY MEENY MURDER MO]   *Archie is describing here a different sort of relapse from what we have seen so far, the kind where Wolfe takes no interest in food at all, which, given his usual attitude toward food, is far more frightening a situation than eating half a lamb in twenty different ways.*

Wolfe, to Fritz entering the office with beer: "Take that back. I don't want it."

"But it will do—"

"Take it back. I shall drink no beer until I get my fingers around that creature's throat. . . . And I shall eat no meat."

"But impossible! The squabs are marinating!"

"Throw them out."

The meals were dismal. Squab marinated in light cream, rolled in flour seasoned with salt, pepper, nutmeg, clove, thyme, and crushed juniper berries, sautéed in olive oil, and served on toast spread with red currant jelly, with 'Madeira cream sauce poured over it, is one of Wolfe's favorite tidbits. He ordinarily consumes three of them, though I have known him to make it four. That day I wanted to eat in the kitchen, but no. I had to sit and down my two while he grimly pecked away at his green peas and salad and cheese. The Sunday evening snack was just as bad. He usually has something like cheese and anchovy spread or *pâté de foie gras* or herring in sour cream, but apparently the meat pledge included fish. He ate crackers and cheese and drank four cups of coffee. Later, in the office, he finished off a bowl of pecans and then went to the kitchen for a brush and pan to collect the bits of shell on his desk and rug. He sure was piling on the agony.

[PLOT IT YOURSELF]

SQUABS MARINATED IN CREAM

6 squabs
2 cups light cream
½ cup all-purpose flour
½ teaspoon salt
¼ teaspoon freshly ground
  black pepper
generous pinch nutmeg

¼ teaspoon powdered clove
1 teaspoon fresh thyme leaves
  (¼ teaspoon dried)
4 crushed juniper berries
¼ cup olive oil
6 slices white bread
1 cup red-currant jelly

Cut the squabs down the back, leaving the backbone intact. Flatten the birds slightly with the palm of your hand and, using a very sharp knife, remove the backbone and ribs. Put the squabs in a bowl and cover with the cream. Set aside for 1 hour. Combine the flour with salt, pepper, nutmeg, clove, thyme, and juniper berries. Remove the squabs from the cream and roll them in the seasoned flour, shaking off the excess. Heat the olive oil in a large skillet and sauté the squabs until browned on both sides and cooked through (about 20–30 minutes). While the squabs are cooking make the sauce (see below) and toast the bread. Spread the toast with the jelly and place the cooked squabs on top. (Serves 6)

MADEIRA CREAM SAUCE:

2 tablespoons all-purpose flour
2 tablespoons butter
1 cup milk

2 tablespoons Madeira
salt and pepper to taste

Melt the butter in a heavy-bottomed saucepan and add the flour. Allow to cook gently for 3 minutes and gradually add the milk. Stir constantly over a low flame until the sauce is thickened. Add the Madeira and salt and pepper to taste. Pour the hot sauce over the squabs and serve immediately.

Another meatless period in Wolfe's life occurred in 1954 in the middle of the Great Meat Shortage when millions of pigs and steers much to the regret of the growers and slaughterers, had sneaked off and hid in order to sell their lives dear, and to Nero Wolfe a meal without meat was an insult. His temper got so bad that I had offered to let him eat me, and it would be best to skip his retort.   [DIE LIKE A DOG]

Fritz was in the kitchen drinking coffee. "Is that Mr. Wolfe up with Horstman?" I asked him.

"And how." That was the only slang Fritz ever used and he always welcomed a chance to get it in. "Now I will just get a leg of lamb and rub garlic on it."

"Rub poison ivy on it if you want to."

The relapse was over.   [FER-DE-LANCE]

LEG OF LAMB

1 leg of lamb, weighing 5 to 6 pounds
2 cloves garlic, crushed
½ cup Dijon mustard
1 tablespoon good soy sauce
1 teaspoon crushed thyme leaves (or ½ teaspoon dried leaves)
¼ teaspoon powdered ginger
1 tablespoon olive oil

Preheat oven to 350°. Trim the fat from the leg of lamb, but do not remove the filament covering the meat. Blend the garlic with the mustard, soy sauce, thyme, and ginger. Gradually beat in the olive oil until the sauce is creamy. Rub over the lamb and set it on a rack in a roasting pan. Roast the lamb for 1 to 1½ hours, depending on your taste for rare or well-done meat. (Serves 6)

8

SNACKS

The dining schedule at West Thirty-fifth Street is strictly observed whenever possible, but there are often occasions when Fritz is called upon to serve an impromptu meal, whether it be to Archie in the kitchen or to a hungry client in the office. Although these snacks often consist of leftovers or informal dishes, they are always superb in quality and served with ceremony.

Wolfe himself is rarely known to partake of snacks in the office; he does, however, snack regularly on Sunday evenings in the kitchen at Archie's breakfast table. These meals often consist of bread, cheese, and one of Fritz's special dishes, such as sausage or pâté (see index for recipes): It was a pleasant scene, the ego-maniac having, as usual, his Sunday-evening snack with the cook. Fritz was on a stool at the long table in the center, steering a dripping endive core to his open mouth. Wolfe, seated at my breakfast table, against the wall, was pouring honey on steaming halves of buttermilk biscuits. A glass and a bottle of milk were there, and I went and poured. [EASTER PARADE]

BUTTERMILK BISCUITS

2 cups all-purpose flour	½ teaspoon baking soda
1 teaspoon salt	4 tablespoons butter
1 teaspoon sugar	¾ cup buttermilk (or more)
3 teaspoons baking powder	

Preheat oven to 450°. Sift together into a large bowl the flour, salt, sugar, baking powder, and baking soda. Cut in the butter with a pastry blender or two knives until the mixture is soft and crumbly. Add the buttermilk and mix until the dough forms a ball, adding more milk if necessary. Turn the dough out onto a floured board and knead for 1 or 2 minutes. Roll out the dough until it is ½ inch thick and cut with a biscuit cutter. Bake on a cookie sheet for 10 to 12 minutes. (Makes 12 biscuits)

On another Sunday evening, Wolfe and I had helped ourselves around seven o'clock, concentrating mainly on a block of head-cheese. I have spent a total of at least ten hours watching Fritz make headcheese, trying to find out why it is so much better than any other I have ever tasted, including what my mother used to make out in Ohio. I finally gave up. It could be the way he holds the spoon when he skims.   [DEATH OF A DOXY]

HEADCHEESE

1 calf's head	10 black peppercorns
1 pair pig's feet	1 tablespoon salt
1 onion studded with 6 cloves	1 quart water
4 sprigs parsley	1 quart dry white wine
1 bay leaf	¼ teaspoon cayenne pepper
1 clove garlic	¼ teaspoon nutmeg
1 carrot, sliced	

Ask the butcher to clean the calf's head and remove the brain and tongue. Reserve both. Place the head, tongue, and pig's feet in a large soup kettle. Add the onion, parsley, bay leaf, garlic, carrot, peppercorns, and salt. Add the water and wine, and bring the liquid to a boil. Skim and reduce the heat; simmer for 4 hours, covered. After 2 hours remove the tongue; trim the end and skin it. Add the brains to the pot for the last 20 minutes of simmering. Remove kettle from heat and drain the head, pig's feet, and brain. The meat should be falling from the bones. Strain the cooking liquid and set it aside. Remove all the meat and cut into ½-inch cubes. Cut the calf's ears and tongue into thin slices. Put all the cut meat into a large mixing bowl; season with cayenne pepper and nutmeg. Mix well. Pack the mixture firmly into a bread pan, add a sufficient amount of the reserved cooking liquid to cover and refrigerate overnight. Unmold onto a serving platter and serve with crackers or French bread. Garnish with watercress and lemon slices.

Because Archie's schedule is a great deal more irregular than Wolfe's he is often obliged to eat a warmed-over meal or a sandwich especially prepared by Fritz: I don't join Wolfe when I arrive in the middle of a meal; we agree that for one man to hurry with meat or fish while the other dawdles with pastry or salad is bad for the atmosphere. Fritz put my things on my breakfast table and brought what was left of the baked bluefish.

[THE DOORBELL RANG]

BAKED BLUEFISH

1 fresh bluefish, 3½ to 4 pounds whole
2 pounds medium-sized fresh shrimp
3 egg whites
1½ cups heavy cream
2 teaspoons salt

1 teaspoon fresh basil (or ½ teaspoon dried leaves)
1 teaspoon fresh tarragon (or ½ teaspoon dried leaves)
2 tablespoons butter
3 tablespoons brandy

Ask the fishmonger to clean the fish as follows, or do it yourself: Scrape off all scales and remove the fins. Cut the fish down the backbone, starting at the neck, and continue to within two inches of the tail. Remove all the innards, including the gills. Do not cut through the belly. Wash the fish in cold water and dry with paper towels. Set aside. Preheat the oven to 375°. Peel, devein, and wash the shrimp; put them through the finest blade of the meat grinder. To the shrimp add the egg whites and beat with an electric hand mixer while you slowly add the cream, salt, basil, and tarragon. Beat until the mixture is very thick. Stuff the bluefish from the back with the shrimp mixture and place in a well-greased baking dish. Make 2 or 3 shallow cuts in the side of the fish. Melt the butter, add the brandy to it, and pour over the fish. Bake for 30 minutes, or until the fish is tender but not dried out. (Serves 4)

Another time, I had phoned from the drugstore on the Grand Concourse, and Fritz had a dish of flounder with his best cheese sauce hot in the oven, with a platter of lettuce and tomatoes and plenty of good cold milk.

[FER-DE-LANCE]

FLOUNDER WITH CHEESE SAUCE

½ pound thin noodles	1 bay leaf
5 tablespoons butter	6 mushrooms
6 flounder fillets, totaling	⅓ pound Fontina cheese
3 pounds	1 egg yolk
2 cups dry white wine	2 tablespoons freshly grated
3 tablespoons chopped shallots	Parmesan cheese

Cook the noodles for 5 minutes in boiling salted water. Drain well, return them to the pot, and stir in 2 tablespoons of the butter. When the noodles are thoroughly coated with butter, spread them in the bottom of a 2-quart casserole. Keep covered and warm. Cut the flounder fillets in half lengthwise. Using your fingers, feel for and remove any hidden bones and trim the edges. Put the fillets in a shallow baking dish. Preheat the oven to 350°. In a saucepan place the fish scraps, wine, shallots, and bay leaf. Peel and stem the mushrooms; add the scraps to the stock. Simmer for 10 minutes. Pour the strained broth over the fillets and bake for 10 minutes. While the fish is cooking, sauté the mushrooms in the remaining butter. Carefully remove the fillets with a large slotted spatula and arrange them on top of the buttered noodles. Return the broth to a saucepan. It should make about 1½ cups; add more wine or water if necessary. Chop the Fontina cheese and add it to the broth. If the sauce seems too thick, add more wine; if too thin, add more cheese. Stir constantly so that the cheese melts evenly. When the sauce is thick enough to coat a spoon, remove from heat and let cool for a few minutes. Add the beaten egg yolk and mix well. Pour the sauce over the fish. Garnish with the sautéed mushroom slices, sprinkle with the Parmesan cheese and put under the broiler for a moment to brown.

When I got back to the old brownstone a little after midnight I was expecting to find on my desk a note telling me to come to Wolfe's room at eight-fifteen in the morning, but it wasn't there. Evidently his imagination and wit hadn't delivered. Fritz's had. In the kitchen there was a dish of lobster cardinal and a saucer with Parmesan ready grated. I sprinkled the cheese on and put it in the broiler, and drank milk and made coffee while it was browning.   [THE MOTHER HUNT]

LOBSTER CARDINAL

6 live lobsters, 1½ to 2
   pounds each
3 tablespoons butter
3 tablespoons all-purpose flour
3½ cups fish stock or
   clam broth

2 tablespoons chopped truffles
6 tablespoons lobster butter
   (see note)
1½ tablespoons grated
   Parmesan cheese

Boil the lobsters for 20 to 25 minutes in water, drain, and with a sharp knife cut each one through the chest and down the tail. Remove all the meat, keeping the body shells intact and discarding the small sac near the head, the black tail vein, and the empty claws. Chop the meat and keep it warm. Dry the inside of the shells with paper towels and reserve. To make the cardinal sauce, melt the butter in a saucepan and add the flour, stirring gently. When the flour has turned golden, add the fish stock, half a cup at a time, stirring until the mixture begins to thicken slightly. Continue to cook until the sauce reduces to about 3 cups. Add the truffles and lobster butter. Continue to stir until the butter has been completely incorporated. Remove the sauce from the heat and reserve ¾ cup. Preheat the broiler, add the lobster meat to the rest of the sauce, put it back on the heat, and simmer until the lobster is thoroughly heated. When it is ready, spoon the mixture into the lobster shells. Spoon the reserved sauce over them and sprinkle with Parmesan cheese. Run the lobsters under the broiler until they are lightly browned on top. (Serves 6)

NOTE: To make lobster butter, pound the claw shells, tomalley, and coral (if any) in a mortar. Blend with 6 ounces (1½ sticks) of sweet butter. Heat the mixture in a saucepan and cook over low heat until the butter is completely melted. Strain through a fine sieve or a double thickness of cheesecloth. Allow the butter to cool and solidify before using.

Fritz had kept some squirrel stew hot for me, and it had long since been put away, with a couple of rye highballs, because the black sauce used for squirrel made milk taste like stale olive juice.   [LEAGUE OF FRIGHTENED MEN]

SQUIRREL STEW

3 squirrels, skinned and cleaned
½ teaspoon paprika

½ teaspoon salt

(Continued)

1 cup all-purpose flour
2 tablespoons butter
1 tablespoon olive oil
6 thin slices Georgia ham
2 large onions, sliced

¼ pound mushrooms, sliced
4 potatoes, sliced
1 teaspoon freshly ground
   black pepper
¾ cup dry red wine

Cut the squirrels into serving pieces. Add the paprika and salt to the flour and dredge the squirrel pieces in it. Heat the butter and oil in a skillet and brown the squirrel on all sides, 2 or 3 pieces at a time. Set aside the cooked meat. Butter a large casserole and line the bottom with 2 slices of ham. Put a layer of squirrel on top, then a layer of onions, mushrooms, and potatoes. Sprinkle the layer with pepper and repeat until all the ingredients are used up. End with a layer of ham. Pour in the wine and cover the casserole. Bake for 1½ to 2 hours, or until the squirrel meat is tender. Serve hot from the casserole. (Serves 4 to 6)

When I finally got back to the old brownstone on West Thirty-fifth Street it was going on ten o'clock. Fritz offered to warm up the lamb loaf and said that it would be edible, but I told him I was too tired to eat. [PLOT IT YOURSELF] *In case you are not too tired, we have included the recipe.*

LAMB LOAF

1½ pounds ground lamb
½ pound ground lean pork
4 eggs
⅔ cup bread crumbs
¼ cup chopped parsley
¼ cup chopped shallots
1 teaspoon fresh basil (or
   ½ teaspoon dried leaves)
1½ teaspoons salt
1 teaspoon freshly ground
   black pepper

½ cup grated Parmesan cheese
2 tablespoons diced green
   pepper
½ cup dry white wine
½ cup clarified butter
3 tablespoons Worcestershire
   sauce
5 medium potatoes
3 ounces butter (¾ stick)
⅛ teaspoon nutmeg

Preheat the oven to 350°. In a large mixing bowl combine the lamb, pork, 2 of the eggs, the crumbs, parsley, shallots, basil, 1 teaspoon of the salt, ½ teaspoon of the pepper, Parmesan cheese, green pepper, and wine. Use your hands to mix the ingredients thoroughly. Shape into an oval loaf and place on a rack in a shallow baking pan. Mix the clarified butter and Worcestershire, and beat briskly. Brush the loaf with the mixture and bake it for 1½ hours. While the loaf is cooking, peel, cube, and boil the potatoes in salted water. When they are tender (about 20 minutes), drain and mash them. Add the butter gradually until it is completely incorporated. Add the remaining 2 eggs, whipping until they are absorbed. Season with salt, pepper, and the nutmeg. When the lamb loaf is cooked, remove it from the oven and place on a heatproof serving platter. Allow to cool for 10 minutes. Using a pastry tube with a fluted end, pipe the potato purée around the loaf, being as decorative as you like. Increase the heat of the oven to 450° and bake the loaf for a few minutes until the purée becomes slightly browned. (Serves 4)

NOTE: This is excellent served with curry sauce made with 2 tablespoons of butter, 2 tablespoons of flour, 1½ cups veal stock, and 1 tablespoon curry powder. Simmer until the desired consistency is achieved.

It was exactly eight o'clock when I mounted the stoop. . . . Wolfe was in the dining room. I stuck my head in the door and said I'd get a bite in the kitchen. Fritz, who always eats his evening meal around nine o'clock, was on his stool at the big center table doing something with artichokes. When I entered he crinkled his eyes at me and said, "Ah, you're back on your feet. Have you eaten?"

"No."

"There's a little mussel bisque—"

"No, thanks. No soup. I want to chew something. Don't tell me he ate a whole duck."

"Oh, no. I knew a man, a Swiss, who ate two ducks." He was at the range, putting on a plate to warm. "Was it a good trip?"

"It was a lousy trip." I was at the cupboard getting a bottle. "No milk or coffee. I'm going to drink a quart of whisky."

"Not here, Archie. In your room is the place for that. Some *carottes Flamande?*"

I said, "Yes, please."

The door swung open and Wolfe was there. It was mutually understood that the rule about talk at meals didn't apply when I was eating alone in the kitchen or office, because it was a snack, not a meal. So when my snack was on my plate and I had chewed and swallowed a man-size morsel of duck Mondor and a forkful of carrots, I told Wolfe, "I appreciate this. You knew I had something on my chest I wanted to unload."

[THE FATHER HUNT]

DUCK MONDOR (see index)

CAROTTES FLAMANDES

1 pound carrots	3 egg yolks
¼ cup cold water	½ cup heavy cream
8 tablespoons butter	1 tablespoon chopped parsley
¼ teaspoon salt	2 tablespoons melted sweet
3 tablespoons sugar	butter
1 tablespoon grated orange rind	

Wash and scrape the carrots, cutting them into 1-inch sections and trimming the ends. Blanch them in boiling water to cover for 5 minutes, drain, and place in a well-buttered casserole. Add the cold water and butter, and season with salt and sugar. Cover the casserole and bring the liquid to a boil. Reduce the heat and continue to cook the carrots for 20 minutes or longer until they are tender. Shake the casserole every 5 minutes or so to prevent the carrots from sticking to the pan. Five minutes before the carrots are done, add the grated orange rind and stir. When the carrots are cooked, remove them from the heat. Mix the egg yolks with the cream, parsley, and melted butter. Add the mixture to the casserole, stirring gently, and put back on a low flame. When the sauce begins to thicken (do not let it boil) , remove from the heat and serve. (Serves 4 to 6)

MUSSEL BISQUE   (see index)

Fritz appeared with a tray and brought it to my desk. There was a bowl of chestnut soup, a cucumber and shrimp sandwich on toast, a roast-beef sandwich on a hard roll, home-baked, a pile of watercress, an apple baked in white wine, and a glass of milk.

[TOO MANY CLIENTS]

CHESTNUT SOUP

2 pounds chestnuts	4 cups chicken stock
1 tablespoon oil	1 egg yolk
6 tablespoons butter	2 tablespoons dry white wine
1 stalk celery, sliced	1 cup light cream
1 leek, sliced	1 cup whipped heavy cream
1 carrot, sliced	(or sour cream)
salt and freshly ground	
black pepper to taste	

To shell the chestnuts, make a slash across the top of each with a sharp knife. Brush them with the oil, place in a shallow pan, and cook for 5 to 10 minutes in a 450° oven until the shells open. Remove the shells and the skin. Melt 4 tablespoons of the butter in a deep heavy pan. Cook the celery, leek, and carrot slowly for 5 minutes in the butter. Season with salt and pepper. Add the shelled chestnuts and pour in the chicken stock. Bring the liquid to a boil and simmer until the chestnuts are soft. Remove the nuts and vegetables with a slotted spoon and purée in a blender or food mill. Return them to the pan with the cooking liquid and add the rest of the butter. Beat the egg yolk well with the white wine and light cream. Add a little of the purée to this mixture; then pour it slowly into the soup, stirring constantly. Correct the seasoning. Serve hot with a tablespoon of whipped cream (or sour cream) in the middle of each bowl. (Makes about 5 cups)

VARIATION:

Add 1 teaspoon fresh chopped tarragon (or ½ teaspoon dried leaves) to the melted butter with the other seasonings. (*Fritz tries this first in* COUNTERFEIT FOR MURDER *and Wolfe approves.*)

CUCUMBER AND SHRIMP SANDWICH (see index)

APPLE BAKED IN WHITE WINE (see index)

Fritz's soups are often used by Wolfe to feed clients, even unwilling ones: The client lowered his hands and the bleary eyes blinked a dozen times. "You'll have to make allowances," he said. "I just left the district attorney's office. I was there all night and no sleep."

"Have you eaten?"

"My god, no."

Wolfe made a face. That complicated it. The mere thought of a man going without food was disagreeable, and to have one there in his house was intolerable. If a man can swallow anything he can swallow Fritz's madrilene with beet juice, and after one spoonful of his lemon-sherry pudding with brown-sugar sauce there's no argument. The cheese and watercress were still on the tray when I took it to the kitchen, but the bowls were empty.

[BLOOD WILL TELL]

MADRILENE WITH BEET JUICE

2 cups chicken stock	salt and freshly ground
2 cups tomato juice	black pepper to taste
½ cup beet juice	1 cup sour cream
¼ cup dry sherry	1 tablespoon chopped chives
½ teaspoon grated onion	3 tablespoons red caviar

Combine the chicken stock, tomato and beet juices, and sherry in a sauce-pan. Add the grated onion. Bring the soup to a boil, stir, and simmer for 15 minutes. Correct the seasoning. Mix the sour cream, chives, and caviar together. Allow the madrilene to cool for a few moments, then serve warm with a tablespoon of the sour-cream mixture in the center of the bowl. (Makes about 4 cups)

LEMON-SHERRY PUDDING   (see index)

Even a hungry woman will move Wolfe to offer sustenance. (As Archie is fond of pointing out, in MIGHT AS WELL BE DEAD, *as elsewhere* the thought of a hungry human, even a hungry murder suspect, even a hungry woman, in his house, is intolerable.) She came and stood at Wolfe's desk, across from him. "I beg your pardon," she said in her low even voice. "I had to take some pills. The food at the hotel is quite good, but I simply can't eat. . . . I haven't eaten much for quite a while. . . ."

"Milk toast," Wolfe said gruffly. "My cook, Fritz Brenner, makes it superbly. Sit down."

"I couldn't swallow it. Really."

"Then hot bouillon," Wolfe said gruffly. "Our own. It can be ready in eight minutes."   [BEFORE MIDNIGHT]

MILK TOAST

6 slices bread (see index)	2 tablespoons butter
2 tablespoons butter	1 tablespoon all-purpose flour
1 cup milk	1 teaspoon sugar
1 cup heavy cream	

Cut the crusts from the bread and toast the slices until golden brown. Spread with butter and arrange on a serving dish. Heat the milk and cream. Make a *beurre manié* of the butter and flour and drop it by bits into the cream and stir until blended. Season with the sugar and pour over the toast. (Serves 2 to 3)

BOUILLON, OUR OWN

3 pounds beef chuck	1 sprig parsley
2 large veal knucklebones	1 teaspoon fresh thyme (or
2½ quarts cold water	½ teaspoon dried leaves)
1 teaspoon salt	1 bay leaf
8 black peppercorns	1 stalk celery, with leaves
4 leeks, sliced	3 egg whites
4 large carrots, sliced	½ cup dry sherry
1 large onion, sliced	

Put the meat and bones in a heavy cast-iron kettle with the water. Bring it to a boil very slowly. Skim off all the fat. Add the salt, peppercorns, leeks, carrots, and onion. Make a bouquet garni with the parsley, thyme, bay leaf, and celery, and add to the pot. Reboil and skim again. Lower the heat and simmer very gently, covered, for 3 hours. Strain the broth and reserve the beef for another use. Allow the strained stock to get cold and remove all the fat. Put the liquid into a pan with the egg whites. Beat with a whisk or electric hand mixer over a slow fire until the mixture comes to a boil. Simmer for 5 minutes, stirring; remove from the heat, and allow to stand for 15 minutes. Soak a double layer of cheesecloth in cold water and wring it out. Line a strainer with the cloth and carefully pour the soup through it. Return to the pan and add the dry sherry. Reheat; add a little more sherry if desired. (Makes about 2 quarts)

Not all women are treated in a chilly manner at the old brownstone, at least not when Archie is around: I would like to think it was my kiss that gave her an appetite, but I suppose it was the assurance from Wolfe that he didn't think her Paul was guilty of murder. She disposed not only of the crackers and milk, but also of a healthy portion of toast spread with Fritz's liver pâté and chives.   [WHEN A MAN MURDERS]

FRITZ'S LIVER PÂTÉ

1 quart salted water	1 stalk celery, minced
1 clove garlic, minced	1 tablespoon chopped shallots
	(Continued)

1 sprig parsley
1 bay leaf
2 pounds chicken livers
½ teaspoon salt
⅛ teaspoon freshly ground
    black pepper
½ teaspoon nutmeg

2 teaspoons dry mustard
4 ounces sweet butter (1 stick)
2 tablespoons cognac
1 tablespoon Marsala
1 truffle, minced
2 tablespoons clarified butter
garnish: pimiento-stuffed olives

Bring the water to a boil. Add the garlic and celery to the water with the shallots, parsley, and bay leaf. Reduce the heat and simmer for 5 minutes. Add the cleaned, halved chicken livers and simmer, covered, for 10 minutes. Remove the livers from the heat, and drain and chop them coarsely. Put them into a blender; add the salt, pepper, nutmeg, dry mustard, the butter cut into chunks, the cognac, and the Marsala. Blend at a low speed until the mixture is thoroughly smooth. Pour the mixture into a bowl, fold in the truffle, and correct the seasoning. Coat a pâté mold or terrine with clarified butter and pack the pâté mixture into it. Cover tightly and refrigerate overnight. When you are ready to serve, unmold the pâté onto a chilled serving dish and garnish with slices of pimiento-stuffed olives. Serve with triangles of fried bread or melba toast rounds. (Makes 2 cups)

When the clients in distress number more than one or two, Fritz usually serves an array of sandwiches on trays in the office. He always makes sandwiches with his own bread (see index) or hard rolls, and the fillings can be anything from minced rabbit meat or Georgia country ham to cucumber and shrimp or homemade pâté and sturgeon.. On one occasion [AND BE A VILLAIN] he even served corned-beef sandwiches, although Archie usually complains that he has to get his corned-beef sandwiches outside, since Wolfe doesn't like to have it in the house.

HARD ROLLS, HOMEMADE

1 package yeast
1¼ cups water
3¾ to 4 cups sifted all-purpose
    flour

1 tablespoon salt
¼ cup corn meal
1 egg white

Dissolve the yeast in ¼ cup of warm water and allow to stand for 5 minutes. Add the yeast to a mixing bowl with 2 cups of the flour and 1 cup of water and the salt. Beat well. Gradually add the remaining flour until a stiff dough is formed. Remove the dough to a floured board, cover it, and let it rest for 10 minutes. Knead for 10 minutes until smooth and elastic. Put the dough in a lightly greased bowl, cover, and allow to rise in a warm place until doubled in bulk. Punch down and allow it to rise again. Remove the dough to the floured board, punch down, and divide into quarters. Cover and rest it again for 10 minutes. Cut each quarter into 2 or 3 equal parts and shape them into ovals. Place the ovals on a baking sheet sprinkled with corn meal. Brush the tops with a mixture of 1 tablespoon of water and the egg white. Let the rolls rise until they double in size. Using a sharp knife, make a shallow cut across the top of each roll. Bake in a 450° oven for about 20 minutes, or until nicely browned. For a very crisp crust, place a pan of water on a lower rack in the oven. (Makes about 10 rolls)

MINCED-RABBIT-MEAT SANDWICHES

1½ pounds minced rabbit meat
   (see index for Civet de Lapin)
¼ cup butter
¼ cup minced shallots
⅓ cup dry white wine
1 cup bread crumbs
2 large eggs, beaten

¼ cup minced parsley
1½ teaspoons dry mustard
1 teaspoon salt
2 tablespoons clarified butter
toasted rolls
lime wedges

Prepare rabbit meat. Melt the butter in a skillet and sauté the shallots until golden. Add the wine, half the bread crumbs, eggs, parsley, mustard, salt, and the rabbit meat. Mix well and shape the meat into 6 patties, rolling them in the remaining bread crumbs. Sauté them in clarified butter until brown on both sides and drain. Serve on toasted rolls with lime wedges.

GEORGIA-COUNTRY-HAM SANDWICHES

Toast slices of Fritz's bread lightly and spread them with Dijon mustard. Put thin slices of Georgia country ham on the toast and top with small slices of pineapple. Run them under the broiler until the pineapple browns. Cover with additional slices of toasted bread.

CUCUMBER AND SHRIMP SANDWICHES

On slices of toast spread a little tartar sauce. Cover with small boiled shrimp and slices of cucumber that have marinated for at least 1 hour in the refrigerator in half a cup of tarragon wine vinegar and a tablespoon of sugar. Top with more slices of tartar-sauced toast.

CORNED-BEEF SANDWICHES

Butter toasted slices of bread and arrange slices of corned beef on top. Spread with Dijon mustard. Add tomatoes and lettuce if desired and a second layer of toast.

On one occasion, Archie is asked to help serve a large group of unexpected visitors. Though he refuses, it is the one piece of evidence we have that he can cook.

Wolfe: "If you men want something hot I can have Yorkshire Buck in twenty minutes if Archie will poach the eggs." They all said no, which suited me fine. I hate to poach eggs.

[THE DOORBELL RANG]

YORKSHIRE BUCK

1 tablespoon butter	1 teaspoon dry mustard
1 pound grated Cheshire cheese	2 dashes Tabasco
1 cup ale	6 slices Canadian back bacon
7 large eggs	3 English muffins
¼ teaspoon salt	2 tablespoons Dijon mustard

Melt the butter in the top of a double boiler. Add the cheese and as it begins to melt, add the ale slowly, stirring constantly. Beat 1 of the eggs and add it, along with the salt, dry mustard, and Tabasco. Continue to stir until all the cheese is melted and the mixture is smooth. Lower the heat and keep hot. Poach the 6 remaining eggs and keep them warm while you fry the bacon lightly on a griddle. Split and toast the English muffins and spread them with a thin coating of Dijon mustard. Put the muffins on a serving plate, pour on the cheese, and top with a slice of bacon, a poached egg, and some more cheese. Serve as hot as possible. Run the muffins under a hot broiler to glaze the tops, if you like. (Serves 6)

9

GUESTS, MALE AND FEMALE

One of Wolfe's favorite sayings, which Archie has quoted at least twice and has probably heard a great deal more than that, is "A guest is a jewel upon the cushion of hospitality." We saw in the previous chapter how he truly acts upon his own convictions, at least where snacks for hungry visitors are concerned. In this chapter we will see the great man's character expand and become greater as he opens his hearth, his dining room, his conversation, and even the achievements of his chef to the client or visitor who happens to be sitting in the office when one-fifteen in the afternoon or seven-thirty in the evening happen to come around. Because the quantities consumed at lunch or dinner in the old brownstone are always large, even if Wolfe is dining quite alone, Fritz is generally prepared to accommodate sudden guests at mealtime. If the number of guests is larger than he can handle with ease, he—like every great chef, except perhaps Vatel, who could not take the pressure—gracefully and quickly adjusts his menu to fit the requirements of the situation. Wolfe often gives him suggestions at these times, but this is usually done for the effect it has on the salivary glands of the prospective diner, for whose sake Wolfe has been known to produce his most eloquent descriptive flights of language.

Wolfe's behavior in the presence of guests, gentlemanly though it is, displays a distinct preference for the company of other gentlemen and a similarly distinct, though low-keyed, hostility to the company of ladies. This reserve, particularly marked by the contrast with Archie's fondness for women, is also shared by Fritz, who, as we shall see, "suspects any woman who enters the house of wanting to take it over."

In this chapter the observant reader will note and admire the extraordinary agility that a man weighing a seventh of a ton can command in the face of a social crisis.

Wolfe: It's time for lunch, and I invite you to join us, and then we'll resume. Clams hashed with eggs, parsley, green peppers, chives, fresh mushrooms, and sherry. Mr. Goodwin drinks milk. I drink beer. Would you prefer white wine?

[CHAMPAGNE FOR ONE]

CLAMS HASHED WITH EGGS

2 dozen cherrystone clams
3 tablespoons butter
6 large mushrooms
1 green pepper
4 large eggs
2 potatoes
1 tablespoon fresh chopped parsley

1 tablespoon fresh chopped chives
2 teaspoons salt
¼ teaspoon freshly ground black pepper
1 tablespoon dry sherry
¼ teaspoon paprika
6 slices bacon

Preheat the oven to 350°. Shuck and mince the clams. Sauté them in butter for about 5 minutes. Slice the mushrooms and chop the green pepper and add them to the pan, cooking until they begin to brown. Remove the clams and vegetables from heat and drain. Beat the eggs. Boil the unpeeled potatoes until tender in salted water. Remove the skins and slice. Combine the eggs and potatoes in a large mixing bowl with the parsley, chives, salt, black pepper, and sherry. Mix well. Fold in the clams, green pepper, and mushrooms, and pour the mixture into a well-buttered baking dish. Sprinkle with paprika and bake for 30 to 35 minutes. Meanwhile, cook the bacon strips until they are crisp. Drain and crumble the bacon and garnish the finished casserole before serving. (Serves 4 as a luncheon dish)

Fritz spoke. "Luncheon is ready, sir."
Wolfe got up. "If you'll join us, Mr. Freyer? There'll be enough to go around. Chicken livers and mushrooms in white wine. Rice cakes. Another place, Fritz."   [MIGHT AS WELL BE DEAD]

CHICKEN LIVERS WITH MUSHROOMS

6 tablespoons butter	1 teaspoon fresh basil (or
1 teaspoon minced shallot	½ teaspoon dried leaves)
1½ pounds chicken livers	¼ pound button mushrooms
2 tablespoons dry white wine	6 slices of bread
1 teaspoon chopped chives	1 cup béarnaise sauce
1 teaspoon fresh chopped chervil	(see note)
(or ½ teaspoon dried leaves)	

Preheat the oven to 400°. Wash the chicken livers, cutting away any membranes, and drain well. Pat dry with paper towel and slice thin. In a frying pan melt 4 tablespoons of the butter and add the shallot, sautéing until light brown. Add the chicken livers, wine, chives, chervil, and basil and cook for 3 minutes, leaving the livers rosy-colored inside. Stem the mushrooms, clean them, and sauté them briefly in the remaining 2 tablespoons of butter. Drain and stir into the livers. Toast the bread, from which the crusts have been trimmed, and arrange the slices on a baking sheet. Divide the liver mixture equally on the pieces of toast, cover each piece with béarnaise, and brown for about two minutes.

NOTE: To make béarnaise sauce, beat 3 egg yolks until thick. Reduce ½ cup of tarragon wine vinegar to 2 tablespoons in a small saucepan and add 2 teaspoons of minced shallots, ½ teaspoon freshly ground black pepper, a pinch of thyme, and 2 tablespoons of hot water. Beat in the egg yolks and set the pan over hot water. Add slowly ½ cup of melted butter, beating constantly until the butter is incorporated into the yolks. Add a few grains of cayenne pepper, 1 teaspoon of fresh chopped tarragon leaves, and a thin slice of lemon. Serve warm but not hot.

RICE CAKES (see index)

With guests Wolfe makes a point of steering the table talk to subjects that he thinks his guests will be interested in. As Fritz was serving the mussels, I was wondering what it would be for these two. It was William Shakespeare. After the skimpy portions of mussels, in white wine with creamed butter and flour, had been commented on, Wolfe asked them if they had read the book by Rowse. They discussed it up one side and down the other. By the time the duck and trimmings had been disposed of, and Fritz had brought the fig soufflé, it looked to me as if Iago was on the ropes.   [A RIGHT TO DIE]

MUSSELS IN WHITE WINE

4 dozen mussels	½ cup chopped celery
2 cups dry white wine	5 tablespoons all-purpose flour
1 bay leaf	1 teaspoon salt
1 carrot	1 cup heavy cream
2 onions	3 tablespoons Marsala
4 tablespoons butter	

Clean the mussels as thoroughly as possible: wash them in several changes of cold water and scrape the shells with a knife to remove the beards. Place the mussels in a large kettle with the wine, bay leaf, sliced carrot, and 1 sliced onion. Cover, bring to a boil, and simmer 5 or 6 minutes until all the shells are open. Remove from the heat, allow the mussels to cool, and remove the meat from the shells. Save all the liquid, including the liquid from the shells. Strain it through a double layer of cheesecloth and reserve. Melt the butter in a skillet. Mince the remaining onion and sauté it in the butter with the chopped celery until soft. Do not brown. Put the onions and celery through the fine blade of a meat grinder or purée in a blender. Sprinkle the mixture with the flour and salt; mix well and return to the kettle. Stir in 1 cup of the reserved liquid and cook slowly over a low flame until the sauce is very thick, stirring constantly. Add the cream and heat, but do not allow the sauce to boil. Add the Marsala and correct the seasoning with salt and pepper. Add the mussels and heat through. (Serves 4 to 6)

VARIATION:

For mussel bisque, use 2 cups of the broth and add 2 cups of milk before adding the cream. Grind or purée the mussels with the onions and celery.

DUCK WITH TRIMMINGS (see index for Duck Mondor)

FIG SOUFFLÉ (see index)

Ordinarily Wolfe is perfectly willing to do most of the talking, with or without company, but that time, from the Neptune *bouchées* right through to the chestnut whip, he not only let the guest, a female guest, take over, he egged her on.

[DEATH OF A DOXY]

NEPTUNE BOUCHÉES

1 cup fish stock or clam juice	½ cup boiled medium shrimp
½ cup butter	1 tablespoon chopped fresh parsley
1 teaspoon salt	½ cup mayonnaise (see index)
⅛ teaspoon white pepper	½ cup smoked salmon
⅛ teaspoon nutmeg	1 tablespoon capers
1 sifted cup all-purpose flour	parsley sprigs
4 large eggs	lemon and lime wedges

Preheat oven to 400°. Put the fish stock, butter, salt, pepper, and nutmeg into a saucepan. When the butter has melted, add the flour, blending with a wooden spoon until the paste has left the side of the pan. Remove from heat. Add 1 egg at a time, beating the mixture until each is completely absorbed. Using a pastry tube, squeeze out 1-inch balls onto a greased baking sheet, leaving 1 inch or more between each ball. Bake for 10 to 15 minutes, or until nicely browned. The puffs should double in size. Remove from oven and cool slightly. Meanwhile make the shrimp and salmon fillings. Put the shrimp through a food mill and add the parsley and enough mayonnaise to bind. In a separate bowl, mash the salmon and mix with the capers and a little mayonnaise. When the puffs have cooled, cut each one open with a sharp knife. Fill each with the shrimp or salmon mixtures, using a pastry tube. Replace the pastry tops. Garnish with sprigs of parsley and lemon and lime wedges. (Makes 18 to 24 bouchées)

CHESTNUT WHIP (see index)

Sometimes, when Wolfe is confronted by a woman at the dining-room table, his conversational hospitality is somewhat strained. In DEATH OF A DOXY, *for instance, he put Julie Jaquette in her place by discussing the difference between imagination and invention in literature:* She did get a word in now and then. Once when his mouth was full of sweetbreads she said, "You're talking over my head on purpose. Show me one thing in one book, and ask me if it's imagination or invention and I'll tell you every time, and let's see you prove I'm wrong." That's no way to talk to a man who is doing his best to prepare you for college.

SWEETBREADS

6 pairs veal sweetbreads	1 sprig parsley
2 onions, diced	1 teaspoon fresh thyme (or
2 carrots, diced	¼ teaspoon dried)
6 tablespoons butter	1 teaspoon salt
6 tablespoons flour	¼ teaspoon freshly ground
1 clove garlic, minced	black pepper
2 cups beef stock	1 cup Marsala
1 bay leaf	1 teaspoon *glace de viande*
1 celery stalk, sliced	(see index)

Wash the sweetbreads and blanch them in boiling water for 3 to 4 minutes. Drain and trim them, removing the outer skin and connective tissue. Sauté the onions and carrots in the butter for about 15 minutes. Stir in the flour and cook for 3 or 4 minutes; then add the garlic and beef stock. Stir over a medium flame until thickened. Add the bay leaf, celery, parsley, thyme, salt, pepper, and sweetbreads. Partially cover the pan and simmer for 30 to 40 minutes. Meanwhile, reduce the Marsala by half over a high flame. When the sweetbreads are cooked, remove them from the pan and cut them into chunks. Strain the sauce and stir in the Marsala and *glace de viande*. Correct the seasoning. If the sauce is too thin, add some butter mixed with an equal part of flour. Return the sweetbreads to the sauce, stir gently, and serve. (Serves 4 to 6)

Fritz's cooking obviously won the lady over where Wolfe's conversation might have put her off. In a thank-you note to Archie, she adds a P.S.: "How is Fritz? Tell him I can still taste that hedgehog omelet. And the sauce with the sweetbreads." (See index for Hedgehog Omelet)

One young lady did not feel so comfortable at the old brownstone, with either Wolfe or Fritz:

"Fritz says you ate only two of his Creole fritters. You don't care for shrimp?"

"I'm sorry. He doesn't like me, and I don't blame him. I'm a nuisance." She sighed deep.

"That's not it. He suspects any woman who enters the house of wanting to take it over."   [KILL NOW, PAY LATER]

CREOLE FRITTERS WITH CHEESE SAUCE

1 pound medium shrimp	1 teaspoon baking powder
½ cup white wine	½ teaspoon salt
½ cup water	⅛ teaspoon cayenne pepper
1 bay leaf	2 large eggs
6 peppercorns	½ teaspoon lemon juice
1 small onion, sliced	1 cup vegetable oil
1 cup all-purpose flour	

Peel and devein the shrimp. Bring the wine and water to a gentle boil and add the bay leaf, peppercorns, and the onion. Add the shrimps and cook for 3 or 4 minutes. Remove them with a slotted spoon, drain (reserving the stock), and chop coarsely. Sift the flour, baking powder, salt, and cayenne pepper. Beat the eggs and stir in the drained poaching stock. Add to the dry ingredients, mix well, and add the shrimp. Add the lemon juice and stir. Heat the oil in a large skillet. Form the shrimp batter into cakes with your hands and fry them gently in the oil until browned on both sides. Drain on brown paper and remove to a warm platter. (Makes 12 fritters)

This is a popular dish at Wolfe's establishment, appearing on at least four occasions; in PLOT IT YOURSELF, *Archie reveals that cheese sauce is served with them.*

CHEESE SAUCE

2 tablespoons butter	¾ cup grated Vermont Cheddar cheese
2 tablespoons all-purpose flour	1 teaspoon tomato paste
1½ cups light cream	2 tablespoons dry sherry, or to taste
few grains cayenne pepper	
1 tablespoon lemon juice	

Melt the butter in a saucepan and stir in the flour. Cook for 2 minutes and gradually add the cream, stirring constantly with a whisk until the sauce begins to thicken. Season with cayenne pepper and lemon juice. Add the cheese and stir until it is melted. Stir in the tomato paste until the sauce is a light pink and add sherry. Serve hot.

Some of her discomfort can be explained by the general atmosphere of a house where the following remark might be made: Wolfe to a client: It was foolhardy to ask her to marry you. You can't know what a woman is like until you see her at her food. I invite you to dine with us. There will be chicken sorrel soup with egg yolks and sherry, and roast quail with a sauce of white wine, veal stock, and white grapes.   [KILL NOW, PAY LATER]

CHICKEN SORREL SOUP (see index for recipe for Germiny à l'Oseille)

ROAST QUAIL VÉRONIQUE

6 quail, dressed
salt and freshly ground
    black pepper
1½ cups cooked wild rice
½ cup melted butter
⅔ cup dry white wine

½ cup veal bouillon
½ cup peeled green seedless
    grapes
12 slices Fritz's bread
½ pound boiled Georgia ham

Preheat oven to 450°. Wash and wipe the quail dry. Rub the insides with salt and pepper. Stuff each bird with the wild rice mixed with a little of the melted butter. Truss with butcher's cord. Put the quail in a shallow roasting pan, brush with butter, and roast for 5 minutes at 450°; lower the heat to 325° and roast for 20 minutes more, basting with additional butter. When done, remove from the pan and keep warm on a platter. Deglaze the pan with the wine and veal bouillon and bring to a boil. Lower the heat, add the grapes, and simmer for 5 minutes. Correct the seasoning. Fry the bread in a little butter and cut into triangles. Arrange the toast on a serving platter and cover with julienned slivers of ham. Place the quail on top and spoon some of the sauce over them. Serve the rest of the sauce in a sauceboat. (Serves 6)

VARIATION:

Omit the bread and ham; put the cooked quail in a casserole dish, cover with the sauce, and heat for 10 or 15 minutes in a medium oven. Remove, heat ½ cup of cognac, and just before serving pour the hot cognac over the quail, ignite, and serve flaming.

Wolfe said to Fritz, "A calamity. We cannot possibly dine at eight as usual. Not dine, that is. We can eat, and I suppose we shall have to. You have filets of beef with sauce Abano."

"Yes, sir."

Wolfe sighed again. "You will have to serve it in morsels, for five persons. By adding some of the fresh stock you can have plenty of soup. Open Hungarian *petits poissons*. You have plenty of fruit? Fill in as you can. It is distressing, but there's no help for it."

"The sauce is a great success, sir. I could give the others canned chicken and mushrooms—"

"Confound it, no! If there are to be hardships, I must share them. That's all. Bring me some beer."

Clara Fox shook her head. "We don't need to eat. Or we can go out for a bite."

"Great hounds and Cerberus!" He was about as close to a tantrum as he ever got. "Don't need to eat! In heaven's name, are you camels, or bears in for the winter?"

Wolfe was the gracious host. He saw that Mike Walsh got two rye highballs and the women a bottle of claret, and like a gentleman he gave Walsh two extra slices of the beef, smothered with sauce, which he would have sold his soul for. But he wouldn't let Walsh light his pipe when the coffee came. He said he had asthma, which was a lie. Pipe smoke didn't bother him much, either. He was just sore at Walsh because he had had to give up the beef, and he took it out on him that way.

[THE RUBBER BAND]

FILETS OF BEEF IN SAUCE ABANO

6 to 12 slices cooked beef filet (see index)

3 hard-cooked eggs

1 teaspoon dry mustard

½ teaspoon salt

½ teaspoon freshly ground black pepper

1½ cups olive oil

½ cup tarragon vinegar

½ cup chopped sour gherkins

1 tablespoon capers

1 tablespoon chopped parsley

1 tablespoon chervil (or 1 teaspoon dried leaves)

½ tablespoon tomato paste

Cook the beef filets according to the cooking instructions for filet of beef in aspic. Grate the egg yolks and blend with the dry mustard, salt, pepper, and ¼ cup of the oil. Beat the mixture to a paste with a wire whisk. Slowly add the remaining olive oil, beating constantly. Add the vinegar and stir vigorously. Stir in the gherkins, capers, parsley, and chervil, and blend in the tomato paste. The sauce should have the consistency of mayonnaise. Cut the egg whites into julienne strips and fold them into the sauce. Pour the sauce over the beef filets and garnish the platter with broiled tomato halves. (Serves 6)

Once in a great while, however, Wolfe is himself put on the receiving end.

"You haven't eaten at all?"

"Of course not."

Wolfe grunted. "That's ridiculous. We have a spare room that is comfortable. Mr. Goodwin will take you to it, and my chef will take you a tray. After your fast you should eat with caution. Have you a preference?"

She cocked her head. "You bet I have, Falstaff. Let the lady enjoy herself. I know about your chef. How about some lamb kidneys *bourguignonne?*   [COUNTERFEIT FOR MURDER]

LAMB KIDNEYS BOURGUIGNONNE

18 lamb kidneys	½ pound mushrooms, minced
½ cup flour	2 cups dry red wine
salt and freshly ground	½ bay leaf
black pepper	1 tablespoon minced watercress
6 tablespoons butter	1 tablespoon minced celery
2 shallots, minced	¼ teaspoon thyme

Soak the kidneys in cold water for 10 minutes. Remove the membranes and connective tissue and cut the kidneys across in half. Season the flour with salt and pepper and dredge the kidneys. Sauté them in 4 tablespoons of the butter and set aside. Add the shallots and mushrooms to the butter. Sprinkle with 2 tablespoons of the seasoned dredging flour and cook over a low heat for 5 minutes, stirring occasionally. Add the wine, bay leaf, watercress, celery, thyme, ½ teaspoon of salt, and a few grindings of black pepper. Stir well and add the kidneys; cover the skillet and simmer gently for 25 minutes. When ready to serve, remove the bay leaf, add the remaining 2 tablespoons of butter, and correct the seasoning. Serve over rice. (Serves 6)

"Bacalhau?" Wolfe demanded.

"Yea. I happened to mention we were having it for dinner and she asked what it was and I told her, and she said salt cod couldn't possibly be fit to eat no matter how it was cooked, not even if it was an adaptation of a Portuguese recipe by you and Fritz." I shrugged my shoulders.

"Skip it. She may be a murderess anyhow."

But because Wolfe did not like the idea of sending anyone from his house hungry, and because of his instinctive reaction to the challenge that salt cod couldn't be made edible, the roomer was not bounced before dinner. Wolfe and I ate together in the dining room as usual; the salt cod with Portuguese trimmings was so good that I had no room for the veal and not much for the walnut pudding.   [PRISONER'S BASE]

BACALHAU

1½ to 2 pounds soaked dried
  cod (see note)
2 large onions, sliced
6 tablespoons butter
1 clove garlic, minced
3 large potatoes
2 tablespoons bread crumbs

10 pitted green olives
10 black olives
4 hard-cooked eggs
½ cup chopped fresh parsley
wine vinegar
olive oil
freshly ground black pepper

Put the cod into a saucepan and add enough cold water to cover. Bring to a boil, reduce the heat, and simmer for 15 minutes, or until the fish is tender. Drain; remove skin and bones. Flake the meat with a fork into large pieces. Sauté the onions in 3 tablespoons of the butter until they are tender and golden in color. Add the garlic. Boil the unpeeled potatoes in salted water. When they are tender (about 20 minutes), remove from the heat, put under running cold water, and remove the skins. Drain and slice into ¼-inch pieces. Preheat the oven to 350°. Grease a 1½-quart casserole with the remaining 3 tablespoons of butter. Arrange a layer of half the potatoes, then half the cod, then half the onions. Sprinkle with a little pepper and repeat the layering. Sprinkle bread crumbs over the top layer. Bake for 15 minutes, or until heated through and lightly browned. Before serving, garnish the top with olives and eggs; sprinkle with parsley. Serve with the wine vinegar and oil in cruets and black pepper in a small dish. (Serves 4)

NOTE: To prepare dried cod, soak in cold water for about 24 hours, or until it is completely moistened. Change the water two or three times. Drain thoroughly.

_____

On one occasion, Wolfe was faced with a most unusual problem —little boys: "Tell Fritz there will be guests at lunch. What do boys of that age eat?"
"They eat everything."

"Tell Fritz to have that."

For lunch Fritz gave us two enormous chicken pies and four watermelons.   [FER-DE-LANCE]

CHICKEN PIE

2 broilers, poached (see index
    for poached truffled
    broilers)
3 tablespoons butter
¼ cup minced shallots
2 tablespoons all-purpose flour

1 cup chicken stock
¼ pound mushrooms
salt and freshly ground
    black pepper
1 9-inch pie crust (see index)

When the chickens have been poached and cooled, remove the skin and bones. Chop the meat, picking it over for tendons, and set aside. Heat 2 tablespoons of the butter in a saucepan and add the shallots, sautéing for 3 or 4 minutes. Add the flour, stirring until it is blended with the butter, about 2 minutes. Gradually add the chicken stock, stirring constantly until the sauce is thickened. In a separate pan sauté the cleaned, sliced mushrooms in the remaining butter and add them to the sauce. Correct the seasoning. Stir the sauce into the chicken and pour into a buttered casserole. Top the casserole with the pie crust and bake at 350° for 20 to 30 minutes until the crust is browned. (Serves 4)

VARIATION:

Sauté a whole black truffle in a little butter and chop fine; add to sauce. Instead of using a pie-crust topping, make forcemeat balls as follows: Grind a whole boned chicken breast in the finest blade of a meat grinder. Blend 1 cup of milk with 1 cup of fine bread crumbs and season with salt, pepper, and nutmeg. Melt 2 tablespoons of butter and add to the crumb mixture with the chicken meat. Beat 2 egg whites until stiff and fold them into the chicken mixture. Form into balls and poach them in boiling chicken stock until they rise to the surface. Dot the chicken pie with the drained balls before baking, and reduce baking time to 15 minutes. (*This variation was served to Saul Panzer in* TOO MANY CLIENTS.)

10

ASSOCIATES FOR DINNER

Somewhere between the category of personal friends and that of clients sits the group of dinner guests who might be termed associates. Characters such as Saul Panzer, Lon Cohen, and Inspector Cramer have appeared in most of the Wolfe stories over the years, and it is not surprising that their appearances have occasionally involved invitations to meals in the old brownstone. Some of these men—Saul Panzer, Orrie Cather, and Fred Durkin —are free-lance detectives hired by Wolfe to assist in various cases; others—Lon Cohen of the Gazette and Doc Vollmer—are occasional sources of information and other forms of assistance. And then there is the New York Police Department—in the persons of Inspector Cramer and Purley Stebbins—which is as often help as hindrance to Wolfe and Archie in the detection of criminals and the solution of crimes.

Saul Panzer, "the best head and foot detective west of the Atlantic," is modest in both size and appearance, and only occasionally sticks around for a meal with Wolfe and Archie. In TOO MANY CLIENTS, *he partook of chicken pie with forcemeat and truffles (see index), and once for dinner, along with clams and broiled turtle steaks, he drank more than half a bottle of Montrachet.*

[THE FATHER HUNT]

TURTLE STEAKS

6 turtle steaks
½ cup butter
1 tablespoon minced shallots
¾ cup Madeira

juice of ½ lemon
salt and freshly ground
    black pepper to taste
chopped watercress

Spread the steaks with butter and broil on one side until evenly browned. Turn and spread more butter on the uncooked side. Broil until done. Remove the steaks to a heated platter and keep warm. Put the broiling pan on top of the stove and brown the shallots in the pan juices, adding more butter if necessary. Add the Madeira and bring to a boil. Add the lemon juice and another tablespoon of butter. Remove from heat and stir until the butter is melted. Correct the seasoning with salt and pepper and pour the sauce over the steaks. Garnish with chopped watercress. (Serves 6)

It is in Saul's apartment, incidentally, that Wolfe tries to make sturgeon fumé à la moscovite *(see index) when holed up during* THE MOTHER HUNT.

Orrie Cather dines more frequently on West Thirty-fifth Street, though he rates rather lower in Wolfe's esteem than Saul does. On one occasion he was treated to shad roe with Creole sauce, a particular favorite of Wolfe's, though at another dinner, the quality of the meal was not up to snuff, and Wolfe remarked to him, "That finnan haddie was too salty, and I'm thirsty. Will you have some beer, Orrie?"

SHAD ROE WITH CREOLE SAUCE (see index)

FINNAN HADDIE

2 pounds finnan haddie
    (smoked haddock)
1 cup milk
1 cup water
¼ cup butter
3 tablespoons flour
2 cups heavy cream
freshly ground black pepper
    to taste

⅛ teaspoon nutmeg
1 tablespoon chopped pimiento
4 hard-cooked eggs
bread crumbs
12 bread triangles fried in
    anchovy butter (see index)

Soak finnan haddie in water to cover for 1 hour. Drain and put into a large saucepan, covering with the milk and water. Bring to a boil, remove from the heat, and let stand for 10 to 15 minutes. When cooled, remove skin and bones, reserving the stock. Melt the butter in a heavy-bottomed saucepan. Stir in the flour and cook over direct low heat until smooth. Add the cream and 1¼ cups of the reserved stock; continue to cook, stirring occasionally, until the mixture is slightly thickened. Season with pepper and nutmeg. When the sauce is thick enough to coat a spoon, remove it from the heat, measure out ¼ cup, and set it aside. Break the finnan haddie into pieces and fold them into the sauce. Simmer gently over low heat for a few minutes until the fish is warmed. Pour the mixture into a shallow casserole; cover with the pimiento and sliced hard-cooked eggs and pour the reserved ¼ cup of sauce over the eggs. Sprinkle the dish with bread crumbs and place under a hot broiler to brown. Serve with the anchovy toast. (Serves 4)

Perhaps it is Orrie's good appetite that appeals to Wolfe and encourages him to invite Orrie to join him for meals. One day, Archie remembers, Fritz was passing a platter of what Wolfe calls hedgehog omelet, which tastes a lot better than it sounds, when the phone rang. . . . Back at the table, I found that the omelet had had no chance either to cool or to shrivel, not with Orrie there to help Wolfe with it. I did get a bite.

[IF DEATH EVER SLEPT]

HEDGEHOG OMELET

6 large eggs	4 strips bacon
¾ teaspoon salt	2 tablespoons blanched slivered
¼ cup blanched chopped	almonds
almonds	5 tablespoons butter
½ teaspoon Grand Marnier	3 tablespoons marmalade

Separate the eggs and beat the yolks until they are fairly thick. Add salt to the yolks. Beat the whites until they hold stiff peaks and fold them into the yolks. Put the chopped almonds into a bowl, add the Grand Marnier, and allow them to stand for 10 to 15 minutes. Fry the bacon until it is crisp; dry on brown paper and crumble. Add the bacon to the egg mixture with the chopped almonds and mix thoroughly. Divide the mixture in half and cook each half separately in the usual manner using 1 tablespoon of the butter (see index for apricot omelet). Before cooking the omelets, sauté the slivered almonds in another tablespoon of the butter and melt the remaining three tablespoons in a separate pan. When the omelets are cooking, spread some marmalade into the center before folding. After they are folded and rolled onto a warm platter, spread them with the melted butter and stick the sautéed almonds into the omelets to give the appearance of bristles. Glaze under a hot broiler and serve immediately. (Serves 2)

VARIATION:

For a breakfast or dessert dish, soak the chopped almonds in lemon or almond extract instead of Grand Marnier and omit the bacon.

Although Saul and Orrie usually eat in the dining room with Wolfe and Archie, Fred Durkin—an Irishman who can tail better than anyone Archie knows except Saul—always eats in the kitchen. As Archie tells it, Fred puts vinegar on things, and no man who does that eats at Wolfe's table. Fred did it back in 1932, calling for vinegar and stirring it into a brown roux for a squab. Nothing was said, Wolfe regarding it as immoral to interfere with anybody's meal until it was down and the digestive process completed, but the next morning he fired Fred and kept him fired for over a month. [WHERE THERE'S A WILL] *On one occasion, Fred made his appearance in the kitchen twenty minutes before noon with pork chops in his pocket for Fritz to cook.*

[THE RUBBER BAND]

PORK CHOPS (see index for Broiled Pork-Loin Wafers)

At one point, however, Fred was treated to fried chicken and mush with Saul and Peter Drossos. This occasion must have been irregular all around, for not only did Fred eat in the dining room, but Fritz was also caught frying chicken, which he never does. Archie usually has to go to a restaurant called the Green Fence near Croton Falls off route 22, where a woman with a double chin fries chicken the way his Aunt Margie did out in Ohio.

FRIED CHICKEN AND MUSH

2 3-pound chickens
2 cups buttermilk (or more)
1½ cups flour
1 teaspoon salt

¼ teaspoon freshly ground
   black pepper
2 cups salad oil

Cut the chickens into serving pieces and soak them overnight in buttermilk. Dry them off with a clean towel. Sift the flour into a flat dish and season with salt and pepper. Dredge the chicken pieces in the flour and dip them in the oil. Dredge again in flour and set aside. Heat the oil (about 1 inch deep) in a large skillet and fry the chicken 3 or 4 pieces at a time, removing the cooked pieces to brown paper to drain. Arrange on a warmed serving platter and serve with mush. (Serves 6)

THE MUSH (see index for Polenta)

Lon Cohen, as an editor on the Gazette, *is one of Archie's most useful contacts and the source of a tremendous amount of valuable information. Though Archie repays him with information, he also sees to it that Lon is well fed, be it at Pierre's restaurant or at Wolfe's table:* At nine o'clock we were back in the office, Lon in the red leather chair and Wolfe and I at our desks, and Fritz was serving coffee and brandy. The hour and a half in the dining room across the hall had been quite sociable, what with clam cakes with chili sauce, the beef braised in red wine, the squash with sour cream and chopped dill, the avocado with watercress and black-walnut kernels, and the Liederkranz. The talk had covered the state of the Union, the state of the feminine mind, whether any cooked oyster can be fit to eat, structural linguistics, and the price of books.   [THE DOORBELL RANG]

CLAM CAKES (see index for Cape Cod Clam Cakes)

BEEF BRAISED IN RED WINE

5 to 6 pounds rump of beef,
   boned
¼ pound salt pork
2 cups red wine

¼ cup wine vinegar
2 teaspoons salt
1 teaspoon black peppercorns
1 large onion, sliced

(Continued)

2 large carrots, sliced
1 stalk celery, sliced
1 clove garlic
4 sprigs parsley
2 bay leaves
2 tablespoons olive oil

2 tablespoons butter
3 tablespoons all-purpose flour
1 tablespoon tomato paste
1 teaspoon fresh rosemary (or
　½ teaspoon dried leaves)
¼ cup cognac

Lard the meat with slices of the salt pork, or ask the butcher to do this for you. Make a marinade with 1½ cups of the wine, the vinegar, salt, peppercorns, onion, carrots, celery, garlic, parsley, and 1 of the bay leaves. Let the meat stand in the marinade for 24 hours in the refrigerator, turning it occasionally. When you are ready to cook, remove the meat, drain it, and dry it thoroughly, reserving the marinade. Heat the oil in a large casserole or Dutch oven and brown the meat on all sides. Remove the meat from the pan and pour out the oil. Melt the butter in the casserole and add the flour, stirring occasionally until the flour turns golden brown. Stir in the tomato paste, rosemary, the other bay leaf, the marinade, and the rest of the wine. Bring the liquid to a boil and add the meat, spooning the liquid over it. Cover the casserole, reduce the heat, and simmer for 2½ to 3 hours. When the meat is tender, remove it to a warm platter. Heat the cognac and pour it over the meat, igniting the cognac with a match. Boil the liquid in the casserole quickly until it is reduced by about half. Skim off the fat, strain the sauce, and serve it with the meat. (Serves 6 to 8)

SQUASH WITH SOUR CREAM AND DILL

1½ to 2 pounds zucchini
1 medium clove garlic, minced
1 medium onion, chopped
1 medium green bell pepper,
　chopped
2 tablespoons olive oil
1 teaspoon fresh dill (or ½
　teaspoon dried leaves)

¼ teaspoon salt
¼ teaspoon freshly ground
　black pepper
1 tablespoon grated Parmesan
　cheese
½ cup sour cream (see index)

Wash the squash but do not peel it. Slice in ⅜-inch rounds. In a heavy skillet over a medium flame, cook the garlic, onion, and green pepper in the oil until they are soft. Add the squash and cook uncovered for 10 to 15 minutes, turning occasionally. The squash should be lightly browned but still crisp. Mix the dill, salt, pepper, Parmesan cheese, and sour cream. Stir into the squash and heat thoroughly but do not boil. (Serves 4)

AVOCADO WITH WATERCRESS AND
BLACK-WALNUT KERNELS

2 ripe avocados	juice of 1 lemon
½ cup black-walnut kernels	¼ bunch young watercress

Shortly before serving, peel and cut the avocados into ½-inch cubes. Mix gently in a small bowl with the walnuts and sprinkle the lemon juice over. Arrange the washed, drained, and chilled watercress on salad plates and place spoonfuls of the avocado mixture on each. (Serves 4)

"I might get something useful from Lon Cohen if I buy him a thick enough steak—and by the way I ought to call him."

"Do so. Invite him to dine with us."

So I phoned Lon, and he came and ate kidneys mountain style and carameled dumplings . . . convenient and economical but it had its drawbacks—namely that I usually dispose of six of those dumplings and this time was limited to four; and Wolfe had to be content with seven instead of ten.   [PRISONER'S BASE]

KIDNEYS MOUNTAIN STYLE

8 lamb kidneys	½ cup red wine
3 tablespoons butter	1 sprig parsley
2 shallots, chopped	1 small stalk celery with
1 clove garlic, minced	leaves, chopped
1 carrot, sliced	1 pinch thyme
2 tablespoons all-purpose flour	salt and freshly ground
1 cup beef broth	black pepper

Split the kidneys lengthwise and remove all fibers and skin. Soak in cold water for 1 hour, changing the water several times. Heat the butter in a saucepan; add the shallots, garlic, and carrot, and let brown slightly. Add the flour, let it brown, and pour in the broth and wine. Add the rest of the ingredients and, when the liquid boils, put in the halved kidneys, which have been drained. Cook until the kidneys are tender. Place the kidneys on a small hot dish and strain the sauce over them. Serve immediately. (Serves 4)

This recipe for kidneys mountain style is an adaptation of a famous dish, rognons aux montagnes, *mentioned on several other occasions, notably in* TOO MANY WOMEN, *where Archie—for good reason—passes it up for a dish of oatmeal. The dumplings are Fritz's own inspired invention.*

CARAMELED DUMPLINGS

1 cup all-purpose flour
2 teaspoons baking powder
½ teaspoon salt
1 large egg
⅓ cup milk (or more)
2 tablespoons minced Italian
    parsley

4 cups beef bouillon (see
    index)
1 cup sugar
¾ cup water

Sift the flour, baking powder, and salt together into a mixing bowl. Sift two times more. Beat the egg with the milk and add the mixture very slowly to the dry ingredients. Add a little more milk if necessary to form a stiff batter. Add the parsley. Heat the bouillon in a large sauce pot. Dip a spoon into the hot bouillon, then into the batter, and drop a spoonful of batter into the simmering liquid. Add more dumplings, leaving ½ inch between each one. Cover and cook for 5 minutes; turn the dumplings and cook 5 minutes longer. While they are cooking, make a caramel with the sugar and water. Stir the sugar and water in a saucepan and cook over a medium heat until the sugar is dissolved and begins to turn an amber color. Remove from the heat but keep it warm. When the dumplings are done, remove with a slotted spoon and drain. Arrange the dumplings on a heated serving platter and spoon the caramel over them. Serve hot. (Makes about 24 dumplings)

Lon's favorite food is steak, however, and Fritz knows it.

It was really a handsome platter. The steak was thick and brown with charcoal braid, the grilled slices of sweet potato and sautéed mushrooms were just right, the watercress was high at one end out of danger, and the over-all smell made me wish I had asked Fritz to make a carbon.

"Now I know," Lon said, "it's all a dream. Archie, I would have sworn you phoned me to come down here. Okay, I'll dream on." He sliced through the steak, letting the juice come, cut off a bite, and opened wide for it. Next came a bite of sweet potato, followed by a mushroom. I watched him the way I have seen dogs watch when they're allowed near the table. It was too much. I went to the kitchen, came back with two slices of bread on a plate, and thrust it at him.

"Come on, brother, divvy. You can't eat three pounds of steak."

"It's under two pounds."

"Like hell it is. Fix me up."

After all he was a guest, so he had to give in.

[THE SECOND CONFESSION]

LON'S STEAK (see index for Planked Porterhouse Steak)

Doctor Edwin A. Vollmer—or Doc—has performed all sorts of services for Wolfe over the years, everything from stitching up heads to delivering phone messages when Wolfe's phone was tapped by the FBI in THE DOORBELL RANG. *In that episode, Archie feels that he must warn Doc of the consequences.* "The trouble is that if someone gets the notion that we get confidential messages through you, your line will be tapped."

"My god, that's illegal!"

"That makes it more fun. You might be obliging and say that you came to take Fritz's blood pressure—no, you haven't got the gadget. You came—"

"I came to get his recipe for *escargots bourguignonne*. I like that better, nonprofessional." He moved to the door. "My word, Archie, it certainly *is* tricky."

ESCARGOTS BOURGUIGNONNE

½ teaspoon minced garlic
2 minced shallots
½ pound butter
2 tablespoons minced parsley
salt and freshly ground
   black pepper

24 canned snails imported from
   France
½ cup dry white wine
24 large mushrooms

Sauté the garlic and shallots in 2 tablespoons of the butter for 5 minutes. Remove from heat and stir in the parsley, salt, and pepper to taste. Blend the mixture with the rest of the butter until the consistency is creamy and smooth. Preheat the oven to 450°. Drain the snails and rinse them in the wine. Wipe the mushrooms with a damp cloth and remove the stems. Place about ½ teaspoon of the butter mixture in each mushroom cap. Add a snail, small end down. Add a bit more butter on top. Put the stuffed mushrooms in a shallow, buttered baking dish and bake for 5 to 8 minutes, or until the butter is bubbling and hot. Serve with a loaf of French bread and a good white wine. (Serves 4 to 6)

Sergeant Purley Stebbins of the Homicide Squad is never really comfortable in the presence of Wolfe and Archie, who as private detectives are often working at cross-purposes with the police. Nevertheless, when his work brings him to West Thirty-fifth Street, he is usually happy to accept their hospitality, especially when it is served up by Fritz. In THE GOLDEN SPIDERS, *he was encouraged to take five or six crescents and two cups of coffee, but —as Archie reminds us—"no man who has ever tasted Fritz's Sunday-morning crescents could possibly turn them down."*

SUNDAY-MORNING CRESCENTS

½ cup milk
1 tablespoon melted butter
1 tablespoon sugar
1 teaspoon salt
½ cake compressed yeast
¼ cup lukewarm water

2½ cups sifted all-purpose
    flour
1 large egg, beaten
½ pound cold butter
2 egg yolks
3 tablespoons light cream

Scald the milk in a saucepan and add the melted butter, sugar, and salt. Pour the milk into a large bowl and allow to cool. Soften the yeast in the lukewarm water and add to the milk, stirring well. Add the flour and the egg, and stir into a soft dough, adding more flour if necessary. Knead the dough on a lightly floured board until it is smooth and elastic. Place the dough in a greased bowl, cover, and allow to rise in a warm place until doubled in bulk. Punch the dough down and chill for 1 hour. Punch it down once again and roll it out into a rectangle about ¼ inch thick. Flatten the chilled butter into a rectangular shape and place it in the center of the dough, leaving about 1 inch of uncovered dough on all sides. Fold the dough into thirds, right side over left, so that three layers are formed. Press the ends together to seal in the butter and roll out into another large rectangle. Fold again in thirds and chill for 30 minutes. Repeat this rolling and folding operation three times, chilling between each. After the last rolling, chill for 1½ hours.

To make the crescents, roll the dough into a rectangle ¼ inch thick and cut the piece into three 4″ squares. Cut these squares in half diagonally to form triangles. Roll up each triangle and curve the ends to form a crescent shape. Put on an ungreased cookie sheet and chill for 30 minutes. Preheat the oven to 400°. Just before baking, beat the egg yolks and cream together and brush the crescent tops. Bake at 400° for 5 minutes, reduce the heat to 350°, and bake for 15 minutes longer, until the rolls are golden brown.

VARIATION:

To make patty shells, roll the dough into a rectangle ½ inch thick and cut the piece into circles 2 inches in diameter. With a sharp knife or a cooky cutter cut out circles 1 inch in diameter, taking care not to cut all the way through the large circle. Remove the smaller circles and bake separately. Arrange all the circles on an ungreased cookie sheet and bake at 350° for 15 minutes until the shells are golden brown.

And Archie once uses Fritz's cooking to allay Purley's suspicions about a particular case:
　　"What kind of a gag is this?"
　　"No gag. I wouldn't dare to trifle with an officer of the law. Call Murphy. If he doesn't satisfy you come and have lunch with us. Peruvian melon, kidney pie, endive with Martinique dressing. . . ."　　　　　　　　　　　　　　　[MIGHT AS WELL BE DEAD]

KIDNEY PIE

3 pounds lamb kidneys
½ cup all-purpose flour
6 tablespoons butter
2 onions, chopped
½ pound mushrooms, sliced
1 teaspoon salt
½ teaspoon freshly ground
　　black pepper
1 bay leaf
1 tablespoon chopped fresh
　　parsley
1 cup red wine
1 tablespoon tomato paste
pastry for single-crust 9-inch
　　pie (see index)

Preheat the oven to 350°. Cut the kidneys into 1½- to 2-inch cubes, removing any fat or membrane. Dredge them in the flour and quickly sauté them in the butter. Stir constantly until they are thoroughly browned. Remove the kidneys to a heated casserole. Lower the flame and put the onions in the skillet; let them cook until transparent. Remove with a slotted spoon and add them to the casserole. Mix the salt, pepper, bay leaf, parsley, red wine, and tomato paste together and pour over the kidneys. Add the mushrooms. Cover the casserole and bake for 1 hour and 35 minutes, adding more wine if necessary. Remove from the oven and keep hot. While the kidneys are cooking, make the pie crust and chill it for 30 minutes in the freezer. Roll the dough into a circle 1½ inches larger than the top of the casserole, and when the kidneys have cooked, remove the casserole cover and replace it with the crust. Bake at 450° for 10 minutes and at 350° for 15 minutes or until the crust is evenly browned. (Serves 4)

ENDIVE WITH MARTINIQUE DRESSING

6 heads endive	1 teaspoon minced fresh
¾ cup olive oil	tarragon
¼ cup tarragon wine vinegar	1 teaspoon minced shallots
½ teaspoon salt	1 teaspoon chopped fresh
⅛ teaspoon freshly ground	chervil (or ¼ teaspoon
black pepper	dried leaves)
½ clove garlic, minced	1 teaspoon minced mushrooms

Wash the endive, dry it thoroughly, and separate the leaves. Wrap the leaves in a clean, dry cloth and refrigerate until use. Combine the vinegar, seasonings, and herbs. Slowly pour the oil into the mixture, beating it until the dressing thickens. Let the dressing rest for 1 hour and beat it again before serving. (Serves 6)

Over the years Wolfe's admiration and respect for Inspector L. T. Cramer has deepened, although Wolfe represses it very well and rarely entertains him at table. Since Cramer spends a good deal of time in the red leather chair in Wolfe's office waiting for the genius to unravel a case, it is not surprising that he is often present when a snack is served.

When I returned to the office with a supply of provender, Cramer was riding Wolfe, pouring it on, and Wolfe was leaning back in his chair with his eyes shut. I passed around plates of Fritz's _il pesto_ and crackers. . . .

In four minutes, Cramer inquired, "What is this stuff?"

Wolfe told him. _"Il pesto."_

"What is in it?"

"Canestrato cheese, anchovies, pig liver, black walnuts, chives, sweet basil, garlic, and olive oil."

"Good god."   [THE ZERO CLUE]

IL PESTO

¼ pound pig liver
2 tablespoons butter
2 cups fresh basil leaves
2 cloves garlic
¼ cup black walnuts
1 teaspoon chopped chives

½ cup grated Canestrato cheese (see note)
1 teaspoon salt
½ teaspoon freshly ground black pepper
¾ cup olive oil

Sauté the sliced pig's liver in the butter; when cool, remove from pan and chop coarsely. In a blender combine the basil, garlic, black walnuts, chives, cheese, salt, pepper, and ¼ cup of the olive oil. Blend at a low speed until a purée consistency is achieved. Slowly add the remaining olive oil, blending at low speed until the oil is completely incorporated and the consistency is that of whipped cream. Add the liver and blend for another 5 seconds and no longer; the texture of the liver should be discernible. Serve as a spread with crackers or as a sauce for spaghetti; in which case the amount of oil should be increased to 1½ cups.

NOTE: Canestrato cheese is a Sicilian grating cheese, very sharp and white, sometimes containing whole black pepper. If it is not available, substitute Cacciocavallo.

11

FRITZ BRENNER

"There are a few great cooks, a sprinkling of good ones, and a pestiferous host of bad ones. I have in my home a good one. Mr. Fritz Brenner. He is not inspired, but he is competent and discriminating. He is also discreet." *These seemingly ungenerous words were spoken by Wolfe in a conversation with Jerome Berin, who is one of the world's few great cooks. Actually, considering Wolfe's customary reserve, this is a description involving the highest kind of praise. Perhaps his only modest statement is that Fritz is not inspired. He certainly is, by Wolfe himself. Whether Fritz Brenner is under pressure or basking in the rare glow of his master's praise, his mind is constantly alert to the nuance, always prepared to meet the nearest challenge. In fact, the two men together probably make up one of the few great cooks, and no discussion of Nero Wolfe the gastronome is complete without at least a chapter devoted to the medium through which he operates. Little is known of Fritz's personal life or his past, if he has either. His room, as described by Archie, tells us little:* Fritz could have had a room upstairs, but he prefers the basement. His den is as big as the office and front room combined, but over the years it has got pretty cluttered—tables with stacks of magazines, busts of Escoffier and Brillat-Savarin on stands, framed menus on the walls, a king-size bed, five chairs, shelves of books (he has 289 cookbooks), a head of wild boar he shot in the Vosges, a TV and stereo cabinet, two large cases of ancient cooking vessels, one of which he thinks was used by Julius Caesar's chef, and so on.　　　　　[THE DOORBELL RANG]

We know that Fritz is Swiss, and perhaps his origin in that neutral country, so conveniently located in the center of Europe, abutting the great culinary nations of France, Italy, and Germany but exclusively belonging to none, explains something of his openness to cuisines of various regions. In any event, Fritz, having been trained in the highest European traditions, is the perfect means by which Wolfe can produce the finest American dishes, to which he is justifiably partial.

We have noted in earlier chapters Fritz's remarkable ability to work under terrific pressure with little apparent reward, but this is, after all, only one of the characteristics of a good cook. His high standards and his perfectionism in achieving them are certainly matched by his ingenuity. In TOO MANY CLIENTS, *for instance, when Archie tells him,* "It's possible that we may have a client, but not likely. It looks more like peanuts. You may have to invent a dish for a king made of peanut butter," *Fritz replies coolly,* "Not impossible, Archie. The problem would be to crack the oil. Not vinegar; it would take too much. Perhaps lime juice, with or without a drop or two of onion juice. I'll try it tomorrow."

Fritz is also proud, and with good reason. When Archie expresses a certain displeasure about the appearance of shad roe for the fifth day in a row, Fritz gives him a look and says, "That is an insult. I pull your nose. My shad roe *aux fines herbes* is a dish fit for a king." *Yet he is not entirely nerveless:* "I told Wolfe I was making *glace de viande,* but he said one of the visitors is a murderer. I want to do my share, you know that, Archie, but I can't make good *glace de viande* if I have to be watching murderers."   [KILL NOW, PAY LATER]

GLACE DE VIANDE

7 to 8 pounds beef shin bones with meat	1 head of celery, chopped
	6 carrots, chopped
7 to 8 pounds veal shin bones with meat	4 to 5 onions, chopped
	4 leeks, chopped
4 to 5 pounds chicken backs and necks	3 quarts water
	2 cups tomato pulp

Have the butcher cut the beef and veal bones into 2- to 3-inch pieces. Place them into a large roasting pan with the chicken parts. Roast in a 450° oven until they are brown; remove the bones and put them in a large kettle. Add the celery, carrots, onions, and leeks to the pot with the tomatoes. Add the water. Simmer the bones and vegetables, covered, for at least 12 hours over a very low flame (use an asbestos pad), skimming off the fat occasionally. Remove the bones, strain out the vegetables, and return the broth to the kettle. Continue to cook, uncovered, until the broth is reduced by half. If more fat rises to the surface, skim it off. Strain the broth again through a double fold of cheesecloth. Return it to the pot and continue to simmer until the broth becomes very thick, like jam. Spoon the mixture into small containers; cool and store in freezer until ready for use. (Makes 1 cup)

Because of Wolfe's reputation as a gastronome, Fritz, too, has achieved a certain amount of fame over the years. In 1958, Lewis Hewitt, the millionaire and orchid fancier, told Wolfe that the Ten for Aristology wanted Fritz Brenner to cook their annual dinner, to be given as usual on April first, Brillat-Savarin's birthday. When Wolfe said that he had never heard of the Ten for Aristology and Hewitt explained that it was a group of ten men pursuing the ideal of perfection in food and drink, and he was one of them, Wolfe swiveled to the dictionary and after consulting it had declared that "aristology" meant the science of dining, and therefore the Ten were witlings, since dining was not a science but an art. After a long argument Hewitt had admitted he was licked and had agreed that the name should be changed, and Wolfe had given him permission to ask Fritz to cook the dinner. The dinner would be at the home of Benjamin Shriver, the shipping magnate, who wrote a letter to the *Times* every year on September first denouncing the use of horse-radish on oysters. [POISON À LA CARTE]   *During that dinner, for which Fritz produced an array of his finest specialities, one of the guests unfortunately is poisoned (the sour cream served to one diner was sprinkled with arsenic), but since the fault was not Fritz's and the dinner was superb, we are including the recipes in this chapter.*

BLINIS WITH SOUR CREAM

GREEN-TURTLE SOUP

FLOUNDER POACHED IN WHITE WINE

MUSSEL AND MUSHROOM SAUCE

ROAST PHEASANT

SUCKLING PIG

CHESTNUT CROQUETTES

SALAD WITH DEVIL'S RAIN DRESSING

CHEESE

BLINIS WITH SOUR CREAM

1½ cups sifted buckwheat flour
1 cup sifted all-purpose flour
2 cups milk
1 yeast cake
½ cup hot water
3 large eggs

3 tablespoons melted butter
½ teaspoon salt
1 teaspoon sugar
¼ cup chopped chives
2 ounces black sturgeon caviar
1 cup sour cream (see note)

Put ¾ cup of buckwheat flour in a large mixing bowl; add the all-purpose flour and 1 cup of the milk, warmed. Dissolve the yeast cake in the hot water and add to the flour mixture. Mix well. Cover the bowl and put in a warm place (about 90°) for 3 hours, or until the dough has doubled in bulk. Beat the dough down and add the remaining ¾ cup buckwheat flour. Cover and allow the dough to rise again (about 2 hours more). Add the rest of the milk and beat the mixture until smooth. Separate the eggs; beat the yolks with the melted butter and add to the batter. Using a whisk or electric beater, whip the egg whites until very stiff and add the salt and sugar. Fold the whites into the batter and allow it to stand for 20 minutes. Lightly grease a griddle and heat it. When it is very hot, drop the batter by spoonfuls to make small cakes; brown on both sides, turning once. Set aside on a warm platter. Put the chives, caviar, and sour cream into separate small dishes. Put a spoonful of caviar into the middle of a cake, or blini, and top it with a spoonful of sour cream. Sprinkle with chives and fold the blini. Arrange the filled blinis on a platter to serve or let each diner make his own at the table.

NOTE: To make sour cream, put one cup of heavy whipping cream into a 1-quart sterilized Mason jar. Add 2 tablespoons of commercial buttermilk, cover the jar, and shake rapidly. Add another cup of heavy cream, cover, and shake once again. Allow the mixture to stand for 24 hours at 75 to 80°. Refrigerate for another 24 hours.

GREEN-TURTLE SOUP

1 pound green turtle meat
2 cups beef bouillon (see index)
2 egg whites
1 teaspoon fresh basil (or ½ teaspoon dried leaves)

¼ teaspoon powdered sage
½ teaspoon fresh marjoram (or ¼ teaspoon dried leaves)
salt and freshly ground black pepper to taste
¼ cup Madeira or dry sherry

Simmer the turtle meat in enough water to cover until it is tender, about 1½ to 2 hours. Remove the meat from the pan, drain, and cut into small cubes—about ¼ inch in diameter. Combine the beef bouillon with the turtle broth. Clarify the broth by adding the beaten egg whites, bringing the liquid to a boil while beating constantly with a wire whisk. Simmer the broth for 5 minutes and let stand off heat for 15 minutes. Strain the broth through a double layer of cheesecloth. Return the clarified broth to the pan and add the herbs and the turtle meat. Reheat without boiling. Correct the seasoning with salt and pepper and add the wine just before serving. (Makes about 4 cups)

FLOUNDER POACHED IN WHITE WINE

6 fillets of flounder, about 3 pounds total	1 sprig parsley
	1 small stalk celery, sliced
1½ cups dry white wine	1 bay leaf
3 cups water	4 black peppercorns
1 onion, sliced	bones, head, and skin of the
1 teaspoon salt	flounder

Trim the flounder fillets and remove any bits of bone that might remain. Make a court bouillon by combining the remaining ingredients and simmering, uncovered, for 15 to 20 minutes. Strain the liquid through cheesecloth and pour into a shallow baking dish. Put in the fish fillets and poach in a 350° oven until the fish flakes at the touch of a fork (about 10 minutes). Remove carefully with a slotted spatula and put on a warmed serving platter. Serve with mussel and mushroom sauce. (Serves 4 to 6)

MUSSEL AND MUSHROOM SAUCE

1 dozen large mussels	6 tablespoons butter
½ cup water	3 tablespoons all-purpose flour
1 small onion, sliced	1 tablespoon chopped parsley
1 sprig parsley	½ teaspoon salt
½ teaspoon fresh thyme (or ⅛ teaspoon dried leaves)	¼ teaspoon freshly ground black pepper
⅓ cup sliced mushrooms	

Steam the cleaned mussels in the water, to which the onion, parsley, and thyme have been added. When the shells open, in about 5 to 6 minutes, remove from heat and cool slightly. Remove the meat from the shells, chop, and set aside. Strain the liquid and reserve. Sauté the mushrooms in 3 tablespoons of the butter. In a saucepan melt the remaining butter and when it is foamy, add the flour, mix well, and do not allow to brown. Add the strained mussel liquid and enough water to make a pint to the butter-flour mixture. Stir, adding the parsley, salt, and pepper. When the sauce begins to thicken, add the mushrooms and mussels. Continue to cook, stirring constantly, until the sauce has the consistency of thick cream. Pour over the fillets of flounder and serve very hot.

ROAST PHEASANT

3 pheasants, 2 to 3 pounds each	10 black peppercorns
1 bottle Hungarian Tokay wine (dry)	salt and freshly ground black pepper
1 bay leaf	6 thin slices salt pork
2 onions, sliced	2 tablespoons all-purpose flour
1 stalk celery, sliced	3 cups cooked wild rice
1 lemon	½ cup raisins
4 cloves	kumquats soaked in brandy

If the pheasants were shot in the wild, hang them for 3 days and then wash and clean them thoroughly. Truss each bird and put into a large enameled pot or stainless-steel mixing bowl. Cover the pheasants with Tokay and add the bay leaf, onions, and celery, the lemon cut in quarters, the cloves, and the peppercorns. Cover the pot tightly and marinate for 20 hours in the refrigerator. Drain the birds and strain the marinade. Preheat the oven to 350°. Tie 2 sheets of the pork around each bird and secure with butcher's cord. Place the birds breast side up on a rack in the roasting pan and roast for 20 minutes per pound. Reserve 2 tablespoons of the drippings and put into a saucepan over a low flame. Add the flour and cook for 3 minutes. Add 2 cups of the strained marinade and stir constantly until thickened. Season to taste. Serve separately. When ready to serve, remove the pork and arrange the birds on a bed of the wild rice mixed with the raisins. Garnish with a ring of brandied kumquats. (Serves 6)

SUCKLING PIG

1 10-pound suckling pig	⅛ teaspoon sage
½ cup chopped celery	⅛ teaspoon nutmeg
¼ cup chopped shallots	6 strips bacon
1 clove garlic, minced	2 large eggs
3 tablespoons butter	½ cup applesauce (optional)
3 cups bread crumbs	maraschino cherries
1 tablespoon chopped parsley	garnish: sausages, kumquats,
1 tablespoon minced chives	parsley or watercress, baked
1½ teaspoons salt	cinnamon crabapples

Wash the pig in cold water and dry with a clean towel. Sauté the celery, shallots, and garlic in the butter for 5 minutes until they are transparent.

Add the cooked vegetables to the bread crumbs with the parsley, chives. salt, sage, and nutmeg. Fry the bacon until crisp; drain and crumble it into the stuffing mixture. Beat the eggs and add them, stirring the whole mixture until well blended. If the stuffing seems too dry, add applesauce. Stuff the pig and tie up the opening, using a skewer and butcher's cord. (If you intend to serve the pig with an apple, put a block of wood in the pig's mouth for roasting.) Preheat the oven to 325°. Cover the tail and ears with aluminum foil to prevent burning. Using a serving fork, puncture the sides, back, and legs of the pig. Rub on some butter and roast for 3½ to 4 hours. Pour off the pan juices every 30 minutes or so, add some water to them, and use to baste the pig. If the pig is browning too quickly, cover with foil. When it is done, remove to a warmed serving platter. Remove the block of wood and insert an apple; put green or red maraschino cherries in the eye sockets. Rub the skin with butter. Make a garland of cooked sausages and kumquats alternating on a string and drape it over the pig's neck. Decorate the platter with parsley or water-cress and baked cinnamon crabapples. (Serves 8 to 10)

CHESTNUT CROQUETTES

1¼ pounds whole chestnuts
1 cup milk (or more)
1 ounce semisweet chocolate
½ cup sugar
4 tablespoons butter
3 egg yolks

oil for deep frying (at 375°)
1 large egg
¼ cup Grand Marnier
1 cup crushed English walnuts
powdered sugar

With the point of a sharp knife cut a small cross on the flat side of each chestnut. Put the nuts in a saucepan, cover with water, bring to a boil, and simmer for 20 minutes. Cool slightly and remove the shells and underlying skin. Put the nuts into a saucepan and cover with milk. Allow to simmer until the nuts are very tender, about 15 minutes. Remove from heat and purée with the milk in a blender or food mill. Put back into the pan and cook for 1 or 2 minutes over medium heat, stirring constantly, to remove excess moisture. Remove from heat. Grate the chocolate and add it to the purée along with the sugar, butter, and beaten egg yolks. Stir briskly until blended and slightly thickened over a low flame. Pour the purée into a baking pan and put into the refrigerator for 3 to 4 hours until thoroughly chilled. When ready to serve, remove from refrigerator and shape the purée into balls with your hands. Heat the frying oil. Beat the whole egg with the Grand Marnier. Dip each ball into the mix-ture and roll in the crushed walnuts. Deep fry the croquettes until they are nicely browned, about 3 or 4 minutes. Drain and sprinkle powdered sugar over all. Serve warm.

SALAD WITH DEVIL'S RAIN DRESSING

3 cloves garlic, peeled
10 English walnuts, shelled
   and toasted
1 teaspoon dry mustard
½ teaspoon cayenne pepper
1 tablespoon minced chives
1 teaspoon salt
1 cup olive oil
¼ cup tarragon wine vinegar
¼ cup dry red wine

greens:

1 head each curly endive,
   romaine, Bibb lettuce
1 small bunch watercress
2 to 3 stalks celery, sliced
   diagonally
½ cup carrot curls
2 small cooked beets, grated

To make the dressing, place all of the ingredients except the greens in a blender and blend at a low speed for 20 seconds. If the walnuts haven't been chopped fairly fine, blend 10 seconds more. If you prefer a less smooth sauce, crush the garlic and walnuts in a mortar until you have a paste, adding a few drops of olive oil to help with the mashing. Then add the dry mustard, cayenne pepper, chives, salt, and olive oil. Whisk for a few moments, then slowly add the vinegar and wine and blend thoroughly. Correct the seasoning. Break the salad greens into pieces and add the watercress, celery, and carrot curls. Pour on the dressing and toss lightly. Sprinkle the grated beets on top. (Serves 6 to 8)

CHEESE*

2 8-ounce packages cream cheese
1 tablespoon grated Romano
   cheese
1 green pepper, minced
½ cup chopped shallots
1 tablespoon caraway seeds
1 teaspoon poppy seeds

3 tablespoons sweet Hungarian
   paprika
2 tablespoons butter
6 anchovies, minced
½ teaspoon dry mustard
2 teaspoons chopped capers
1 tablespoon cognac

Bring the cream cheese to room temperature and blend in the grated Romano cheese. Add the green pepper to the cheese with the shallots, caraway and poppy seeds, and paprika. Blend well. Soften the butter and add to the mixture with the anchovies, mixing well. Stir in the mustard, capers, and cognac. Fill small crocks with the cheese, cover tightly, and store in the refrigerator for at least 1 week before serving. (Makes about 3 cups)

Although Fritz's dinner was undoubtedly a great culinary success, the unfortunate murder by poisoning was a bit too much for

---

* Made by Bill Thompson in New Jersey under Fritz's supervision.

him. When Archie asked him about it the following morning, Fritz leveled his eyes at Archie and said, "Archie, that is never to be mentioned. That terrible day. *Épouvantable.* My mind was here with you. I don't know what I did, I don't know what was served. I will forget it if possible."

"Hewitt said on the phone that they stood and applauded you."

"But certainly. They were polite. I know I put no truffles in the *Périgourdine.*"

"Good god. I'm glad I wasn't there. Okay, we'll forget it. May I have a carrot? It's wonderful with milk." He said certainly and I helped myself.

It would not do to end this chapter of Fritz's on such a low note, so we are taking this opportunity to insert a special favorite of his—a dish that has not yet appeared in the Wolfe stories but one that we are assured meets with a warm welcome whenever it appears on Wolfe's table.

FRITZ'S FROGS' LEGS

30 frogs' legs
2 cups dry white wine
¼ cup chopped chives
½ cup dry sherry
2 tablespoons butter

2 tablespoons all-purpose flour
1 cup cream
salt and freshly ground white
    pepper to taste

Trim and clean the frogs' legs. Put them into a saucepan and cover with the wine, into which you have stirred the chives, saving a few bits for a garnish. Simmer the frogs' legs for about 15 minutes or more, depending on the size of the legs. When they are tender, drain them thoroughly, removing the chives. Put them in a bowl and pour the sherry over them. Let stand for 1 hour. Meanwhile, make a thick white sauce with the butter, flour, and cream. Season with salt and pepper. Put the frogs' legs with the sherry into a casserole and pour the sauce over them. Cover the casserole and simmer over very low heat for 15 or 20 minutes. Serve very hot. (Serves 4 to 6)

12

DISHES COOKED BY OTHERS

All the foregoing chapters have dealt with dishes prepared exclusively by Fritz Brenner, culminating with his highest professional achievement as invited chef for the dinner of the Ten for Aristology. This chapter and those that follow will be devoted to dishes cooked by others—including Wolfe himself. Every recipe included has received Wolfe's approval or praise, and we have reason and, in some cases, evidence, to believe that many of them, if not all, have at one time or another been adapted by Fritz and incorporated into his own repertoire.

As we all know, Wolfe rarely leaves home, and then only under the most extreme pressure. During these infrequent trips, he has often had to put up with ordinary (meaning inferior) cooking, but once in a great while he enjoys himself. In DEATH OF A DUDE, *Wolfe spent over two weeks in Montana as the guest of Lily Rowan, a long-time friend of Archie's whose taste in food is sometimes a little precious* but who occasionally strikes it rich.*

Lily said, "The fricassee with dumplings is made by a Mrs. Miller whose husband has left her four times on account of her disposition and returned four times on account of her cooking and is still there."

We babbled on. The fricassee came, and the first bite, together with dumplings and gravy, made me marvel at the hellishness of Mrs. Miller's disposition to drive a man away from that.

"Archie, I must thank you"—Wolfe put his napkin down—"for suggesting the fricassee. It is superb. Only female Americans can make good dumplings, and not many of them."

[SOME BURIED CAESAR]

* Lily has been known to serve at a single luncheon mushroom chowder, lobster soufflé, avocado salad, and pineapple mousse.   [A RIGHT TO DIE]

CHICKEN FRICASSEE WITH DUMPLINGS

1 4 to 5 pound chicken	1 teaspoon salt
1 celery stalk, sliced	3 tablespoons butter
1 small onion, sliced	3 tablespoons all-purpose flour
1 small carrot, sliced	½ cup heavy cream
6 black peppercorns	1 egg yolk
1 bay leaf	1 teaspoon lemon juice

Cut the chicken into serving pieces and place them in a large pot. Add the celery, onion, and carrot to the chicken with the peppercorns and bay leaf. Cover with cold water. Bring to a boil, cover, and simmer until the chicken is tender, about 1 hour. Add the salt. Melt the butter in a saucepan and add the flour. Cook for 3 minutes and gradually pour in 2 cups of the strained chicken stock, stirring constantly until the sauce is thickened. Blend the cream and egg yolk and add to the sauce. Heat thoroughly and season with lemon juice and more salt if needed. Arrange the chicken pieces on a warm platter and pour the sauce over. (Serves 4)

DUMPLINGS

½ pound fresh spinach	1 large egg
1 cup ricotta cheese	3 tablespoons melted butter
½ cup grated Parmesan cheese, plus 2 tablespoons	½ cup all-purpose flour
1 teaspoon salt	2 cups chicken stock
¼ teaspoon freshly ground black pepper	

Wash, trim, and blanch the spinach in salted water. Drain well and chop fine. Mix well with the cheeses, salt, pepper, egg, and half the butter. Refrigerate for 1 hour. Shape the dough into balls, roll them in flour, and drop, a few at a time, into gently boiling chicken stock. As soon as they rise to the surface, remove with a slotted spoon to a hot buttered baking dish. Preheat the broiler. Sprinkle the dumplings with the additional Parmesan cheese, drizzle with the melted butter, and broil under a hot flame until the cheese browns. (Makes 12 dumplings)

This is one recipe for which we have evidence of Fritz's approval. In MIGHT AS WELL BE DEAD, *Archie describes a Sunday dinner of chicken fricassee and dumplings, Methodist style. "Fritz is not a Methodist but his dumplings are plenty good enough for angels."*

Another impressive Montana feast consisted of "Mr. Stepanian's favorite dish, a *hunkiev beyandi.* He says it was originally Armenian, but the Turks have claimed it for centuries. It's kebab served with eggplant stuffed with a purée which the Turks call *imam baildi,* 'swooning imam.' Onion browned in oil, tomatoes, garlic, salt, and pepper." [DEATH OF A DUDE]

HUNKIEV BEYANDI

1½ pounds lamb, boned
1 green pepper, diced
2 medium onions, diced
3 tablespoons olive oil
2 medium tomatoes
1 teaspoon dill weed (or
    ½ teaspoon dried leaves)

salt and freshly ground
    black pepper to taste
½ cup or more beef bouillon
    (see index)
2 cups eggplant puree (see
    below)
Italian parsley sprigs

Cut the lamb into 1-inch cubes. Sauté the pepper and onions in the olive oil in a large saucepan. Add the meat and continue to cook until the cubes are browned on all sides. Peel, seed, and slice the tomatoes and add them to the pan; cook for 5 minutes more until their juice is rendered. Season with the dill, salt, and pepper. Cover the pan and continue to simmer for 1 to 1½ hours, or until the meat is tender. Stir occasionally and add a little beef bouillon as necessary. When cooking is completed, put the meat into the center of a large serving platter and arrange the eggplant purée around the meat. Garnish with sprigs of parsley.

VARIATION:

You may substitute shish (or seekh) kebab (see index) for the stewed lamb above.

EGGPLANT PURÉE

3 medium eggplants
2 tablespoons olive oil
¼ pound mushrooms, chopped
1 onion, grated
2 tablespoons butter
2 tablespoons all-purpose flour

1 cup milk
1 tablespoon chopped fresh
    parsley
salt and pepper to taste
⅓ cup grated Gruyère cheese

Trim the stem ends of the eggplants and put them in a hot oven (400°) for 20 minutes, turning them from time to time so that they cook evenly.

Allow the skins to blacken and burn slightly. When the flesh is soft, remove the eggplants from the oven and allow to cool. Peel them and chop the flesh very fine. Put the pulp in a cheesecloth-lined strainer and allow to drain. Heat the olive oil in a skillet. Cook the mushrooms in the oil until all the moisture has evaporated. Add the onion and cook it with the mushrooms for 3 minutes. Remove from heat and set aside. In a large saucepan melt the butter, add the flour, and stir until the flour turns golden. Slowly add the milk and continue to stir until the mixture has thickened. Add the eggplant pulp, mushrooms, onion, parsley, salt, and pepper. Cook for 10 minutes, blending well. Add the cheese and stir the purée until the cheese has melted.

One of the highlights of Wolfe's Montana trip was the Montana trout deal, served up by a Mrs. Greve. As Archie tells it, the first real Montana trout deal—that is, the first one cooked by a paleface—was probably at the time of the Lewis and Clark expedition, fried over a campfire in a rusty pan with buffalo grease. Since then there have been hundreds of versions, depending on what was handy. There's an oldtimer in a hardware store in Timberburg who says that for the real thing you rub bacon grease on a piece of brown wrapping paper, wrap it around the trout, with the head and tail on and plenty of salt and pepper, and put it in the oven of a camp stove as hot as you can get it. The time depends on the size of the trout. Mrs. Greve got her version from an uncle of hers who was probably inspired by what he had left at the tail end of a packing-in trip. She has changed two details: she uses aluminum foil instead of wrapping paper, and the oven of her electric range instead of a camp stove. It's very simple. Put a thin slice of ham about three inches wide on a piece of foil, sprinkle some brown sugar on it and a few little scraps of onion, and a few drops of Worcestershire sauce. Lay the trout on it, scraped and gutted but with the head and tail on, and salt it. Repeat the brown sugar and onion and Worcestershire, wrap the foil around it close, and put it in a hot oven. If some of the trout are eight or nine inches long and others are fourteen or so, the timing is a problem. Serve them in the foil. [DEATH OF A DUDE] *Archie has obviously memorized all of this for a reason, and we can assume that it was to give Fritz the whole account verbatim on his return to New York. Wolfe returns the favor with his own deal,* truite montbarry *(see index), which is indication enough of his hard-to-win approval.*

Wolfe's reluctance to leave home was obviously outweighed by certain aspects of Montana's cuisine: When, two years back, I had returned from a month's visit to Lily Rowan on the ranch she had bought in Montana, the only detail of my trip that had really interested Wolfe was one of the meals I described. At that time of year, late August, the young blue grouse are around ten weeks old and their main item of diet has been mountain huckleberries, and I had told Wolfe they were tastier than any bird Fritz ever cooked, even quail or woodcock. Of course, since they're protected by law, they can cost up to five dollars a bite if you get caught.   [RODEO MURDER]

BLUE GROUSE

6 grouse (raised on mountain huckleberries, if possible)
1 teaspoon salt
½ teaspoon freshly ground black pepper
6 stalks celery, chopped
1 medium apple, peeled and chopped
6 tablespoons chopped shallots
3 tablespoons butter
2 tablespoons chopped parsley
1 teaspoon powdered sage
12 slices bacon
1 cup dry red wine
½ cup beef bouillon (see index)
½ cup currant jelly

Trim the grouse and pat dry with clean toweling. Season with the salt and pepper. Sauté the celery and apple with 4 tablespoons of the shallots in the butter for 5 minutes. Add the sage and parsley and blend well. Stuff the grouse with this mixture and truss. Place a piece of bacon (or thin sheet of pork fat) over each bird. Roast in a 425° oven for 15 minutes. Remove to a hot platter. Sauté the remaining 2 tablespoons of shallots in the pan juices over a low heat until they are slightly brown. Add the wine and bouillon and bring the mixture to a boil. Simmer for 5 minutes and add the currant jelly; continue to simmer until the jelly has dissolved. Serve the sauce separately with the grouse. (Serves 6)

One of the most startling examples of Wolfe's accepting another's recipe with pleasure occurs when an extraordinary young woman, by the name of Maryella Timms, actually manages to work her way into Fritz's kitchen and not only that, but to cook dinner as well. When Fritz comes to the office to speak with Wolfe about some trouble he is having with the corned-beef hash, she speaks up:

"Excuse me," she said, "but corned-beef hash is one of my specialities. Nothing in there but meat, is there?"

"As you see," Wolfe grunted.

"It's ground too fine," Maryella asserted.

Wolfe scowled at her. I could see he was torn with conflicting emotions. A female in his kitchen was an outrage. A woman criticizing his or Fritz's cooking was an insult. But corned-beef hash was one of life's toughest problems, never yet solved by anyone. To tone down the corned flavor and yet preserve its unique quality, to remove the curse of its dryness without making it greasy—the theories and experiments had gone on for years. He scowled at her but he didn't order her out.

"This is Miss Timms," I said.

"Ground too fine for what?" Wolfe demanded truculently. "This is not a tender fresh meat, with juices to lose—"

"Now you just calm down." Maryella's hand was on his arm. "It's not ruined, only it's better if it's coarser. That's far too much potatoes for that meat. But if you don't have chitlins you can't—"

"Chitlins!" Wolfe bellowed.

Maryella nodded. "Fresh pig chitlins. That's the secret of it. Fried in shallow olive oil with onion juice—"

"Good heavens!" Wolfe was staring at Fritz. Fritz was frowning thoughtfully. "It might do," he conceded. . . .

Wolfe turned to me in swift decision. "Archie, call up Kretzmeyer and ask if he has pig chitlins. Two pounds."

"You'd better let me help," Maryella said. "It's sort of tricky. . . ."

The hash was okay. It was good hash. Wolfe had three helpings, and when he conversed with Maryella, as he did through most of the meal, he was not only sociable but positively respectful.   [CORDIALLY INVITED TO MEET DEATH]

CORNED-BEEF HASH

1½ pounds boiled corned beef
4 medium potatoes
1 onion, minced

½ green pepper, minced
1 to 2 pounds chitlins,
    cooked as below

Grind the corned beef in a meat grinder, using the finest blade. Boil the unpeeled potatoes in salted water; when tender, cool slightly, remove the skins, and chop. Put the potato pieces through the grinder as well.

Preheat oven to 350°. Add the minced onion and green pepper to the mixture. Add the cooked chitlins and mix well. Pack the hash mixture into a buttered casserole and bake until the crust is nicely browned, in about 20 to 25 minutes. (Serves 4)

CHITLINS FOR CORNED-BEEF HASH

2 pounds pig chitlins	1 stalk celery, sliced
2 cloves	1/4 cup red wine vinegar
1 bay leaf	1/2 cup olive oil
1 hot red pepper, chopped	1/2 teaspoon onion juice
1 onion, sliced	

In a large enameled pot or bowl, cover the chitlins with cold water and let soak for 4 hours. Drain and wash the chitlins five or six times in running water, removing as much fat as you can. Place in a large kettle and add the cloves, bay leaf, red pepper, onion, celery, vinegar, and enough water to cover. Bring to a boil and continue to cook until tender (about 2 to 3 hours). Drain and cut into small pieces 2 to 3 inches long. Put 1/2-inch layer of olive oil in a large skillet and add the onion juice. Add the chitlins, a handful at a time, and cook until golden. Use in corned-beef hash.

Maryella's hash made such an impression on Wolfe, in fact, that the next day found them together in the kitchen: "We had a discussion about spoon bread, and there are two batches in the oven. Two eggs, and three eggs. Milk at a hundred and fifty degrees, and boiling." I turned without answering, went to the hall and got my hat, slammed the door from the outside, walked to the corner and into Sam's place, and climbed on to a stool at the counter. I didn't know I was muttering to myself, but I must have been, for Sam, behind the counter, demanded, "Spoon bread? What the hell is spoon bread?"

SPOON BREAD (*Two Ways*)

5 tablespoons butter	2 cups boiling water
1 cup white corn meal	1 cup milk
1 teaspoon salt	3 large eggs
1/3 cup raisins soaked in 1/4 cup Kirschwasser (optional)	

Melt the butter over low heat and set aside. Combine the corn meal, salt, and raisins in a mixing bowl and stir in the boiling water. Continue to stir until the mixture is smooth;, then let it rest for 5 to 10 minutes. Preheat the oven to 425°. Heat the milk until it just reaches the boiling point and slowly beat it into the corn meal. Add the eggs 1 at a time, beating thoroughly after each addition. Stir in the melted butter and pour the batter into a buttered baking dish. Bake for 25 to 30 minutes and serve hot with butter, maple syrup, or currant jam.

VARIATION:

Instead of boiling the milk, heat it to a temperature of 150° before beating it into the corn-meal batter. Omit 1 egg.

Maryella's success with Wolfe was more than impressive. It was, in fact, unprecedented and extraordinary: Wolfe was standing by the long table, watching Fritz rub a spice mixture into slices of calves' liver, and watching with him, standing beside him, closer to him than I had ever seen any woman or girl of any age tolerated, with her hand slipped between his arm and his bulk, was Maryella. Wolfe gave me a fleeting glance. "Back, Archie? We're doing mock terrapin. Miss Timms had a suggestion." He leaned over to peer at the liver, straightened, and sighed clear to the bottom.

MOCK TERRAPIN

1¼ to 1½ quarts of stock (see below)
1 pound calves' liver
½ teaspoon minced thyme leaves (or ¼ teaspoon dried leaves)
1 pinch powdered cloves
½ teaspoon minced chervil (or ¼ teaspoon dried leaves)

4 tablespoons butter
¼ pound ham
1 shallot, minced
2 teaspoons sugar
4 tablespoons flour
juice of 1 lemon
1 tablespoon Madeira
thin lemon slices

Put the stock into a saucepan and bring to a gentle simmer. Slice the calves' liver thin. Rub the liver with a mixture of the thyme, cloves, and chervil, which have been blended with 1 tablespoon of the butter. Allow to stand for 30 minutes. Chop the ham. Melt the remaining butter in another saucepan and sauté the liver, ham, and shallot for about 5 minutes; add them to the simmering stock. Sprinkle on the sugar and stir well. Make a thin paste of the flour and ¼ cup of the stock and add it slowly to the soup. Simmer for 20 minutes and then blend in the lemon juice and Madeira. Garnish with lemon slices. (Serves 4 to 6)

STOCK FOR MOCK TERRAPIN

½ calf's head (or 3 to 4 pounds veal bones)
2 cups water or consommé
1 cup dry white wine
2 stalks celery, sliced
½ cup sliced yellow onions
1 cup tomato pulp
1½ tablespoons tomato paste
½ teaspoon chopped thyme leaves (or ¼ teaspoon dried leaves)
½ teaspoon chopped basil (or ¼ teaspoon dried leaves)
1½ teaspoons salt

Put the calf's head into a large soup pot and add the water or consommé and wine. Bring to a boil, lower the heat, and add the remaining ingredients. Simmer for 2½ hours. Strain the stock, remove the grease, and use as directed.

In 1937 Wolfe was invited by the exalted group of master chefs who call themselves Les Quinze Maîtres to be guest of honor at a dinner being held at Kanawha Spa, in West Virginia, where Louis Servan, an old friend of Wolfe's and one of the fifteen masters, was head of the cuisine. The group met every five years on the home ground of the oldest of their number, each member being allowed one guest. Archie goes as the guest of Marko Vukcic, enduring a fourteen-hour train ride with Wolfe and coaching him in his speech, "Contributions Americaines à la Haute Cuisine." *One of the reasons compelling Wolfe to make such a trip, aside from the tremendous honor involved, is the possibility of obtaining Jerome Berin's famous recipe for* saucisse minuit *which Wolfe has coveted for many years. When Wolfe and Berin meet on the train, Wolfe employs his most persuasive arguments and offers a good deal of money, but Berin refuses to yield the secret. Finally, Wolfe is obliged to solve a murder in order to pry it out of Berin, and that solution is the story of* TOO MANY COOKS. *In the course of the mystery and the struggle to obtain Berin's recipe, Wolfe and Archie are treated to various dishes cooked by the other masters, all of which are superb, but the highlight of the meeting is Wolfe's special dinner served on the final night, to which the last chapter in this book is devoted.*

For luncheon on the first day several of them prepared dishes, and Phillip Laszio [*of the Hotel Churchill, New York*] did the salad, and he had announced that he was going to make Meadow-brook dressing, which he originated. They all know that he mixes the sugar and lemon juice and sour cream an hour ahead of time, and that he always tastes in spoonfuls.

MEADOWBROOK SALAD DRESSING

1 cup sour cream (see index)
½ teaspoon sugar
¼ teaspoon dry mustard
1 teaspoon lemon juice

½ cup mayonnaise (see index)
½ teaspoon capers
3 watercress sprigs

Put the sour cream in a bowl and add the sugar and dry mustard. Blend well and gradually add the lemon juice, stirring constantly. Chill in the refrigerator for 1 hour. Just before serving add the chilled mayonnaise and the capers. Mince the watercress. Spoon the dressing over prepared greens and sprinkle with the watercress. (Makes 1¾ cups)

The dinner that evening was elegant as to provender but a little confused in other respects. The soup, by Louis Servan, looked like any consommé, but it wasn't just any. . . .

CONSOMMÉ

1 5-pound fowl
2 quarts water
1 teaspoon salt
8 black peppercorns
4 leeks, sliced
4 large carrots, sliced
1 large onion, sliced

1 stalk celery, with leaves
1 sprig parsley
1 teaspoon fresh thyme (or ½ teaspoon dried leaves)
1 bay leaf
3 egg whites
1 truffle

Follow the instructions for making and clarifying bouillon in the recipe on page 109. Just before serving, correct the seasoning and drop julienned slices of truffle into the tureen.

The fish, by Leon Blanc [*of the Willow Club, Boston*], was little six-inch brook trout, four to a customer, with a light-brown sauce with capers in it, and a tang that didn't seem to come from lemon or any vinegar I had ever heard of.

BROOK TROUT WITH BROWN BUTTER AND CAPERS

16 fresh brook trout, 6 to 7
    inches long
2 teaspoons salt
1 teaspoon freshly ground
    black pepper
1 cup all-purpose flour
½ cup butter, plus 2
    tablespoons

1 tablespoon lemon juice
1 teaspoon fresh tarragon
    leaves (or ½ teaspoon dried
    leaves)
dash Tabasco
capers

Clean the trout, leaving heads and tails on. Sprinkle with salt and pepper and roll lightly in flour. Heat 2 tablespoons of the butter in a skillet, lay in the trout, being careful not to crowd them, and sauté to a golden brown, turning frequently. Arrange in a row on a hot platter. For the sauce, heat ½ cup butter in a saucepan and continue to cook over a low flame until it is light brown. Put the tarragon leaves in the lemon juice, let stand for a few minutes, and strain them out. Add the lemon juice to the butter. Add a dash of Tabasco and a few capers and correct the seasoning. Let the sauce come to a boil. Pour over the trout and serve. (Serves 4)

The entrée, by Pierre Mondor [of Mondor's, Paris], was of such a nature that I imitated some of the others and had two helpings. It appeared to be a famous creation of his, well known to the others, and Constanza told me that her father made it very well and that the main ingredients were beef marrow, cracker crumbs, white wine, and chicken breast.

QUENELLES BONNE FEMME

⅔ cup raw breast of chicken
2 egg whites
½ teaspoon salt
⅛ teaspoon white pepper
¼ cup heavy cream
1½ cups dry white wine
1 cup water
4 tablespoons beef marrow
¾ teaspoon chopped fresh
    parsley
2 large eggs

4 tablespoons sifted cracker
    crumbs
⅛ teaspoon paprika
salt to taste
3 tablespoons butter
1 shallot, chopped
6 medium mushrooms, sliced
2 tablespoons all-purpose flour
¾ cup strong chicken broth
2 tablespoons sour cream (see
    index)

Put the chicken breast through the finest blade of a meat grinder, then through a sieve, and add, gradually, the egg whites, salt, white pepper, and enough heavy cream to make it the right consistency to mold into ovals with the aid of two teaspoons. Drop the ovals into gently boiling white wine and water mixed in equal parts (1 cup each should be enough), and cook until firm, about 10 minutes. Remove with a slotted spoon and lay gently on a hot shallow baking dish. Work the marrow with a wooden spoon until creamy. Add the parsley, whole eggs, cracker crumbs, paprika, and a few grains of salt. Drop the mixture by teaspoonfuls into the same boiling liquid used for the *quenelles*. Drain and arrange on the baking dish, alternating with *quenelles*. To make the sauce, melt 3 tablespoons of butter in a saucepan and add the shallot and mushrooms. Before they begin to brown, add the flour. Pour in ½ cup wine and the chicken stock. Simmer for five minutes, add the sour cream and cook just long enough to blend everything perfectly. Pour the sauce over the *quenelles* and marrow balls and brown in a very hot oven or under a broiler. (Serves 4)

> *This dish is a favorite on West Thirty-fifth Street. Fritz has his own version (see index for Mondor patties), and Pierre Mondor, one of Wolfe's closest friends, even cooked the dish himself in Wolfe's kitchen on one occasion.* [THIS WON'T KILL YOU] *Once, when Wolfe is obliged to feed a group of women, he has Fritz make Mondor patties for them, and all indications are that this is Wolfe's pet name for the* Quenelles Bonne Femme. [MURDER BY THE BOOK]

The roast was young duck Mr. Richards, by Marko Vukcic. This was one of Wolfe's favorites, and I was well acquainted with the Fritz Brenner–Nero Wolfe version of it.

ROAST DUCK MR. RICHARDS

1 large duck, 4½ to 5 pounds
1 tablespoon minced shallots
2 sprigs parsley
½ teaspoon salt
few grains cayenne pepper
freshly ground black pepper
1 cup strong chicken broth

½ teaspoon fresh tarragon (or ¼ teaspoon dried leaves)
1 tablespoon fresh chopped parsley
½ teaspoon fresh thyme (or ¼ teaspoon dried leaves)
¼ cup cognac

Preheat oven to 500°. Remove giblets and liver from the duck and chop with the shallots and parsley sprigs. Season with a little salt and cayenne and put back into the duck, which has been well cleaned and rubbed with salt and black pepper. Truss carefully, pricking the skin in several places, and lay on a rack in a roasting pan in the very hot oven for 15 minutes. Reduce heat to 400° and continue cooking until the duckling is done, 70 to 80 minutes, basting occasionally with the chicken broth, which has been seasoned with tarragon, parsley, and thyme and from which the herbs have been strained. Also baste with the pan juice. There should be at least ½ cup or more of basting and duck juices in the roasting pan when the duck is done. Arrange the cooked duck on a hot platter, pour a little warmed cognac over it, and set fire to it. As the flames die down, pour over it the pan juices, from which you have skimmed the fat. Carve at once. (Serves 4)

The salad, by Domenico Rossi [*of the Empire Café, London*], was attended by something of an uproar. . . . Rossi noticed that Pierre Mondor wasn't pretending to eat, and wanted to know if perchance he had discovered things crawling on the lettuce. Mondor replied, friendly but firm, that the juices necessary to impart a flavor to salad, especially vinegar, were notoriously bad companions for wine, and that he wanted to finish his Burgundy.

Rossi said darkly, "There is no vinegar. I am not a barbarian."

"I have not tasted it. I smell salad juice, that is why I pushed it away."

"I tell you there is no vinegar! That salad is mostly by the good God, as He made things! Mustard sprouts, cress sprouts, lettuce! Onion juice with salt! Bread crusts rubbed with garlic!"

ROSSI SALAD

mustard sprouts	1 cup olive oil
escarole	juice of 3 lemons
sorrel (or spinach)	1 teaspoon salt
watercress sprouts	1½ teaspoons freshly ground
Boston lettuce	black pepper
young nasturtium leaves	1 teaspoon onion juice
1 cup chapons (see note)	2 hard-boiled eggs

Trim and break the greens into small pieces; wash them thoroughly and dry on a clean towel. Place the greens in a large salad bowl and chill them while you make the chapons and dressing. Blend the oil, lemon juice, salt, pepper, and onion juice. Pour over the salad greens and toss until they are all well coated. Chop the eggs very fine and sprinkle over the top, along with the chapons. Toss well and serve immediately.

NOTE: To make the chapons, cut stale bread into small cubes and fry them in olive oil and minced garlic until brown.

At one luncheon during the four-day meeting, Leon Blanc had this to say about the rabbit cooked by Louis Servan: "This civet de lapin is in fact perfection, except for a slight excess of bouquet garni, possibly because the rabbits were young and tender-flavored."

CIVET DE LAPIN

3 tablespoons butter
2 tablespoons diced bacon
1 wild rabbit
few drops of vinegar
1 teaspoon salt
½ teaspoon freshly ground
    black pepper
2 tablespoons all-purpose flour
1 cup chicken stock

¾ cup red wine
1 bouquet garni (1 sprig
    parsley, 1 small bay leaf,
    1 sprig thyme)
2 tablespoons minced shallots
½ clove garlic, mashed
4 small white onions
6 mushrooms, sliced

Heat the butter in a heavy pot and add the diced bacon. Clean, skin, and disjoint the rabbit, saving the blood and adding the vinegar to keep it from coagulating. Rub the rabbit with salt and pepper, dust with flour, and brown in the butter and bacon fat. When the meat is nicely browned, pour on the stock and wine and add the bouquet garni, shallots, garlic, salt, and pepper if necessary. Cover tightly and simmer gently for 90 minutes. Parboil the onions in salted water for 10 minutes, drain, and add them to the pot. Add the mushrooms. Let the pot simmer for another 30 minutes. Remove the bouquet garni and thicken the sauce with the blood of the rabbit. Garnish with sprigs of parsley. (Serves 4)

NOTE: If the rabbit is small or particularly young, remove the bouquet garni after 90 minutes.

At another point during the meeting, Archie notes that some of the cooks were working on the oeufs au cheval and some of us were eating what was left of the duck and other things.

OEUFS AU CHEVAL

4 slices white bread	¼ cup grated Parmesan cheese
2 tablespoons butter	¼ teaspoon paprika
1 ounce *pâté de foie gras*	2 tablespoons melted butter
4 large eggs	
salt and freshly ground	
black pepper to taste	

Preheat the broiler. Trim the crusts from the bread and make the slices circular in shape. Melt the butter in a skillet and fry the bread on both sides until it is a delicate brown. Drain on brown paper. Spread each round with *pâté de foie gras*. Fry the eggs very gently in the butter and season with salt and pepper. Slip them on top of the *pâté*. Sprinkle with Parmesan cheese and a dash of paprika, moisten with a little melted butter, and leave under the broiler until they brown slightly.

Wolfe lifted one of the covers, bent his head, gazed, and sniffed. "*Piroshki?*"

He lifted other covers, bent, and smelled, with careful nods to himself. He straightened up again. "Artichokes *barigoule?*"

"I think, sir, he called them 'drigante.' "

PIROSHKI VALLENKO (by Sergei Vallenko of Château Montcalm, Quebec)

2 tablespoons butter	1 cup cold cooked minced veal
6 mushrooms, peeled and sliced	2 chicken livers, chopped
1 teaspoon chopped yellow onion	1 hard-cooked egg, chopped
1 teaspoon all-purpose flour	salt and freshly ground black pepper to taste
⅓ cup chicken broth	½ recipe puff pastry (see index)
½ teaspoon chopped fresh parsley	¼ cup milk

Preheat oven to 375°. Melt the butter in a saucepan and add mushrooms and onion. Just before they begin to brown add the flour. Pour in the broth; add the parsley, veal, chicken livers, egg, salt, and pepper. Let simmer until all the broth is absorbed. Roll the puff pastry to a thickness of ⅛ inch and cut it in rounds the size of a saucer. Put a spoonful of meat on each round, fold the pastry into a semicircle, and press down and seal the edge with a fork. Brush each roll with a little milk and bake for 15 minutes, or until the pastry is a good brown and well risen. (Makes 12 *piroshki*)

ARTICHOKES DRIGANTE

4 artichokes	2 tablespoons all-purpose flour
1 medium tomato	1 cup light cream
4 tablespoons butter	dash nutmeg
salt and freshly ground	½ cup grated Parmesan cheese
black pepper to taste	2 tablespoons melted butter

Boil the artichokes in salted water for 25 minutes. Drain, remove the leaves and burr, and lay the hearts in a flat baking dish. Preheat the oven to 450°. Peel and slice the tomato about ½ inch thick. Sauté the tomato slices in 2 tablespoons of the butter until they are a nice brown; season with salt and pepper, and lay a slice on each artichoke heart. Make a cream sauce with the remaining 2 tablespoons of butter, the flour, and cream. Season with salt, pepper, and a dash of nutmeg. Pour the sauce over the artichokes and sprinkle generously with the cheese. Moisten with the melted butter and brown in a hot oven. (Serves 4)

After another memorable meal, Wolfe speaks to the host chef: "I'm glad of this opportunity to express my admiration, Mr. Crabtree. Mr. Servan tells me that the shad-roe mousse was handled entirely by you. Any chef would have been proud of it. I noticed that Mr. Mondor asked for more. In Europe they don't have shad roe."

SHAD-ROE MOUSSE POCAHONTAS   (see index)

At one point during the festivities, Archie reports to Wolfe: "After the digestion of dinner, there is to be a test. The cook will roast squabs, and Mr. Laszio, who volunteered for the function, will make a quantity of *sauce printemps*. That sauce contains nine seasonings, besides salt: cayenne, celery, shallots, chives, chervil, tarragon, peppercorn, thyme, and parsley." *The experiment, during which each chef was instructed to taste the nine dishes of sauce and name the single seasoning omitted from each, was designed to test the relative sensitivity of each man's palate. It also set up a situation in which Phillip Laszio himself was murdered.*

SAUCE PRINTEMPS

4 tablespoons butter	2 shallots, chopped
¼ cup diced bacon	12 mushrooms, sliced

¼ cup cognac
1 cup dry red wine
1 cup strong chicken broth
1 tablespoon chopped fresh
    parsley
1 tablespoon chopped fresh
    chervil (or 1 teaspoon
    dried leaves)
1 teaspoon chopped celery
½ teaspoon chopped chives

few tarragon leaves (or
    ¼ teaspoon dried leaves)
pinch thyme
few grains cayenne pepper
few crushed black peppercorns
salt
2 tablespoons blood from
    the squab
few drops vinegar

Melt 3 tablespoons of the butter in a heavy saucepan and fry the bacon
until crisp together with the shallots and mushrooms. When the whole
is a rich brown, pour on the cognac, set fire to it, and as the blaze dies
down add the wine and chicken broth. Add the parsley, chervil, celery,
chives, tarragon, thyme, cayenne, peppercorns, and salt. Correct the seasoning with salt. Let the sauce simmer for 15 minutes very gently. Strain
and cook another 4 minutes. During this time, thicken the sauce first
with the butter, then with the blood from the birds which has been carefully saved in a bowl and blended with a few drops of vinegar to prevent
congealing. Serve hot with roast quail, squab, young grouse, or pheasant.
(Makes 2 cups)

*Jerome Berin is immediately suspected of Laszio's murder because
of his well-known and long-lived hatred for the victim, and when
Wolfe manages to clear him and to name the real murderer,
Berin's gratitude is such that he gives the* saucisse minuit *recipe
to Wolfe, though he demands from Wolfe a vow never to reveal
the recipe to another soul, with the exception of Fritz. When
Berin died in 1938, the victim of a Fascist bomb in Barcelona,
where he had gone to fight for the Loyalists and the freedom of
the Spanish people, Wolfe was released from his vow and has
permitted its disclosure here. No proportions are given, however.
Mr. Berin told Wolfe that they should vary with the climate, the
season, the temperaments involved, the dishes to be eaten before
and after, and the wine to be served. Mr. Berin's usual preference
was an inexpensive Spanish wine, the Rioja of the Marquis de
Murrieta, bottled on the estate at Ygay.*

SAUCISSE MINUIT

onions	beef broth	cloves	pheasant
garlic	thyme	bread crumbs	salt
goose fat	rosemary	bacon	black pepper
brandy	ginger	pork	pistachio nuts
red wine	nutmeg	goose	pigs' intestines

Chop up some onions and a clove of garlic and brown them lightly in a generous amount of goose fat. Pour in enough brandy to cover the onions, and twice as much good red wine as brandy, and as much strong beef broth as wine. Add a pinch of thyme and one of rosemary, the slightest dusting of ginger and nutmeg, and a mere threat of cloves. Let simmer gently for 10 minutes and add enough sifted bread crumbs to make a soft, runny mush. Cook gently for 5 minutes. Add chopped boiled bacon, coarsely chopped roast fresh pork, twice as much coarsely cut up roast goose as pork, and as much coarsely cut up roast pheasant as goose. Season with salt and a generous quantity of freshly ground black pepper, add a few roasted pistachio nuts, and let simmer to the consistency of fresh sausage meat. Get it perfectly cold. Wash and scald the pigs' intestines thoroughly. Fill with the cold stuffing, tying at intervals to form sausages. Broil on a slow fire, having pricked the skins to prevent bursting.

> *Some five years after this precious recipe was obtained by Wolfe, we find Fritz putting it to good use in* BLACK ORCHIDS. *As Archie tells it:* I went to the kitchen and put two bowls of crackers and milk where they belonged, meanwhile chinning with Fritz and getting sniffs of the sausage he was preparing. Eating crackers and milk and smelling *saucisse minuit* simultaneously is like sitting with your arm around a country lass while watching Hedy Lamarr raise the temperature.

13
RUSTERMAN'S
RESTAURANT

"Restaurant? I know nothing of restaurants; short of compulsion, I would not eat in one were Vatel himself the chef." *Wolfe makes this statement in* THE RED BOX, *and he sticks to it always, with the single exception of Rusterman's Restaurant in New York City, which is, as Archie puts it,* "the only place where Wolfe really likes to eat except at home, owned and operated by Marko Vukcic, the only man in New York who called Wolfe by his first name. . . . The only outside interest that Wolfe permits to interfere with his personal routine of comfort, not to mention luxury, is Rusterman's. When Vukcic died, leaving the restaurant to members of the staff and making Wolfe executor of his estate, he also left a letter asking Wolfe to see to it that the restaurant's standards and reputation were maintained; and Wolfe had done so, making unannounced visits there once or twice a week, and sometimes even oftener, without ever grumbling—well, hardly ever."

Wolfe went once to spend an hour in the kitchen, and twice he raised hell—once about a Mornay sauce and once about a dish which the menu called *suprêmes de volaille en papillote*.

[THE BLACK MOUNTAIN]

SUPRÊMES DE VOLAILLE EN PAPILLOTE

2 whole chicken breasts
½ cup all-purpose flour
salt and white pepper
5 tablespoons clarified butter
1 tablespoon chopped shallot
¼ pound mushrooms, minced

½ cup dry white wine
½ cup chicken broth
½ cup heavy cream
few drops lemon juice
1 tablespoon chopped fresh
 parsley

Preheat the oven to 400°. Bone and split the chicken breasts; remove the tendons and pat the *suprêmes* into an oval shape. Dredge them with flour, shaking them so that only a very thin coating of flour remains. Sprinkle with salt and pepper. Heat the clarified butter in a skillet over a low flame. Sauté the shallot for 1 or 2 minutes and add the mushrooms. Push the mushrooms to one side and add the *suprêmes*, sautéing for 3 minutes on each side. Be very careful not to let them brown. Remove to a warm platter. Add the wine and chicken broth to the pan, raise the heat, and boil until the liquid is reduced by half. Lower the heat. Add the cream and stir until the sauce is thickened slightly. Taste for seasoning off the heat; add a few drops of lemon juice and stir to blend. Cut out 4 circles of parchment paper, butter them, and place a *suprême* in the center of each circle. Pour over a spoonful of sauce and dust with parsley. Fold over the paper and seal the edges. Put the *papillotes* on a cookie sheet and bake for 12 minutes, or until the paper is puffed and slightly brown. (Serves 4 as a first course or for luncheon)

There were only a few customers scattered around the tables, since it was nearly nine-thirty and by that hour the clientele were inside busy with *perdrix en casserole* or *tournedos Beauharnais*.

[THE BLACK MOUNTAIN]

PERDRIX EN CASSEROLE

6 partridge, with their livers
6 chicken livers
½ cup minced celery
½ cup minced onions
12 tablespoons butter (¾ cup)
2 cups fresh bread crumbs
½ teaspoon nutmeg
1 tablespoon chopped fresh
 parsley

½ teaspoon salt
¼ teaspoon freshly ground
 black pepper
⅛ teaspoon fresh thyme leaves
2 cups chicken broth
½ cup dry white wine
¼ pound button mushrooms

Preheat oven to 350°. Clean and mince the partridge and the chicken livers. Cover and set aside. Sauté the celery and onions in 4 tablespoons of the butter; when they are soft, but not brown, add the livers. Add the bread crumbs, nutmeg, parsley, salt, pepper, and thyme. Blend thoroughly and divide into 6 equal portions. Stuff each cleaned partridge with the mixture, truss, and brush each with 1 tablespoon of melted butter. Put the partridge into a large casserole and bake for 30 minutes until browned on all sides. Turn each bird over every 10 minutes or so. When they are browned, cover the casserole and cook for 30 minutes longer. While they are cooking, put the broth and wine in a saucepan and reduce over high flame to about 1½ cups. Sauté the mushrooms in the remaining 2 tablespoons of butter. Add the broth and mushrooms to the casserole, cover, and cook for 10 minutes. Serve from the casserole. (Serves 6)

VARIATION:

Substitute ripe olives for mushrooms in the sauce. In DEATH OF A DOXY, Archie notes that when partridge in casserole are served for dinner, olives have been omitted, as they are here. Nevertheless, the reference does imply that olives can be used and that there was a good deal of give-and-take between Rusterman's and the kitchen on West Thirty-fifth Street.

TOURNEDOS BEAUHARNAIS

6 tournedos (see note)	½ cup Madeira
6 slices bacon	château potatoes (see note)
¼ cup clarified butter	6 artichoke hearts, cooked
1 tablespoon minced shallots	18 asparagus tips, cooked
1 tablespoon minced watercress	18 mushroom caps
½ cup beef stock or bouillon	

Wrap a slice of bacon around each piece of meat and sauté the *tournedos* in clarified butter for 4 to 5 minutes on each side. Remove to a warm serving platter. Add the shallots and watercress to the pan and cook for 2 to 3 minutes, adding more butter if necessary and scraping up any bits of meat. Add the stock and Madeira to deglaze the pan; bring to a boil and simmer for a few minutes, stirring occasionally. Surround the *tournedos* with alternating mounds of château potatoes, artichoke hearts, asparagus tips, and mushrooms. Pour the sauce over the meat and serve. (Serves 6)

NOTE: Be sure that the *tournedos* are sliced 1 inch thick from the front end of a beef tenderloin. To make château potatoes, peel and cut 2 pounds of potatoes into balls the size and shape of large green olives. Sauté the potato balls in clarified butter, turning them occasionally, until they are golden brown.

While investigating the death of a delivery boy in MURDER IS
CORNY, *Archie had to spend some time in Rusterman's back alley:*
I couldn't be seen from the windows of the restaurant kitchen
because the glass had been painted on the inside so boys and
girls couldn't climb onto the platform to watch Leo boning a
duck or Felix stirring goose blood into a *sauce Rouennaise.*

BONED DUCK WITH SAUCE ROUENNAISE

2 ducks, 5 pounds each	1½ cups cooked wild rice
½ pound shrimps	2½ cups dry white wine
4 tablespoons butter	salt and freshly ground
½ cup diced celery	black pepper to taste
2 tablespoons diced shallots	1 to 2 cups chicken broth
¼ cup sliced mushrooms	2 small onions, chopped
2 navel oranges	2 sprigs parsley, chopped
1 cup bread cubes	1 stalk celery, chopped

Have the butcher bone the ducks. Reserve the liver for the sauce. Parboil
and chop the cleaned shrimps. In the butter sauté the celery, shallots, and
mushrooms over a low flame for 5 minutes. Add the shrimps and cook for
3 minutes longer. Preheat oven to 350°. In a mixing bowl stir together
the oranges, which have been peeled, sectioned, and chopped, with the
bread cubes, rice, and ½ cup of the wine. Add the cooked celery, shallots,
mushrooms, and shrimps. Add salt and pepper to taste. Divide the mixture in half. Place the boned ducks skin side down and wipe them dry
with a clean cloth or paper towel. Sprinkle with salt and pepper and
spread each duck with an even layer of the stuffing. Roll the ducks like
a jelly roll and secure with butchers' cord or wrap with cheesecloth, tying
off both ends. Put the two rolled ducks into a large baking pan and pour
the rest of the wine and 1 cup of the broth over them. Add the onions,
parsley, and celery to the pan. The broth should come halfway up the
ducks. Cover the pan and cook for 2 to 2½ hours. From time to time
skim off any accumulated fat and add more broth as needed. When ready
to serve, remove the duck rolls to a platter, discard the cord or cheesecloth wrapping, and allow to stand for 10 to 15 minutes. When slightly
cooled, slice and serve with *sauce Rouennaise.* (Serves 6)

SAUCE ROUENNAISE

3 tablespoons butter	1 tablespoon flour
6 tablespoons minced shallots	2 cups chicken broth
2 tablespoons minced	⅛ teaspoon freshly ground
mushrooms	black pepper

1 bay leaf
2 teaspoons tomato paste
½ cup red wine

• 2 duck livers
¼ cup cognac

In 2 tablespoons of the butter sauté 4 tablespoons of the shallots and all the mushrooms for 5 minutes. Stir in the flour and continue to cook, stirring constantly, until the mixture is lightly browned. Slowly add the broth and stir until it boils. Add the pepper, bay leaf, and tomato paste. Cook over a low heat for 20 minutes, strain, and set aside. In another saucepan melt the remaining tablespoon of butter; add the remaining 2 tablespoons of shallots and cook for 5 minutes. Add the wine and simmer until the liquid is reduced by half. Add the reserved brown sauce and allow it to simmer for 10 minutes. While the sauce is cooking, wash the livers and chop fine. Add them to the sauce, stir well, and simmer for 5 minutes more. Remove from heat and blend in the cognac. Serve with the stuffed boned ducks.

In 1965, Archie wrote that Rusterman's has lost some of the standing it had when Marko Vukcic was alive. Wolfe is no longer the trustee, but he still goes there about once a month and Felix comes to dine at the old brownstone now and then for advice. When Wolfe goes, taking Fritz and me, we eat in the small room upstairs, and we always start with the queen of soups, *Germiny à l'oseille*.   [THE DOORBELL RANG]

GERMINY À L'OSEILLE

⅓ cup sliced onions
3 tablespoons butter
½ pound sorrel
½ teaspoon salt
5 cups chicken consommé

salt and white pepper to taste
2 egg yolks
⅓ cup heavy cream
¼ cup dry sherry

Slice the onions and shred the sorrel. Melt the butter in a large kettle and cook the onions in it slowly for about 5 minutes. Do not allow them to brown. Add the sorrel (reserving a bit for the garnish) and salt and cook, covered, for 5 minutes more. Add the chicken consommé and when it comes to a boil, simmer for 5 minutes. Remove from the heat and purée in a blender or run the soup through a fine sieve. Correct the seasoning. Keep the soup hot over a low flame. In a mixing bowl combine the egg yolks and cream. Beat with a whisk and slowly add a cup of the hot soup, beating constantly. Gradually pour this mixture into the soup kettle, beating with the whisk. Add the sherry. Reheat for a minute or two but do not allow the soup to boil. Garnish each bowl with a few slivers of sorrel. (Makes 5 cups)

VARIATION:

You may use spinach instead of sorrel, but you must then change the name of the soup to *Germiny à l'épinards*.

Archie occasionally takes a client or personal guest to Ruster-man's, where most people have "to reserve a table in advance and then pay six bucks for one helping of guinea hen." For Archie, however, there was a little question of etiquette. As a matter of business it would have been proper to tell her that neither Nero Wolfe nor I was ever allowed to pay for anything we or our guests ate at Rusterman's. But such a remark didn't seem to fit with squabs à la Moscovite, mushrooms Polonaise, salade Beatrice, and soufflé Armenonville.   [THE DOORBELL RANG]

SQUABS À LA MOSCOVITE

6 squabs	1 tablespoon minced shallots
2 teaspoons salt	1 tablespoon chopped parsley
1 teaspoon freshly ground black pepper	1 tablespoon minced mushrooms
½ cup clarified butter	6 tomatoes
2 large eggs	1 teaspoon paprika
2 tablespoons water	1 cup sour cream (see index)
1 cup bread crumbs	1 small truffle

Cut the squabs down the back, leaving the breast side intact. Flatten the birds slightly with the palm of your hand and, using a very sharp knife, remove the backbone and ribs. Rub with some of the salt and pepper. Beat the eggs with the water. Put the bread crumbs into a shallow dish. Dip the squabs first in the eggs, then in the bread crumbs, and sauté them on both sides in the clarified butter until golden. Remove to a warm serving platter and put in a holding oven. To the butter remaining in the skillet add the shallots, parsley, and mushrooms. Peel, chop, and seed 3 of the tomatoes and add to the pan. Turn the heat up and bring the mixture to a boil. Simmer for 5 minutes, stirring constantly. Add the paprika, 1 teaspoon of salt, and ½ teaspoon pepper, and simmer 3 minutes more. Gradually stir in the sour cream and taste for seasoning. Strain the sauce through a fine sieve and pour over the waiting squabs. Grate the truffle and sprinkle over the birds. Garnish with broiled tomato halves. (Serves 6)

VARIATION:

Instead of rubbing the squabs with salt and pepper, marinate them for 1 hour in heavy cream and use this marinade instead of the sour cream called for above. Omit the bread crumbs and roll the squabs in flour seasoned with salt, pepper, nutmeg, clove, thyme, and crushed juniper berries. Omit the tomatoes and when you stir in the cream, add ¼ cup of Madeira. Serve on fried bread slices spread with red currant jelly and pour the sauce over.

MUSHROOMS POLONAISE

1 pound small mushrooms	1 tablespoon chopped parsley
½ cup butter	¼ cup white bread crumbs
2 hard-cooked egg yolks	

Clean and stem the mushrooms. Melt 2 tablespoons of the butter in a saucepan and sauté the mushrooms over a low heat for 5 minutes, or until they become golden. Drain and put on a warm serving dish. Grate the egg yolks and sprinkle them over the mushrooms with the parsley. Keep the dish warm while you prepare the remaining butter in another saucepan, melting it and cooking it very gently until it turns golden brown. Stir in the bread crumbs and cook them for another minute or two until they turn golden. Pour the butter and crumb sauce over the mushrooms and serve hot. (Serves 4)

SALADE BEATRICE (see index for Beet and Watercress Salad)

SOUFFLÉ ARMENONVILLE (see index for Fig Soufflé)

14

NERO WOLFE
COOKS

*In this chapter are included recipes for dishes that Wolfe has at
one time or another in the stories actually cooked himself or
described in such detail that we know he has cooked it, instead
of relying on his reliable Fritz. As Archie says,* "with or without
Fritz to help, he could turn out a dish of *couronne de canard au
riz à la Normande* without batting an eye. I had to concentrate
to poach an egg." *Unless Wolfe is trying to prove a particular
point, as with spoon bread, or to play house, as Archie calls it,
by cooking his own eggs* au beurre noir, *Wolfe rarely cooks at
home. When away from home, however, confronted by the
possibility of someone else's inedible fare, he has been known
to fend for himself.*

In THE MOTHER HUNT, *Archie and Wolfe are holed up in Saul
Panzer's apartment, and Wolfe resorts to raiding the cupboards
for sustenance.*

"Speaking of fuming, the sturgeon is quite good, and I would
like to try it *fumé à la Moscovite.* When you go for papers could
you get some fennel, bay leaf, chives, parsley, shallots, and
tomato paste?

"At a delicatessen Sunday morning? No."

"A pity. Get any herbs they have."

A licensed private detective, and he didn't even know what
you can expect to find in a delicatessen.

STURGEON FUMÉ À LA MOSCOVITE

6 slices smoked sturgeon
(5 to 6 ounces each)
1 bay leaf
1 sprig fennel
1 sprig dill
1 cup milk (or more)
3 tablespoons butter
1 tablespoon minced shallots
¼ cup sliced mushrooms
1 tablespoon minced chives

1 tablespoon minced Italian
parsley
1½ cups sour cream (see
index)
1½ tablespoons tomato paste
salt and pepper to taste
2 teaspoons lemon juice
12 bread triangles fried in
anchovy butter (see index)
3 hard-boiled egg yolks

Put the sturgeon in a baking pan with the bay leaf, fennel, dill, and enough milk to cover. Bring to a boil, remove the pan from the heat, and allow it to stand for 3 minutes. Carefully remove the sturgeon, drain and dry it, and set it aside. Discard the milk. Melt the butter in a skillet and add the shallots and mushrooms, sautéing over a low heat until lightly browned. Add the chives and parsley and cook 2 minutes more. Add the sour cream and tomato paste, stirring well; heat through but do not allow to boil. Correct the seasoning. Remove the sauce from the heat and add the lemon juice. Set aside. Arrange each piece of sturgeon on two of the bread triangles and spoon on some of the sauce. Grate the egg yolk and sprinkle on as a garnish. Serve the rest of the sauce separately. (Serves 6)

In THE BLACK MOUNTAIN, *Wolfe and Archie travel to Montenegro, where Wolfe was born. Undoubtedly inspired by the fresh air and ingredients of his homeland, Wolfe makes his own version of the local pasta dish:* In the kitchen I found Wolfe concentrated on cuisine, with his shirt sleeves rolled up. We ate at a little table in the kitchen. There was just one item on the menu, dished by him out of a pot. After three mouthfuls, I asked him what it was. A pasta called tagliarini, he said, with anchovies, tomato, garlic, olive oil, salt, and pepper from the cupboard, sweet basil and parsley from the garden, and Romano cheese from a hole in the ground. I wanted to know how he had found the hole in the ground and he said—offhand, as if it were nothing—by his memory of local custom. Actually, he was boiling with pride, and by the time I got up to dish my third helping I was willing to grant him all rights to it.

TAGLIARINI

4 cups semolina flour	2 teaspoons olive oil
3 large eggs	¼ cup warm water
1½ teaspoons salt	

Sift the flour onto a board or into a large bowl. Make a well in the center of the flour. Beat the eggs with the salt and add them to the flour with the oil. Using your hands, work the flour into the eggs. Gradually add the water, 1 tablespoon at a time, until the dough becomes soft and can be compacted into a ball. Dust the pastry board with flour and knead the dough for about 15 minutes until it is smooth and elastic. Cut the ball of dough into 4 parts. Using a rolling pin, roll each piece of dough into a rectangular sheet as thin as you can manage it. Flour the sheets and roll them up or fold into a cylinder. Using a sharp knife, cut each roll crosswise, making each piece less than ¼ inch wide. As each sheet is cut, gently unfold the noodles and spread them out to dry. Cook them in a large pot of boiling salted water. Test them often and serve *al dente* with the following sauce.

SAUCE FOR TAGLIARINI

2 tablespoons olive oil	3 tablespoons fresh parsley leaves
2 cloves garlic	¼ pound well-aged Romano cheese
6 large tomatoes	
2 anchovy fillets	
freshly ground black pepper	
6 leaves fresh basil (or ¼ teaspoon dried leaves)	

Heat the olive oil in a large skillet. Mash or mince the garlic cloves and sauté them in the oil for a minute or two. Add the tomatoes, which you have peeled, seeded, and juiced. Simmer over a low flame for 20 minutes or longer, until the tomato juice has evaporated and the tomato pulp is very soft. Mince the anchovy fillets and add them to the pan with the basil, parsley, and pepper. Cook for 10 minutes longer. Correct the seasoning. Remove from heat and put the sauce through a fine sieve. Serve very hot over the tagliarini and sprinkle grated Romano cheese over the top.

At Lily Rowan's ranch in Montana, Nero Wolfe returns the favor of the "real Montana trout deal" with one of his own.

Archie sets the scene for the event by presenting himself and the ingredients to Spiros Papps, whose kitchen Wolfe will use:

"My name is Archie Goodwin, and I came here by invitation to bring fourteen things: parsley, onions, chives, chervil, tarragon, fresh mushrooms, brandy, bread crumbs, fresh eggs, paprika, tomatoes, cheese, and Nero Wolfe. That's only thirteen so I must have left out one. They are ingredients of baked brook trout Montbarry, except the last; Mr. Wolfe is not exactly an ingredient." *We assume that the missing ingredient is the one Wolfe calls for below.*

"I need some trout. I know there are more and larger trout in the river, but there are some in the creek, and the size I prefer. If you and Miss Kadany and Mimi will take the day for it you can reasonably expect to be back by five o'clock with enough for my purpose. Can't you?"

Lily was squinting. "That depends on your purpose."

"That's my favor. Yours for me is to get the trout. Mine, for you, is to serve a real Nero Wolfe trout deal at your table. It can't be true *truite Montbarry* because some of the ingredients are not at hand, but I'll manage. If you will?"

[IMMUNE TO MURDER]

THE REAL NERO WOLFE TROUT DEAL

10 brook trout, 6 to 7 inches long	1 tablespoon minced tarragon (or ½ teaspoon dried leaves)
2 tablespoons brandy	¼ pound mushrooms
1 medium onion, minced	4 large tomatoes
1 tablespoons minced parsley	½ teaspoon paprika
1 tablespoon minced chives	2 large eggs
1 tablespoon minced chervil (or ½ teaspoon dried leaves)	½ cup bread crumbs
	¼ cup grated Parmesan cheese

Clean the trout and rub them inside and out with the brandy. Add half the onion to the parsley, chives, chervil, and tarragon. Clean the mushrooms and chop; squeeze their juice into the herbs. Stir this mixture well and stuff the trout with it. Peel, chop and seed the tomatoes. In a saucepan, cook the tomato pulp and the rest of the onion over a low heat until it becomes mushy; add the mushrooms and cook another 5 minutes. Season with paprika and, if you want a very smooth sauce, put through the fine blade of a meat grinder or purée in a blender. Set aside and keep warm. Beat the eggs in a shallow bowl and combine the bread crumbs and cheese in another shallow dish. Dip each trout first into the egg and then into the bread crumbs, until they are thoroughly coated. Place the breaded trout in a generously buttered baking dish and bake in a 350° oven for 10 to 12 minutes until they are tender and golden brown. Remove to a warm serving dish and cover with the hot tomato sauce.

> *Before the trout deal, however,* Wolfe had done four things: packed most of his belongings, inspected every shelf and cupboard in the storeroom, but not the freezers, to get ingredients for a real Nero Wolfe trout deal, and made a casserole of eggs *boulangère* for our early lunch.

EGGS BOULANGÈRE

2 pounds potatoes	6 large eggs
(5 to 6, medium size)	salt and freshly ground
6 tablespoons butter (or more)	black pepper to taste
4 tablespoons minced shallots	1 to 2 cups light cream
⅓ cup grated Parmesan cheese	2 tablespoons cognac

Peel, wash, and slice the potatoes very thin. In a large skillet sauté the potatoes and shallots in the butter; add more butter if necessary and cook until the potatoes are nicely browned. Preheat the oven to 375°. Butter a casserole and spread the potatoes and shallots evenly over the bottom. Sprinkle on the cheese and carefully break the eggs, laying them on top of the potatoes. Season with salt and pepper and cover the eggs with cream until just the yolk is showing. Dribble the cognac over the dish. Bake for 10 minutes, or until the eggs are set. (Serves 3 to 6)

> *Back on West Thirty-fifth Street, Inspector Cramer threatens Wolfe with his constant surveillance, and Wolfe manages to set him straight once again:*
> "If you go up to your plants, I go along. If you go to the kitchen to mix salad dressing—"
> "You don't mix salad dressing in the kitchen. You do it at the table and use it immediately."   [OVER MY DEAD BODY]

NERO WOLFE'S SALAD DRESSING

3 hard-cooked eggs	½ teaspoon minced anchovies
4 tablespoons olive oil	½ teaspoon minced gherkins
¼ teaspoon minced chives	salt and freshly ground
¼ teaspoon minced tarragon	black pepper
(or a few flakes of dried)	2 tablespoons lemon juice

In a mixing bowl, mash the yolks of the eggs with half the olive oil until it forms a paste. Gradually add the remaining oil, beating constantly. Add the chives, tarragon, anchovies, and gherkins. Chop the egg whites very fine and add to the dressing. Mix thoroughly. Add the lemon juice and use immediately on a variety of greens which have been washed, drained, and torn into pieces just before serving time. (Makes ½ cup)

> *This dressing should take exactly eight minutes to make. In* WHERE THERE'S A WILL, *Wolfe allowed the pressure of business to accelerate the tempo of Sunday dinner, a very rare occurrence, and made the dressing in six minutes instead of the usual eight.*

On the train to Kanawha Spa for the meeting of Les Quinze Maîtres, Wolfe is obliged to defend American cooking to Jerome Berin, who is chef of the Corridona in San Remo. Since American cuisine is the subject of Wolfe's forthcoming speech at the meeting of Les Maîtres, Wolfe is well prepared. And, if one follows his descriptions [TOO MANY COOKS], *so would the dishes be.*

"I am told," Berin said, "that there is good family cooking in America; I haven't sampled it. I have heard of the New England boiled dinner and corn pone and clam chowder and milk gravy. This is for the multitude and certainly not to be scorned, if it is good. But it is not for masters."

"Indeed." Wolfe wiggled a finger at him. "Have you eaten a plank porterhouse steak, two inches thick, surrendering hot red juice under the knife, garnished with American parsley and slices of fresh limes, encompassed with mashed potatoes which melt on the tongue, and escorted by thick slices of fresh mushrooms faintly underdone?"

"No."

PLANKED PORTERHOUSE STEAK

1 porterhouse steak,
    2 inches thick
	salt and freshly ground
	    black pepper to taste

2 cups mashed potatoes	¼ cup chopped fresh parsley
¼ cup melted butter	6 slices lime

Procure a porterhouse steak of fine-grained texture, bright red in color and well marbled with fat. Trim off the excess fat and wipe with a clean cloth. Heat a wire broiler, grease it with some of the fat, and broil the steak over a hot charcoal fire for 3 minutes on each side. Take a well-seasoned oak plank which has never been washed but which has been kept scrupulously clean by being scraped with a dull knife and wiped with good olive oil. Lay the steak on the plank, surround with a border of fluffy mashed potatoes, and put in a hot oven (450°). After 9 minutes, brush the potatoes over with the melted butter and salt and pepper the steak. Return to the oven for 5 minutes, remove, paint with butter, sprinkle with parsley, garnish with the slices of lime, and serve at once. (Serves 4)

"Or the Creole Tripe of New Orleans?"

CREOLE TRIPE

3 cups fresh honeycomb tripe
¼ pound salt pork
1 carrot, sliced
1 stalk celery, sliced
1 clove garlic, minced
1 tablespoon chopped fresh
    parsley
1 medium yellow onion, sliced
3 whole cloves

1 bay leaf
1 sprig thyme, chopped
2 pig's feet
salt and freshly ground
    black pepper
few grains cayenne pepper
¼ cup cognac
1 cup flour

Cover the tripe with salted water, bring to a boil, and drain. Cover with fresh boiling salted water and cook for 15 minutes. Drain. Preheat the oven to 350°. Line an earthenware pot with slices of salt pork. Fill with the tripe in layers, alternating with the vegetables and herbs and seasoning with the salt, pepper, and cayenne. Lay the pig's feet, which have been cut in two lengthwise, on top of all, season with salt and pepper, and put a slice of salt pork on top. Pour the cognac over and put on a close-fitting lid, sealing it with a flour paste (made by mixing the flour with a little water). Cook for 5 hours. Unseal; remove celery, carrot, and garlic; and serve very hot in the cooking pot. (Serves 6)

"Or Missouri Boone County ham, baked with vinegar, molasses, Worcestershire, sweet cider, and herbs?"

BOONE COUNTY MISSOURI HAM

12 pound Missouri ham
whole cloves
1 quart cold water
1 cup cider vinegar
1 cup black molasses

2 teaspoons Worcestershire
    sauce
1 cup cider
½ teaspoon fresh thyme (or
    ¼ teaspoon dried leaves)

Scrub the ham thoroughly and soak it for 24 hours in cold water. Preheat oven to 350°. Remove the skin with a thin, sharp knife, taking off as little of the fat as possible. Stick cloves ½ inch apart all over the fat side. Place in a large roasting pan with 1 quart of cold water, the vinegar, molasses, Worcestershire, cider, and thyme. Cover the roaster and bake for 2 hours. Lower the heat to 300° and continue cooking for another 2½ hours. Remove the cover and bake 30 minutes longer uncovered. Take from the oven and allow to cool with the cover on. (Serves 12 to 16)

"Or chicken in curdled egg sauce, with raisins, onions, almonds, sherry, and Mexican sausage?"

CHICKEN IN CURDLED EGG SAUCE

1 fowl, weighing 5 pounds
3 pints cold water
1 carrot
1 onion stuck with 2 cloves
1 celery stalk
1 bay leaf
1 teaspoon salt
½ teaspoon freshly ground
   black pepper
2 tablespoons butter
2 tablespoons minced shallots
1 Mexican sausage, sliced
½ cup chopped almonds

¼ cup raisins
2 teaspoons chopped fresh
   Italian parsley
¼ teaspoon cinnamon
¼ teaspoon powdered cloves
rind of 1 lemon
salt
chili powder
few grains cayenne pepper
½ cup sherry
4 egg yolks
1 tablespoon all-purpose flour
juice of 1 lemon

Clean the chicken, disjoint it as for frying, cover with the water, and add the carrot, onion, celery, bay leaf, and salt and pepper. Cover and cook slowly until the chicken is tender, about 1½ hours. Remove the vegetables and keep the chicken hot in the broth while preparing the sauce. Heat the butter in a saucepan and add the shallots and sausage. As the shallots begin to brown, add the almonds, which have been rolled fine, the raisins, parsley, cinnamon, and cloves. Cook for 2 minutes and pour in 3 cups of the broth in which the chicken was cooked. Add the lemon rind, salt, chili powder, and cayenne and simmer for 5 minutes. Beat the egg yolks with the flour and the sherry and pour into the boiling broth, stirring constantly. Let thicken for 1 or 2 minutes and add the lemon juice. Arrange the chicken on a hot platter and pour the sauce over after removing the lemon rind. (Serves 4)

"Or Tennessee opossum?"

TENNESSEE OPOSSUM

1 opossum	¾ cup bread crumbs
salt and freshly ground black pepper	1 teaspoon chopped parsley
4 tablespoons butter	¼ cup beef broth
½ onion, chopped fine	1 teaspoon Worcestershire sauce

Skin and clean the opossum and rub inside and out with salt and pepper. Melt 3 tablespoons of the butter in a frying pan and in it brown the onion with the chopped liver of the opossum. When the meat is well browned, add the bread crumbs, parsley, salt, pepper, and enough beef broth to moisten. Preheat the oven to 450°. Stuff the cavity of the opossum with this mixture and sew up with a cotton string. Put into a baking pan with 2 tablespoons water and roast for 15 minutes. Lower the heat to 350° and continue cooking until the dish is tender and a rich brown. Baste frequently with a mixture of ½ cup water, 1 tablespoon butter, 1 teaspoon Worcestershire, and salt and pepper.

"Or lobster Newburgh?"

LOBSTER NEWBURGH

2 cups boiled lobster meat	3 egg yolks
1 cup light cream	½ cup dry sherry
2 tablespoons butter	salt and cayenne pepper

Cut the lobster meat into good-sized pieces. Melt the butter in a saucepan or chafing dish and add to it the cream. Let boil gently for 30 seconds and add the lobster. When the cream has again reached the boil, add the well-beaten egg yolks, to which the sherry has been added. Season to taste with salt and cayenne and let thicken for a minute or two, stirring constantly. Serve with a dish of hot buttered toast. (Serves 4)

"Or Philadelphia snapper soup?"

PHILADELPHIA SNAPPER SOUP

meat of snapper turtle	1 stalk celery
1 large veal knuckle	½ cup all-purpose flour
¼ pound chicken fat	1 pinch thyme
1 sliced carrot	1 pinch marjoram
2 medium yellow onions	1 bay leaf

(Continued)

2 whole cloves	2 cups good sherry
3 quarts chicken broth	salt and freshly ground
3 chopped tomatoes	black pepper to taste
2 hard-cooked eggs	lemon slices
3 slices lemon	Tabasco

Cut the turtle meat and the veal knuckle into pieces. Put the knuckle, chicken fat, carrot, onions, and celery into a baking pan over a low flame on top of the stove. When the fat is beginning to brown, add the flour and continue cooking until a light brown. Add the herbs and spices and turn all into a soup pot with the broth. Add the tomatoes and simmer gently for 4 hours. Strain. Meanwhile, cook the turtle meat for 5 minutes in the sherry with the lemon slices and Tabasco. Add meat and sherry, removing the lemon slices, to the soup. Season with salt, pepper, and Tabasco and add the chopped hard-cooked eggs. Add more sherry to taste. (Makes 2½ quarts)

"But I see you haven't." Wolfe pointed a finger at him. "The gastronome's heaven is France, granted. But he would do well, on his way there, to make a detour hereabouts. I have eaten *tripe à la mode de Caen* at Pharamond's in Paris. It is superb, but no more so than Creole tripe, which is less apt to stop the gullet without an excess of wine. I have eaten bouillabaisse at Marseilles, its cradle and its temple, in my youth, when I was easier to move, and it is mere belly fodder, ballast for a stevedore, compared with its namesake at New Orleans. If no red snapper is available—"

BOUILLABAISSE OF NEW ORLEANS

½ green pepper, chopped	2 dozen small lake shrimp
1 clove garlic, chopped	½ cup all-purpose flour
2 tablespoons chopped scallions	2 tablespoons butter
3 tablespoons olive oil	slices of French bread
2 cups beef broth	1 pinch Spanish saffron
¾ cup dry white wine	salt and freshly ground
1 pinch thyme	black pepper to taste
2 pounds red snapper	

Chop the green pepper, garlic, and scallions very fine. Heat the olive oil in a soup pot and add the vegetables. Cook for 2 minutes over a low flame; add the broth, wine, and thyme. Continue to cook for 15 minutes. Remove bones and skin from the red snapper, cut the meat into 5 or 6 pieces, roll each piece in flour seasoned with salt and pepper, and drop into the boiling sauce. Prepare the shrimp in the same way. Cook gently for 15 minutes. Cut the crust from the slices of French bread, fry them in the butter, and drain on brown paper. Lay the bread on a hot platter. Add Spanish saffron to the fish mixture and correct the seasoning. Let it boil up once and serve on the toast. (Serves 4)

> Wolfe lifted his brows. "Yes?" Wait till you taste oyster pie, à la Nero Wolfe, prepared by Fritz Brenner. In comparison with American oysters, those of Europe are mere blobs of coppery protoplasm."

OYSTER PIE NERO WOLFE

3 tablespoons butter
2 shallots, minced
3 tablespoons flour
3 dozen oysters, with their liquor
1 tablespoon finely chopped celery
2 teaspoons finely chopped chervil (or 1 teaspoon dried leaves)
1 teaspoon finely chopped fresh parsley

1 teaspoon soy sauce
1/4 teaspoon salt
1/4 teaspoon freshly ground black pepper
3 thin slices Georgia ham
1/2 recipe puff pastry (see index for Sunday-morning crescents)
2 tablespoons milk

Melt the butter in a saucepan, add the shallots, and as soon as they are tender but before they begin to brown add the flour. When well blended, pour in the oyster liquor and add the celery and herbs, the soy sauce, salt, and pepper. Let the mixture simmer for 5 minutes. Lay the oysters and ham, cut in small pieces, in a large deep baking dish, cover with the sauce, and put on a top crust of puff pastry. Brush the top with milk and bake for 5 minutes at 450°. Lower the heat twice at 5 minute intervals until 350° is reached. Continue baking until crust is a delicate brown and well risen. (Serves 4)

15

THE KANAWHA
SPA DINNER

*If Wolfe's eloquence was not enough to convince Jerome Berin
and the other Quinze Maîtres of the excellence of American
cuisine, surely his speech and the dinner that preceded it did so
without arousing even the slightest murmurs of disbelief or
raising a skeptical eyebrow. The complete text of Wolfe's speech
is not available, but we know from Archie's reports that it was
partly historical* ("he had reached the part about the introduc-
tion of filé powder to the New Orleans market by the Choctaw
Indians on Bayou Lacombe, so I knew he had got to page 14")
and partly informative ("Similar results have been achieved by
the feeding of blueberries to young chickens. The flavor of a
four-months-old cockerel, trained to eat large quantities of blueberries from infancy, and cooked with mushrooms, tarragon, and
white wine—") *and partly polemical* ("or, if you would add another American touch, made into a chicken and corn pudding,
with onion, parsley, and eggs, is not only distinctive, it is unique,
and it is assuredly haute cuisine.")

CHICKEN WITH MUSHROOMS AND TARRAGON

2 whole chicken breasts, boned
   and split (from chickens
   raised on blueberries, if
   possible)
¼ teaspoon salt
¼ teaspoon white pepper
5 tablespoons butter
1 tablespoon minced shallots
½ lb. sliced mushrooms

1 teaspoon chopped tarragon
   leaves (or ½ teaspoon dried)
buttered waxed paper cut to
   the dimensions of baking
   casserole
¼ cup chicken broth
¼ cup white wine
1 cup heavy cream
lemon juice to taste

Preheat the oven to 400°. Sprinkle the chicken breasts with salt and pepper. Heat the butter in a heavy casserole, with a cover, until it foams. Stir in the shallots and sauté 1 minute. Add mushrooms and tarragon and sauté 2 minutes more (do not allow to brown). Add the chicken breasts, rolling them quickly in the butter. Lay the buttered paper over the chicken, cover the casserole, and place it in the oven. Cook 7 minutes, or until meat springs back when pressed. Remove the chicken to a platter and keep it warm. Pour the chicken broth and wine into the casserole and boil the liquid on top of the stove over high heat until it is syrupy. Add the cream and boil rapidly, stirring, until the sauce thickens. Taste for seasoning and add more salt and pepper, if needed, and drops of lemon juice to taste. Pour the sauce over the chicken and serve immediately. (Serves 4)

CHICKEN AND CORN PUDDING (see index)

Undoubtedly his most persuasive argument, however, lay in the dishes themselves. Following, therefore, is the entire menu of Wolfe's specially selected and prepared dinner for the masters.

OYSTERS BAKED IN THE SHELL

TERRAPIN MARYLAND

BEATEN BISCUITS

PAN-BROILED YOUNG TURKEY

RICE CROQUETTES WITH QUINCE JELLY

LIMA BEANS IN CREAM

AVOCADO TODHUNTER

SALLY LUNN

PINEAPPLE SHERBET

SPONGE CAKE

OYSTERS BAKED IN THE SHELL

8 oysters to a person	chervil
freezing salt	thyme
salt and freshly ground	butter
black pepper	lemon juice
bacon	Tabasco
chives	Worcestershire sauce
parsley	horse-radish

Fill layer-cake tins (1 for each person) with freezing salt and put in a hot oven until the salt is thoroughly heated. Half-sink 8 oysters on the half shell into the salt of each tin and season them with salt and pepper. Run through a meat grinder some bacon, with a little chives, parsley, and chervil, and a very little fresh thyme, and then pound until the mixture becomes a paste. Dot the paste over the oysters and place in a very hot oven (500°) until the oysters curl up at the edges. Serve in the tins in which they were baked, with a little bowl of sauce at each place. For the sauce, melt some butter in a double boiler and season with lemon juice, Tabasco, a very little Worcestershire sauce, salt, and a dash of horse-radish. Each oyster is dipped into the sauce as eaten.

TERRAPIN MARYLAND

1 terrapin	salt and freshly ground
¼ pound butter	black pepper
1 cup dry sherry (or more)	

Use the terrapin eggs and liver, and all the meat portions of the terrapin except the white meat, which is tough and tasteless. Cut the meat into medium-sized pieces. Melt the butter in a chafing dish, add the terrapin and sherry, and cook until tender. Add salt and pepper to taste, and more sherry if necessary. (Serves 4)

BEATEN BISCUITS

1 quart all-purpose flour	1 tablespoon lard
1 teaspoon salt	1 tablespoon butter
1 teaspoon sugar	milk

Sift the dry ingredients together, rub in the shortening, and add enough milk to make a stiff dough. Knead thoroughly. Place on a firm block or table and beat with a mallet for 30 minutes, keeping the dough in a round mass and turning it with the palm of the hand after each blow. When the dough is perfectly smooth, roll out to ½-inch thickness, cut with a small biscuit cutter, prick with a fork, and bake in a fairly slow oven (275°) until a light brown. (Makes 18 to 20 biscuits)

PAN-BROILED YOUNG TURKEY

1 10-week-old turkey	1 cup boiling water
5 tablespoons soft butter	
salt and freshly ground black pepper	

Procure a well-fed turkey 10 weeks old. Clean it and split it and wipe it off with a damp cloth. Massage with 2 tablespoons of the butter, the salt, and the pepper. Place the turkey in a hot well-greased broiler and cook, finishing one side before starting the other, to a good brown. Take out of the broiler and rest in a roasting pan. Dot with 1 tablespoon of the butter and pour over it ¾ cup boiling water. Finish cooking in a moderately hot oven (375°) until done, basting several times. Just before serving pour into the pan ¼ cup boiling water and the remaining 2 tablespoons of butter; let it boil up quickly and serve on a hot platter with the sauce poured over it. (Serves 4 to 6)

RICE CROQUETTES

½ cup rice	2 egg yolks
½ cup boiling water	quince jelly
½ teaspoon salt	1 cup bread crumbs
1 cup scalded milk	½ cup parsley sprigs
2½ tablespoons butter	

Wash the rice well in several waters. Put it in a double boiler with the boiling water and the salt and steam until all the water is absorbed. Pour in the milk and cook until the rice is soft. Remove from fire and add 1½ tablespoons of the butter and the slightly beaten egg yolks. Mix well, spread in a shallow pan, and leave in the refrigerator until perfectly cold. Take small squares of jelly, form the rice mixture around them, roll them in bread crumbs, and fry in deep fat. Drain on brown paper and serve as soon as cooled, on a hot platter, surrounded with the parsley fried in 1 tablespoon of butter. (Serves 4)

LIMA BEANS IN CREAM

2 cups lima beans   salt
1 tablespoon butter   ¼ cup heavy cream

Put fresh, tender lima beans in a saucepan and pour onto them enough
boiling water to cover. Add the butter and salt to taste. Cook for 6
minutes, well covered; then remove cover, raise heat, and finish cooking
quickly until the water is absorbed. Pour in the cream, let boil once and
serve. (Serves 4)

AVOCADO TODHUNTER

4 ripe avocados   1 teaspoon lime juice
2 cups watercress leaves   1 teaspoon grapefruit juice
1 teaspoon lemon juice   1 teaspoon pineapple juice
1 teaspoon orange juice   1 teaspoon shredded ice

Halve the avocados and remove the seeds; do not peel them. Pinch or cut
off the watercress leaves singly, keeping no stems, and distribute them
into the avocados, which should be fairly well filled. After straining the
fruit juices through a double layer of cheesecloth, put them into a small
atomizer with the shredded ice and shake until the ice is melted. Spray
the watercress leaves thoroughly just before the avocados are to be eaten.
Serve on nests of nasturtium leaves. (Serves 8)

SALLY LUNN

1 cup milk   ¼ cup hot milk
3 tablespoons butter   2 large eggs
2 cups all-purpose flour   4 tablespoons sugar
   (or more)   1 teaspoon salt
¾ yeast cake   3 tablespoons butter

Bring the milk to the boiling point; add the butter and pour into a mixing bowl. Sift in enough flour to make a soft dough and add the yeast
dissolved in the hot milk. Beat the eggs until very light; add sugar and
salt and beat again. Combine with the dough and sift in enough more
flour to make the dough fairly stiff. Knead on a bread board and put back
in the bowl to rise in a warm place. Let rise until double its bulk. Preheat oven to 425°. Again turn the dough onto the bread board and
knead. Put small pieces of dough in buttered muffin tins, bake in a hot
oven, and serve as soon as done, about 10 minutes. (Serves 12 to 14)

PINEAPPLE SHERBET

1 large ripe pineapple   sugar
juice of 2 oranges   water
juice of 4 lemons

Use a large handsome pineapple with plenty of foliage. Cut off the top
to form a lid and scoop out the inside of the fruit. Grate or grind the
pineapple pulp. Make a strong lemonade with the oranges, lemons,
sugar, and water. Add the pineapple pulp and let it stand for 30 minutes.
Strain. Freeze until firm, then fill the pineapple with the sherbet, piling
it high, and perching the foliage on top. (Serves 4)

SPONGE CAKE

6 egg whites   grated rind ½ lemon
1 cup sugar, sifted twice   1 cup all-purpose flour
5 egg yolks   ¼ teaspoon salt
1 tablespoon lemon juice

Preheat the oven to 325°. Beat the whites until stiff but not dry and beat
in half the sugar. Beat the yolks in a separate bowl until they are thick
and lemon-colored. Add the lemon juice and rind and beat again. Beat
in the remaining sugar and continue beating until smooth. Combine the
two mixtures. Sift the flour three times and add the salt; fold it into the
batter. Pour the batter into an ungreased cake tin with a funnel in the
middle. Cut through the batter with a knife several times to break the
air bubbles. Bake for 1 hour. Turn the pan upside down on a cake
cooler and let it stand until cold. Loosen the cake with a spatula and let
the cake drop out of the pan by its own weight.

INDEX

Index

C

D

E

For a complete list of books available from Penguin in the United States, write to Dept. DG, Penguin Books, 299 Murray Hill Parkway, East Rutherford, New Jersey 07073.

For a complete list of books available from Penguin in Canada, write to Penguin Books Canada Limited, 2801 John Street, Markham, Ontario L3R 1B4.

THE GREAT DETECTIVES

Edited by Otto Penzler

Otto Penzler has persuaded the greatest living masters of mystery to reveal what they have never before told about their heroes, to answer the questions that their books leave unanswered: How did you conceive of your investigator? Was he (or she) drawn from real life? What characteristics most account for his success? What new information can you disclose about his background, tastes, private life? From Brett Halliday on Michael Shayne to Carolyn Keene on Nancy Drew, from Christianna Brand on Inspector Cockrill to Dell Shannon on Lieutenant Luis Mendoza, twenty-six authors replied, giving us the last word on their detectives—the truth behind the fiction. "The most insightful and entertaining presentation of detective-story writers and their fictional heroes that any mystery fan could hope for"—Stanley Ellin.